Hamlyn
Modern
World
Encyclopedia

Hamlyn
Modern
World
Encyclopedia

GONDOLA

Hamlyn
London·New York·Sydney·Toronto

Acknowledgements

Authors

Peter Arnold
Rosalind Carreck
Jennifer Cochrane
Neil Curtis
Gillian Denton
Richard Denton

Paul Gettens
Sebastian Graham-Jones
Jonathan Green-Armytage
Martin Hayman
Margaret Histed
Ken Roscoe

First published 1980 by The Hamlyn Publishing Group Limited

First published 1984 as a Hamlyn Gondola Book by
The Hamlyn Publishing Group Limited
London · New York · Sydney · Toronto
Astronaut House, Feltham, Middlesex, England

© Copyright The Hamlyn Publishing Group Limited 1980
This edition © Copyright The Hamlyn Publishing Group Limited 1984

ISBN 0 600 34713 3

Printed in Italy

Our Planet

Photographs
Ardea – J. Gooders 34 right; A. N. Browne 16 top right, 16 bottom right, 16 centre top; Camera Press – R. Hamilton 58 top; J. Allan Cash 53, 59 centre below; Daily Telegraph Colour Library – A. Ben-Horin 37 bottom left, M. Turner 50 right, J. Urry 37 top; W. F. Davidson 23 inset, 26 bottom; Deep Sea Drilling Project 32 bottom left and right; Mary Evans Picture Library 34 left; Geological Museum, London – D. A. Swanson 21 centre right; Hamlyn Group Picture Library 17, 18, 31, 45 bottom; Institute of Geological Science 19 top, 24 bottom; Italian State Tourist Office 26 top; B. P. Kent 21 left, 22; Keystone Press Agency 64; NASA 8; Photri 29, 32 centre, 33 top, 33 bottom, 45 top, 46 centre, 49; Popperfoto 43 bottom right, 51 top, 54 right, 58 bottom, 59 top right; G. R. Roberts 16 centre bottom, 21 top right, 23, 61 bottom, 62 top, 62 centre, 62 third from top; Spectrum Colour Library 37 bottom right, 39 bottom right, 47 right, 55 bottom, 57; Tony Stone Associates 42 bottom; M. Vautier 54 bottom left, de Cool 46 bottom, de Nanxe 39 centre right, 59 bottom right; Woodmansterne – J. E. Guest 9, 32 top; ZEFA – W. F. Davidson 19 bottom, 28, R. Halin 61 top, G. Heilmann 46 top, J. Herman 41 top, Hetz 41 bottom, J. Heydecker 50 left, H. Kramarz 39 bottom left, A. Liesecke 49, 51 bottom, G. Marche 43 top, Orion Press 59 centre above, J. Pfaff 16 top left, G. Riccatto 21 bottom right, H. Scmied 47 left, 55 top, P. J. Sharpe 24 top, L. Sitensky 43 bottom left, Starfoto 16 bottom left, 39 top right, Vontin 42 top, Ziesmann 54 top left.
Illustrations
Tudor Art Agency Ltd, Creative Cartography Ltd.

Science and Technology

Photographs
Aerial Phenomena Research Organisation Inc 87; Barr & Stroud Ltd 98; Bibliotheque Royale, Belgique 99; British Broadcasting Corporation 101 centre; British Museum 106 bottom right; Central Electricity Generating Board 94–95 below; CGR 114 inset; CIBA-Geigy (UK) Ltd 110 bottom; Daily Telegraph Colour Library – M. Freeman 104 below, B. Martin 116 top right, S. Skelly 117 right, A. Woolfitt 65; Deutsche Fotothek, Dresden 125 top; Electricity Supply Board (Eire) 95 right; Ford Motor Co Ltd

93 below left; Guy's Hospital 114; Hale Observatories 66–67 top, 86 top; Hamlyn Group Picture Library 99 right, 116 bottom; M. Holford 85 top, 88 top; Hughes Aircraft Corporation 97; IBM 105 centre; Imperial War Museum 125 bottom; Japan Information Service 109; Keystone Press Agency, P. Köch 93 top left, 93 right; Linotype Paul Ltd 107; MacClancy Press 125 centre; Mansell Collection 106 top, 112; Ministry of Agriculture, Fisheries and Food 111; Ministry of Defence 122, 122 inset, 124, 127, 128 bottom (Crown copyright); NASA 73 top, 78 bottom, 79, 80, 81, 94 bottom, 110 top; National Coal Board 88 bottom, 89 bottom; National Maritime Museum 94 top; Novosti Press Agency 75 bottom – J. Batchelor 123; Phoebus – J. Batchelor 123; Photri 101 top, 121; Popperfoto 116 top left, 120; Rolls Royce Ltd 128 top; Ann Ronan Picture Library 102, 106 bottom left; Science Museum 104 top (Crown copyright); Scifotos 69, 75 top, 83 centre; Jane Scott 108; Shell 90 top; Smith and Nephew Optics Ltd 115 bottom; Space Frontiers 68, 71, 72, 73 bottom, 79, 83 bottom; H. Steeper Ltd 115 top; Vitatron (UK) Ltd 115 centre; World Health Organization – J. Mohr 113, 118, 119; ZEFA – B. Benjamin 105 bottom left, G. Kalt 86 bottom, P. Pfaff 89 top, Photri 78 top, M. Pitner 91 bottom, G. Sommer 105 bottom right.
Illustrations
Linden Artists Ltd.

Transport and Travel

Photographs
Barnaby's Picture Library, London 139 right, 153 top; British Airways 134 top, 138, 139 left, 142; British Petroleum Co Ltd, London 149 top; Austin J. Brown, Bristol 132 centre; Central Office of Information, London 160 bottom; Dallas/Fort Worth Airport 136; Flight International, London 140–141, 144 bottom, 153 bottom; Ford Motor Co Ltd, South Ockendon 157 left, 157 centre, 157 right, 158–159; Globtik Management Ltd, London 148; Hamlyn Group Picture Library 156 top; David Hodges, London 150; Hoverlloyd, London 144 top; Robin Lush, Winsford 141, 150 bottom, 151 left, 151 bottom; Mansell Collection, London 130 top, 150, 150 centre; Novosti Press Agency, London 134 lower centre; Overseas Containers Ltd, London 145 bottom, 147 top, 147 bottom; Rolls-Royce Ltd, Derby 143 top left, 143 bottom; Royal Navy Photographs, Gosport 146; Science Museum, London

156 centre; Smithsonian Institution, Washington 130 bottom; Spectrum Colour Library, London 152 top; Tony Stone Associates, London 149 bottom; Swissair, London 129; John Taylor, Cheam 132 top, 132 bottom, 134 upper centre, 134 bottom, 135, 143 top right; ZEFA, London 140; ZEFA – Hrdlicka 152 centre left; ZEFA – J. Pfaff 160 top; ZEFA – J. Schörken 152 centre right; ZEFA – Peter Thiele 145 top.
Illustrations
John Batchelor.

The Natural World

Photographs
Heather Angel 199, 201 right, 205, 225 top, 226 inset, 229 top, 230 bottom, 231, 236, 249 bottom, 250, 253; Aquila Photographics 220; Biofotos: I. Took 225 bottom; Cambridge Scientific Instruments Ltd. 196; Bruce Coleman Ltd. 237 bottom, D. Bartlett 228 centre, J. and D. Bartlett 239 bottom right, J. M. Burnley 240 bottom, 249 top left, B. Coates 239 top, F. Eriza 240 top, C. B. Frith 237 centre, M. Grant 217 top, D. C. Houston 248 top, H. Reinhard 217 bottom, L. Lee Rue III 249 top right; Daily Telegraph Colour Library: F. Dalgety 242 left; Hamlyn Group Picture Library 242 right; B. Hawkes 238 right, 240 bottom; D. P. Healey 235 centre; E. A. Janes 210 bottom, 252; Frank W. Lane: G. Moon 238 left; Natural History Photographic Agency: D. Baglin 237 top right, J. and M. Bain 212 top right, 214 top, A. Bannister 209 top, 227 bottom, 229 bottom, N. A. Callow 247, S. Dalton 193, 214 bottom, 228 top, 230 top, 235 top, R. Erwin 241 centre, J. B. Free 216 top, B. Hawkes 205 top, 214 centre, E. A. Janes 205, 212 bottom, 245, P. Johnson 213 top, J. Kroener 219 top right, K. G. Preston-Mafham 206 bottom left, 206 bottom right, 213 bottom, E. Murtonaki 208, B. Newman 201 left, M. Savonius 204, 209 bottom, 210 centre right, 215, K. H. Switak 210 bottom right, M. W. F. Tweedie 216 bottom, B. Wood 232, W. Zepf 210 top right; Natural Science Photos 219 bottom, P. H. Ward 248 inset, C. E. Williams 246; Oxford Scientific Films 212 top left, 224, 227 top right, 241 bottom, 243 bottom; RIDA Photo Library: David Bayliss 221, R. N. Golds 239 bottom left, M. Harrison 237 top right, D. J. Taylor 218–219 top; Seaphot: C. Petron 226; Suttons Seeds Ltd. 197; Syndication International 243 inset.
Illustrations
Tudor Art Agency Ltd.

Arts and Entertainment

Photographs
British Broadcasting Corporation 283 top, 286; Camera Press (Colin Davey) 288 right; Daily Telegraph Colour Library (Richard Strong) 273; E.M.I. 288 top left; Fratelli Fabbri 265; Giraudon 259, 260 right; Sonia Halliday 270; Hamlyn Group Picture Library 257, 258 top, 258 bottom, 260 left, 261 top, 261 bottom, 263 top, 263 bottom, 264 top, 264 bottom, 266, 274–275, 280 top, 285; Japan Information Centre 271; Keystone Press Agency 268; Mansell Collection 287 top; Metro-Goldwyn-Mayer Pictures Ltd 283 bottom right; National Theatre 275 top left, 275 top right; Rank Film Distributors 284; Rex Features Ltd 278, 279, 280 centre, 280 bottom, 283 bottom left, 283 centre; Royal Shakespeare Theatre (Holte Photographics Ltd) 275 bottom; Reg Wilson 287 bottom, 288 bottom.
© SPADEM, Paris 258 bottom, 261 top, 262 bottom, 263 bottom 264 bottom.
© ADAGP, Paris 257, 260 left, 261 bottom, 263 top.
Cosmopress, Geneva 262 top.
VAGA, New York 265.
Illustrations
Carlo Torra, Ray Burrows.

Commerce and Industry

Photographs
British Airways 309 top right; British Steel Corporation 301 below left; J. Allan Cash 299 centre; Courtaulds 304; Courtesy of the Archives, the Coca-Cola Co 297; Daily Telegraph Colour Library: A. Howarth 289, 292 right; Hamlyn Group Picture Library 291 top, 293 left, 305 bottom; ICI 304 top and bottom; Lansing-Bagnall 307 bottom; Levi Strauss 310; Mansell Collection 293 right, 302 left above; J. Mowlem & Co. Ltd. (M. T. Walters Association Ltd.) 293 centre; National Westminster Bank 313; Plessey 305 left; Popperfoto 291 bottom, 314; Shell 298 top; Spectrum Colour Library 294 top, 295 bottom, 303 top right, 307 top, 309 top left; Stock Exchange 312; Suzuki 303 bottom right; Wimpey Group Services 293 left; ZEFA: J. Bitsch 295 below, H. Kramarz 303 bottom left, S. Kübe 309 bottom right, H. Nowak 299 top right, Orion Press 296, Starfoto 306 top; Zimco 301 top.
Illustrations
Terry Allen Designs Ltd.

Contents

Our Planet 9

This introductory section examines the world we live in, from the formation of our planet millions of years ago, to the political and economic groupings of countries today. The structure of the Earth is fully explained and each continent is discussed in detail, with full colour maps complementing the text.

Science and Technology 65

Man's achievements in the world of science and technology; his exploration of space including the first moon landing, advances in medicine, telecommunications, weapon technology and fuel science are detailed. Clear diagrams also explain the workings of lasers, jet engines and atomic power.

Transport and Travel 129

The history of aviation, including details of how an airport functions, opens this exciting section. Trains, from the first steam locomotive to the latest advanced passenger trains, are described as are the advances in car production. Modern container ships, passenger liners and oil tankers are also included.

The Natural World

The fascinating world of living creatures is examined—from the smallest land plant to the giant blue whale. Plant and animal groups are explained and described, with pictorial examples. The evolution of life, from prehistoric times, adds to the depth of knowledge contained within these pages.

Arts and Entertainment

An absorbing look at the many developments this century has seen in the fields of painting, literature, theatre, music and ballet. Popular entertainment today is also considered, with descriptions of how a film is made and how a television studio works adding to the interest of this highly illustrated section.

Commerce and Industry

The complex world of economics is clarified for everyone, with pictures, maps, diagrams and a simple text explaining international trade, big business, money, banks and insurance.

Index

Our Planet

Contents

The Earth in space

Our planet seems to us to be very large and solid because we are so tiny by comparison, but compared to the Universe and all its forces, the Earth is really rather a fragile little body. It is only one planet in a system of planets which we call the *Solar System* because they all revolve around a central star which we call the Sun. The Sun however, is only one of many millions of stars in a larger system called a galaxy – in fact you are looking at our galaxy when you look up at the night sky and see the stars of the *Milky Way*. To put ourselves further in perspective: the Earth has a radius of little more than 6000 kilometres (less than 4000 miles) but our galaxy is 80 000 light years across (a light year is the distance travelled by light in one year and light travels at nearly 300 000 km/second or 186 000 ml/sec). What is more, there are many millions of galaxies in the Universe!

Human beings have always wondered how their planet came into existence and many theories have been put forward over the centuries. Nowadays, cosmologists (scientists who study the Universe) are generally agreed that the Universe formed by what they call the *Big Bang*. Their idea is that about 10 000 million years ago, a very dense mass of matter exploded into expanding matter and radiation which then formed the galaxies. This theory has generally superseded the *Steady State* theory put forward by the famous English astronomer Fred Hoyle and others, which maintained that the Universe has always existed in a steady state because matter is being created as fast as the Universe is expanding.

From this Universe, a little less than 5000 million years ago, our Solar System was born. Many scientists believe that there was a cloud of dust and gas which, by gravitational pull, began to come together. The contraction caused the centre of the cloud to heat up until eventually it became hot enough to trigger the nuclear reaction which we know today as sunshine. Around the Sun the planets themselves, including our Earth, were formed. The planets of the Solar System are Mercury, Venus, Earth, Mars, Jupiter, Saturn, Uranus, Neptune and Pluto. Mercury is nearest to the Sun, Pluto is the furthest away –

THE EARTH IN SPACE

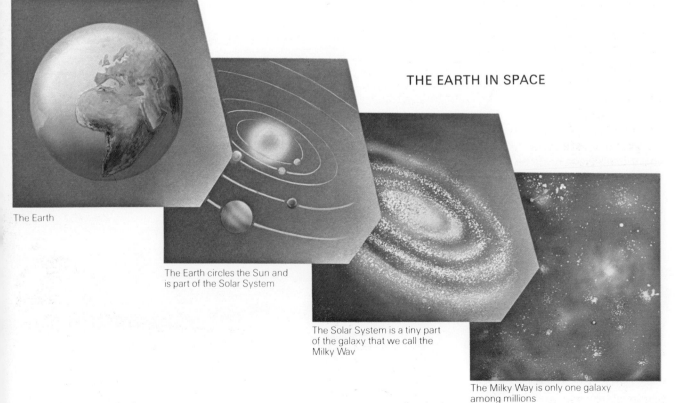

The Earth

The Earth circles the Sun and is part of the Solar System

The Solar System is a tiny part of the galaxy that we call the Milky Way

The Milky Way is only one galaxy among millions

5910 million kilometres (3672 million miles). The planets move around the Sun at different rates. Pluto takes 248 years to complete its circuit, Neptune 165 years and Mars 687 days.

The Earth in motion

The Earth, together with its twin planet, or satellite, the Moon, moves in an elliptical orbit around the Sun at the rate of one complete circuit every 365¼ days. It is because this period of rotation is not exactly 365 days that every four years we need to have a leap year of 366 days. This makes up for the quarter day lost in a normal 365 day year. The Earth also spins around on its own axis, making one complete revolution every 24 hours. This spinning causes our days and nights: half of the Earth faces the Sun and receives daylight while the other half faces away and is in darkness. As the Earth moves round from west to east, different parts of the planet receive daylight.

The Earth's axis is tilted at an angle of 23° and therefore on its journey around the Sun there is a period in June when the northern hemisphere is tilted towards the Sun. This gives rise to the northern summer, while winter is occurring south of the Equator. Six months later, the southern hemisphere is tilted towards the Sun, and so experiences summer, while winter is in progress north of the Equator. So the movement of the Earth around the Sun causes the seasons, and the movement of the Earth on its own axis brings about day and night.

THE EARTH'S ORBIT

It takes the Earth 365 days, 5 hours, 48 minutes and 46 seconds to complete each orbit around the Sun. The Earth travels around the Sun at a speed of 106 000 kph (66 000 mph)

As the Earth moves around the Sun, it is also spinning on its own axis, taking about 24 hours to complete an entire revolution. As the Sun's rays shine steadily from one direction, the spin of the Earth has the effect of creating day and night on the Earth's surface

THE SEASONS

June 21st — the North Pole is tilted towards the Sun and it is summer in the northern hemisphere, winter in the southern

March 21st — spring in the northern hemisphere and autumn in the southern

September 23rd — autumn in the northern hemisphere and spring in the southern hemisphere

December 21st — the South Pole is tilted towards the Sun. It is summer in the southern hemisphere

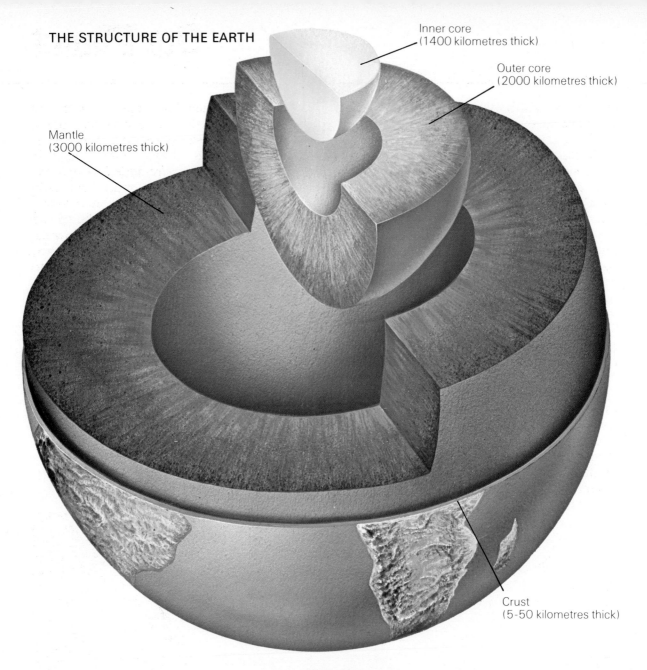

Inner core
(1400 kilometres thick)

Outer core
(2000 kilometres thick)

Mantle
(3000 kilometres thick)

Crust
(5-50 kilometres thick)

The structure of the Earth

People once thought that the Earth was flat and that you could fall off the edge. Most of us now think of the planet as a sphere although it is more accurately described as an *oblate spheroid*, being flattened at the poles and bulging at the Equator. It is quite useful to think of the Earth and its atmosphere as being rather like an onion – that is a ball made up of layers, although, unlike an onion, each layer is made of a different material.

One of the stories created by the writer Jules Verne describes a journey to the centre of the Earth, but at the Earth's centre it would certainly be rather uncomfortable because the *inner core* of our planet is thought to be made of an alloy of nickel and iron at a pressure some four million times greater than that which we experience at the surface. Surrounding this inner core is an *outer core* which seems to be liquid and is made of nickel and iron together with a lighter element such as silicon or sulphur.

It is very difficult to discover what it is like within the Earth. Information has been collected from the study of earthquake waves, which react differently in rocks of different densities and different degrees of solidity. Volcanoes also provide evidence as they throw up to the surface materials from great depths. There is one other source of information –

meteorites which fall from space and are thought to represent the composition of the Universe as a whole.

Outside the core is the *mantle*. The evidence we have from the way in which earthquake waves pass through the mantle suggest that it is solid but it is likely that the upper part is more plastic in consistency. The composition of the mantle seems to be similar to that of a rock found at the Earth's surface called *peridotite* which contains iron, magnesium, silicon, and oxygen.

Finally, surrounding the mantle, the Earth has a very thin skin known as the *crust* which is probably nowhere more than 50 kilometres (30 miles) thick. The crust is at its thickest under the world's mountain belts.

The atmosphere

Surrounding the solid ball of the Earth itself is a thin envelope of gases and water vapour which we call the *atmosphere* – this is the air we breathe. The Earth has not always had an atmosphere like the one which we enjoy today and, of course, most planets do not have a breathable atmosphere at all.

The heating that took place as the Earth was formed meant gases were set free from the evolving planet but we would certainly not think of this first atmosphere as 'air'. It was probably composed of the gases hydrogen and carbon monoxide, plus water vapour. The carbon monoxide together with some carbon dioxide which was also present may

then have reacted with the hydrogen leaving an atmosphere of methane and hydrogen. Later, other volcanic gases were added so that the Earth's atmosphere gradually became more like it is today.

However, it was the spread of plants on to the land which made the final difference, providing sufficient oxygen to support animal life. By a process called *photosynthesis* green plants use the Sun's energy to convert carbon dioxide taken in from the air, and water from the soil, into the sugars and starches that provide the energy to make their stems, flowers, leaves and roots.

This enormous crater in Arizona, USA, was caused by a meteor falling from space. The crater is well over 1000 metres across and 170 metres deep.

Photosynthesis produces oxygen as a by-product, so as plant life spread, the excess carbon dioxide in the air was replaced by oxygen. At present there is a state of balance: plants take in carbon dioxide and release oxygen, animals breathe in oxygen and expel carbon dioxide.

The air is now made up of 78 per cent nitrogen, 21 per cent oxygen, 0.9 per cent of the noble gas, argon, 0.03 per cent carbon dioxide (although there are fears that this is increasing as a result of industrial pollution and the removal of huge areas of forest), and smaller amounts of other gases. Of course, there is also water vapour in the air but this varies in amount.

Weather and climate

The Earth is kept warm by the energy it receives from the Sun as sunshine, but temperatures vary from place to place and from season to season.

Temperature variations

Rays of sunlight travel from 150 million kilometres (93 million miles) away, and when they reach the Earth they are parallel rays. The curve of the Earth means that the rays are vertical at the Equator but at quite a low angle when they reach temperate latitudes. As the rays lose heat passing through the atmosphere, the more direct the journey, the greater the heat which penetrates through to the surface of the Earth. The vertical rays in equatorial latitudes mean

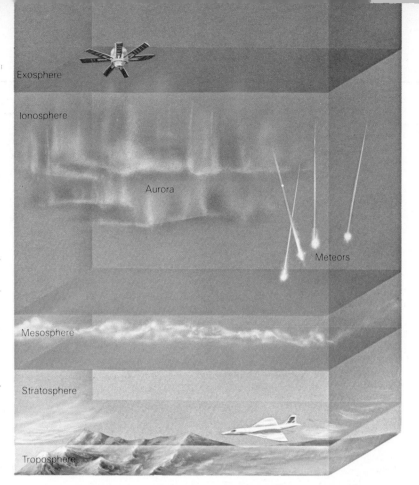

it is much hotter at the Equator than it is in the regions where the Sun's rays strike at a low angle. It is these variations in temperature that are largely responsible for the changes in the weather.

Air pressure

Although we do not notice it, the air is really quite heavy and exerts a considerable pressure on the Earth. On average, a column of air from sea-level to the top of the atmosphere, and measuring about a square centimetre, would weigh about a kilogram (average air pressure could also be expressed as 14 pounds per square inch). The air pressure is not uniform all over the Earth – if it was, we would not have weather as we know it. Nor is the pattern a simple one. Where the Earth is warmest – at the Equator – air rises and creates a low

The atmosphere does not have the same consistency throughout. It is divided into layers, each with its own characteristics.

pressure region known as the *equatorial low pressure* or *doldrum belt*. The main mass of air which rises from the doldrums falls near the tropics, creating regions of high pressure which are known as the *tropical highs* or *horse latitudes*. The falling air near the tropics cannot just disappear, but travels across the surface of the Earth. Some of the major planetary winds have their origin in this falling air.

In addition to the falling air of the tropics there is also falling air in the Arctic and Antarctic because it is so cold. From these two high pressure areas, winds blow out into temperate latitudes and meet air blowing out from the tropical highs. Where the

The Sun's rays strike different parts of the Earth at different angles. Where they strike vertically they give most warmth.

tropical air meets the cold polar air, friction creates a whirling air mass which will eventually form a *depression*.

As a general rule it is true to say that winds blow from areas of high pressure to areas of low pressure, but this is complicated by the rotation of the Earth which means that in the northern hemisphere winds are deflected to the right and in the southern hemisphere to the left. In fact the circulation of the atmosphere is even more complicated because the Earth is not warmed uniformly. This warming is affected by such factors as the water content of the air, how much dust or other pollution is present, what sort of surface the sunshine is falling on to and so on.

Precipitation

To the pattern of air pressure and temperature is added precipitation in all its forms – rain and snow are the most common examples. The process which causes rain to fall is complicated but generally rain falls as a result of the condensation into larger droplets of the moisture that is always present in the air. Firstly moisture condenses into what we call clouds and then, when the droplets reach a critical size, they fall as rain, or as snow when the temperature is low.

Weather charts and forecasts

As the weather affects all our lives, people have spent a great deal of time and money trying to forecast the weather to come. A typical weather chart has lines on it rather like the contours on an ordinary map. These lines are called *isobars* and they represent lines of equal air pressure in the same way that contours represent lines of equal height. Where contours are close together, a steep-sided hill or valley is represented; similarly, if the isobars on a weather chart are close together, the air-pressure gradient is very steep and the wind will tend to be very strong as it blows from high to low pressure and is then deflected by the rotation of the Earth.

A weather chart may also have odd-looking spiky or bumpy lines on it. These represent fronts or boundaries between different air masses.

GENERAL CIRCULATION OF AIR FOR NON-ROTATING EARTH

North Pole
Cold   Cold
Cool   Cool
Northerly surface winds
Warm   Equator   Warm
Southerly surface winds
Cool   Cool
Cold   Cold
South Pole

Prevailing Winds

Trades

Westerlies

Polar Easterlies

North Pole
High
Low   60°N
High (Horse latitudes)   30°N
Low
Doldrums   Equator
High (Horse latitudes)
Low   30°S
60°S
Low
South Pole

GENERAL CIRCULATION OF AIR FOR ROTATING EARTH

An air mass is a pocket of air which has uniform characteristics of temperature and humidity throughout; in other words it might feel warm and damp or hot and dry and so on. Where two of these air masses collide, that is, at a *front*, there is an abrupt change in the weather. At a warm front, where warm air impinges on cold air, there is a wide band of cloud preceded by a belt of rain, but at a cold front the weather is often showery with thunderstorms developing along the line of the front itself. So a weather chart can tell us a lot about the weather to come.

Right : A typical synoptic chart for the northern hemisphere.

Below : Different cloud types

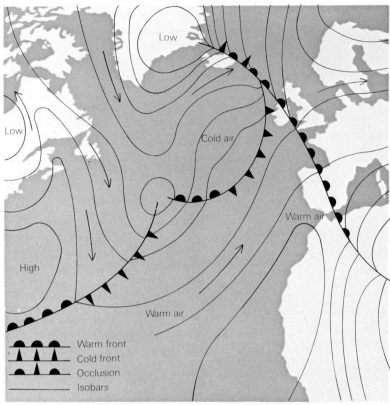

Above : Cirrus

Below : Cumulus

Above : Cirrocumulus

Below : Cumulonimbus

Above : Stratocumulus

Below : Nimbostratus

The composition of the Earth

Having looked at the Earth's atmosphere, let's come back down and examine a little more carefully the elements that make up our planet. Analyzing such bodies as meteorites, which are thought to represent the composition of the Universe as a whole, we find that the Earth is largely made up of iron, oxygen, silicon, and magnesium in that order of abundance. Analyzing the crust, on the other hand, which, after all, is where all our raw materials come from, we find that oxygen makes up nearly half of it followed by silicon, aluminium, and iron.

These elements take the form of *rocks* and rocks are made up of *minerals*.

Minerals and crystals

A mineral can be regarded as a solid material with a fixed chemical composition and having elements that are similar throughout. This is how rocks differ from minerals. Minerals always have the same composition and structure no matter where they are found, while rocks are usually made up of a mixture of minerals. Granite, for example, is made up mostly of three minerals, quartz, feldspar and mica, but the three minerals are not always present in the same proportions.

Most minerals are made of *crystals* which are very regularly shaped, the shape reflecting the internal atomic structure of the substance. The many different crystal shapes can be grouped together into seven basic systems. Discovering to which system a crystal belongs helps to identify the mineral. The seven systems are defined by their *symmetry* which can be worked out quite easily. The following exercise will help you to know what to look for.

Cut a potato into a cube shape and then cut that cube in half – one half is an exact mirror image of the other half and the line along which you have cut is a *plane of symmetry*. Take another potato cube and hold it by two opposite corners in your finger and thumb; if

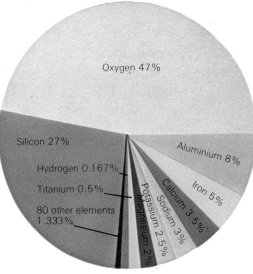

PROPORTIONS OF THE ELEMENTS IN THE EARTH'S CRUST

Below and over page : The seven crystal systems and some common minerals that crystallize in each of them :

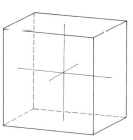

Cubic (Pyrite)

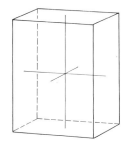

Tetragonal (Cassiterite)

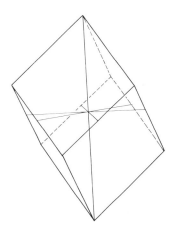

Trigonal (Tourmaline)

In the pie chart: Oxygen 47%, Silicon 27%, Hydrogen 0.167%, Titanium 0.5%, 80 other elements 1.333%, Magnesium 2%, Potassium 2.5%, Sodium 3%, Calcium 3.5%, Iron 5%, Aluminium 8%

you now rotate it you will see the same shape repeated three times – this is an *axis of symmetry*. The centre of that cube would be a *centre of symmetry* because the cube has three sets of parallel faces. The basic symmetry of all crystals can be worked out using just these three simple facts.

Cubic crystals all have four threefold axes of symmetry. *Tetragonal crystals* have one fourfold axis. *Trigonal crystals* have one threefold axis. *Hexagonal crystals* have one sixfold axis. *Orthorhombic crystals* have three twofold axes. *Monoclinic crystals* have one twofold axes and *triclinic crystals*, which are the least symmetrical, have no axes of symmetry at all but they do have a centre of symmetry.

There are many hundreds of different minerals, although most rocks are largely composed of minerals called *silicates*. Silicates are combinations of silicon and oxygen with various metals, mainly aluminium, iron, calcium, sodium, potassium and magnesium. Feldspar, for example, is a potassium aluminium silicate. To be sure of the identity of a lot of minerals quite complicated tests in a laboratory are needed but for general field work there is a number of physical and chemical properties that can be determined with a few simple tests.

Identifying minerals

One of the first things that you might notice about any mineral is its colour, but beware for this can be misleading. Some minerals exist in more than one colour and others may weather to different colours. Looking at the colour of the powdered mineral can be helpful, however. The easiest way to do this is to scratch the mineral on a piece of unglazed porcelain which is called a *streak plate*. Be careful to note the difference between a mineral which gives no streak because it is too hard and one which gives a white streak. A mineral such as haematite (an iron mineral) is characterized by its blood-red streak.

Minerals vary greatly in their hardness and this is quite easy to test by scratching the sample with other objects of known hardness. There is a standard scale of hardness called *Mohs' scale* (named after the German mineralogist Friedrich Mohs) with which all minerals can be compared. On this scale the softest mineral, talc, is given a hardness of 1, while diamond, the hardest known mineral, has a

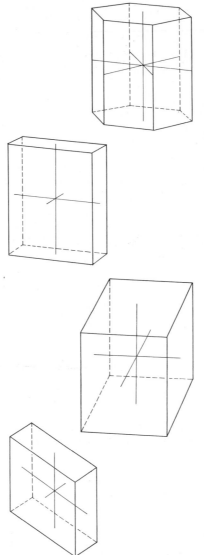

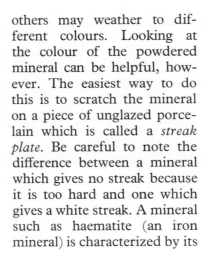

Hexagonal (Beryl)

Orthorhombic (Topaz)

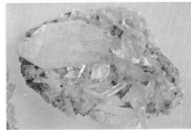

Monoclinic (Gypsum)

Triclinic (Kyanite)

hardness of 10. A finger nail, a copper coin, a steel blade, and a piece of glass provide a rough-and-ready measure of hardness. As a very rough guide, a fingernail will scratch up to hardness 2, a copper coin up to about 5, glass $5\frac{1}{2}$, and a penknife to hardness 6.

Minerals can also be distinguished by the way they break. Quartz, for example, fractures with the broken edges having a shell-like pattern known as a *conchoidal fracture*. Others (a good example is calcite) will break cleanly along planes related to their internal structure. This property is called *cleavage*.

Minerals are the basic building blocks of nature and it is from these that the rocks that we are familiar with are made.

Igneous rocks

By far the greater part of the Earth's crust is made of two important rocks; these are the *granites* which make up the continental crust and the *basalts* which are to be found in the ocean basins. Both of these rocks are *igneous* in type, that is, they were formed at high temperatures within the Earth's crust. Granite is found in the USA, Canada, Scandinavia and England – particularly in Devon and Cornwall. Here, Dartmoor, Bodmin Moor, St Austell and the Scilly Isles are all made of the same granite which can be shown to be continuous at depth. Basalt forms the Giant's Causeway in Co. Antrim, Northern Ireland, and is widely distributed in India, Iceland and Hawaii.

Above : The jointed basalt of the Giant's Causeway, Northern Ireland.

Below : A granite tor, Dartmoor, England.

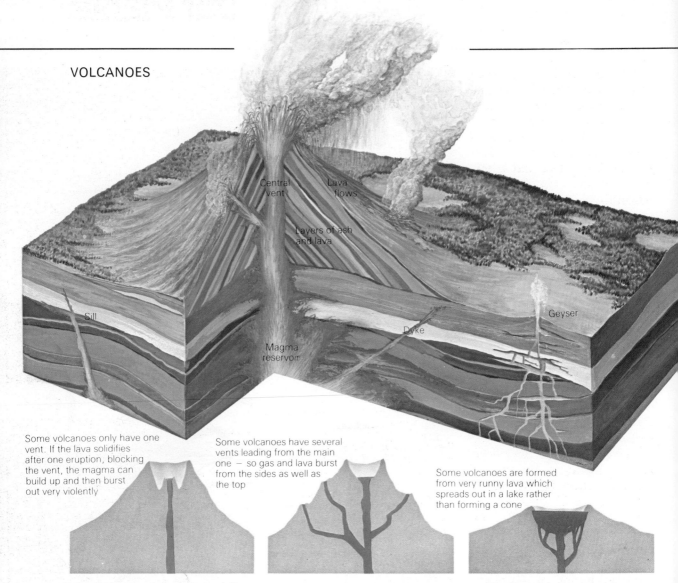

Central vent

Lava flows

Layers of ash and lava

Sill

Geyser

Dyke

Magma reservoir

Some volcanoes only have one vent. If the lava solidifies after one eruption, blocking the vent, the magma can build up and then burst out very violently

Some volcanoes have several vents leading from the main one – so gas and lava burst from the sides as well as the top

Some volcanoes are formed from very runny lava which spreads out in a lake rather than forming a cone

Looking at a piece of basalt and a piece of granite, the most obvious difference is that the granite is quite pale coloured whereas the basalt is almost black (although it can weather to a reddish or greenish colour). This is because the granite is made of light minerals such as quartz and the basalt is made of darker iron and magnesium silicates. Looking a little more closely shows that the basalt mineral grains are much smaller than those of the granite. This is because the basalt has cooled from a high temperature more quickly (although still taking a very long time) than granite, which has cooled more slowly from a lower starting point. The longer rock takes to cool and solidify, the longer crystals have to form and grow before the rock sets hard.

Extrusive and intrusive rocks

The reason for this difference in cooling time brings to light an important difference in the way in which these two igneous rocks are formed. The Hawaiian basalts, for example, are volcanic in origin, that is, they were spewed out in their molten state from a volcano. On the other hand, granite rocks welled up in the Earth's crust to cool very slowly, insulated from the cooling atmosphere by the overlying rocks. The rocks above the granite may then have been eroded away to expose the granite at the surface. These granite rocks are called *intrusive*, while volcanic rocks like basalt are called *extrusive*.

There are many other types of igneous rocks apart from granite and basalt. They contain a variety of minerals and they may be formed in a variety of ways. The molten material which lies below the surface of the Earth is called *magma*. Whenever magma forces its way to the surface, it forms extrusive rocks in some shape or form. The molten rock which spreads out over the Earth's surface and solidifies is called *lava*. The lava which forms a volcano may be thick and pasty, in which case the cone of the volcano will be steep sided and some of the eruptions may be explosive as gas pressure builds up below the almost solid rock until the volcano finally blows its top. Krakatoa is perhaps the most famous of this type of eruption. In 1883 the noise of Krakatoa exploding could be heard 5000 kilometres (3000 miles) away. On the other hand the lava may be quite runny, in which case it spreads out over a huge area forming no cone at all and cooling to produce a plateau of rock. The volcanoes of Iceland are of this type.

Not all magma flows from a volcano as molten rock, or lava. Expanding gases blow some of it out in the form of ash and lumps of solidified lava called bombs. The pumice that you might have in your bathroom is volcanic rock which has cooled into a rather sponge-like material because of the gas bubbles trapped inside it. Lava, too, can vary in form and have a blocky appearance which is then given the name *aa* or it may be ropy, when its is called *pahoehoe*.

Intrusive rocks may also be found in different forms, depending on the composition of the original magma and the conditions under which it is emplaced. In fact, the shapes of igneous intrusives depend

Volcanic features:
Above: An active volcano off North Island, New Zealand.

Right: Cascades of lava pouring over Alae crater, Hawaii, burning the trees from the forested slopes of the crater.

Below: Pahoehoe lava in Idaho, USA. This lava cools to form a rock with a rope-like surface.

Below right: A basaltic lava field in Iceland. Basalts are generally found in the form of lava flows which may be extensive.

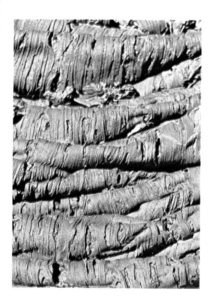

to a large extent upon the relationship of the magma with the rocks into which it has intruded. These rocks are often referred to as the *country rocks* and they can be greatly affected by the heat (and to some extent the pressure) exerted upon them by the intrusion. Perhaps the best known forms in which intrusive rocks appear are *dykes* and *sills*. Dykes occur when the magma has forced its way into the country rock cutting across any bedding planes. Sills, on the other hand, have managed to find the paths of least resistance, by moving along existing bedding planes.

Sedimentary rocks

Igneous rocks are the source from which all other rocks are formed. The process by which igneous rocks come eventually to form *sedimentary rocks* can be observed on a very small scale by examining a very old brick wall or even the stone wall of an ancient cathedral which hasn't been renovated. Looking closely you will probably see that the bricks are beginning to crumble and may even have small plants finding a niche in the tiny amounts of soil that have started to form.

Weathering and erosion
You are actually looking at the process of *weathering and erosion* on a small scale. Acids in the rainwater are eating away at the stone. The sudden expansion and contraction that is caused by the heating and cooling by day and night may cause stone to flake. Water freezing and thawing in crevices can have the same effect. In desert areas, sand grains picked up by the wind wear away at the rocks, acting like the sand-blasting machines that are used today to clean old buildings.

Above : Muldrow Glacier, Alaska. The effects of moving ice on a landscape can be tremendous.

Right : Motueka river, New Zealand, in its mature stage.

Right inset : The wind can only carry eroding agents (e.g. sand) to a low level, so wind eroded rocks can look like this.

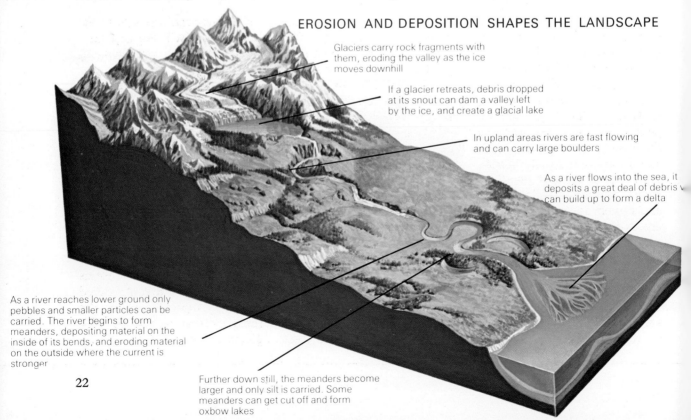

EROSION AND DEPOSITION SHAPES THE LANDSCAPE

Glaciers carry rock fragments with them, eroding the valley as the ice moves downhill

If a glacier retreats, debris dropped at its snout can dam a valley left by the ice, and create a glacial lake

In upland areas rivers are fast flowing and can carry large boulders

As a river flows into the sea, it deposits a great deal of debris [which] can build up to form a delta

As a river reaches lower ground only pebbles and smaller particles can be carried. The river begins to form meanders, depositing material on the inside of its bends, and eroding material on the outside where the current is stronger

Further down still, the meanders become larger and only silt is carried. Some meanders can get cut off and form oxbow lakes

This weathering is the first stage in the formation of sedimentary rocks. Next, the rock debris is carried from its source by the process called erosion. The most common agent of erosion on land is running water, that is, water trickling downwards from where it fell as rain and eventually joining with other trickles to form rivers and streams. In upland areas rivers are fast flowing and are constantly wearing away the rock into deep channels. In these areas the river has enough energy to transport quite large boulders downstream, breaking them and smoothing and rounding them as they are carried. Further downstream where the river flows more slowly, these boulders are dropped and only pebbles are carried and rolled onwards until finally only the smallest particles of silt are carried out to sea.

Frozen water is also an agent of erosion. Glaciers, caused by pressure squeezing surplus ice downhill, can carry sediment with them as well as having a dramatic effect on the shape of the valleys in which they are flowing. It is easy to recognize a glaciated valley. Firstly, the valley will be U-shaped rather than the normal V-shape of a river valley. Also, the valley will have been carved so deeply that the small rivers or tributaries flowing into the main valley will fall as waterfalls from their own *hanging valleys*.

The ways in which glaciers drop the debris they carry vary. Where the glacier has melted at its sides and at its snout, depositing large fragments of rock and finer sediment, the piles of debris are called *moraines*. Fine particles of rock deposited by the ice are called *till*, and consist of clay and sands. When this material is lithified, or hardened, it forms *tillite*. Mounds of till can form hillocks called *drumlins*. Perhaps one of the most interesting features of a glaciated region is the *glacial erratic*. This is the large block of one kind of rock that is broken off and carried far from its source ultimately to rest on a completely different type of bedrock.

The wind can also be a powerful eroding agent, particularly in desert areas, which are defined by the amount of precipitation (snow or rain) that falls rather than their temperature. Where wind-borne sand has worn away at

Above : A sea stack of red sandstone, Devon, England.

Below : A fern fossilized in rock, found in a colliery, Yorkshire, England.

weakly resistant rocks, a kind of elongated cock's comb feature can form – this is called a *yardang*. Larger pebbles are also sometimes affected by the sand blasting so that the side of the pebble facing the wind is worn away and flattened. Because they are relatively small the pebbles may be turned over to face the other way and another side may be affected. In this way, three-sided stones called *dreikanter* may be produced.

The sea is perhaps most important as the place in which the sediments that have been produced by the other agents of weathering and erosion are finally brought to rest. But it is also an agent of erosion in its own right. If you have been to the seaside, you have probably seen many of the features of erosion produced by the sea's waves and tides. For example, the pounding of the sea against a cliff can set up tremendous pressures in the cracks in the rock and eventually erode it away leaving a kind of shelf of rock called a *wave-cut platform*. And arches can be formed by the sea cutting away at weaknesses in the rock. Sometimes whole pillars of rock called *sea stacks* may be left behind as the sea works landwards.

Compressed layers

For the most part, debris created by weathering and erosion is eventually deposited in the sea. Rock fragments are carried into the seas by the rivers and come to rest on the ocean bottom. The sediments are deposited in layers which are evident later as the bedding planes that can be clearly seen

in exposures of sedimentary rocks. These layers are the result of lulls in the rate of sedimentation or are evidence of changes in the type of material that has been laid down.

As the sediments are buried beneath thicker and thicker layers of overlying material, changes take place which eventually result in the formation of a sedimentary rock. The actual processes are complicated but basically the sediment is compacted as the pressure increases and the individual grains become cemented together.

Material that has travelled the least distance usually goes to make up *conglomerates* (that is pebbles which become cemented together), which are really old beach and river-bed deposits. Material which has had the longest journey produces clay. Sand becomes, quite naturally, sandstone. Sometimes the original ripple marks of waves on the sand are preserved in the rock. Shale, sometimes called mudstone, is mainly clay that has hardened into rock, and it splits very easily. Clay itself is really sediment which has not become solid.

There is another important type of sedimentary rock, that forms from the remains of tiny sea creatures. Many of the animals that live in the sea, particularly the myriad microscopic ones, have shells or skeletons containing calcium carbonate which sink to the ocean floor on the death of the creature. Countless millions of these tiny objects eventually build up to form the *oozes* which are found in the deep seas. Eventually they can be compressed into rock. In some cases calcium carbonate and other salts go into solution only to be precipitated out later forming rocks. Calcium carbonate sediments give us chalk and other limestones.

Other sedimentary deposits are very important to man, for example coal. Coal is the compressed remains of plant life and often the remains of plants can be seen in pieces of coal.

The coal found in the British Isles dates back about 300 million years ago. Oil, found in 'traps' beneath the surface of our planet, has formed from the remains of vast numbers of microscopic animals.

TIDES AND WAVES

On most shores you will notice that the sea level changes throughout the day. These ups and downs of the seas are called tides.

Why should tides occur? Everything on the Earth's surface is attracted towards the Earth by a force called *gravity*. The Moon and the Sun also have a gravitational pull of their own. As the Moon passes around the Earth it attracts the waters of the oceans on the side facing it, pulling them away from the Earth, and causing them to bulge. On the opposite side from this 'tidal bulge', there is another one because on that side, the land is nearer the Moon than the waters, and the land is pulled away from the seas, leaving a bulge behind. These two bulges remain in the same position in relation to the Moon, but the rotation of the Earth means that each of them appears to move around the Earth. As a result, a tidal bulge passes the same place on Earth about every 12 hours. These bulges are called high water, and the gaps between them are called low water.

There are two other factors which help in the formation of the tides. You know that if you cause the water in your bath to rock, it may rise and fall against the side of the bath for some time. In the same way, once the tides have begun, the waters tend to continue to rock up and down and they are given an extra push by the attraction of the Moon. The Sun also tends to attract the Earth's oceans towards itself, but because it is so much further away the attraction is less important. At certain times of the year, however, the Sun, the Moon, and the Earth are all in a straight line. When this happens, the attraction of the Sun is added to the attraction of the Moon and tides are extra high.

Waves are almost wholly the result of wind blowing across the surface of the water. The wind drags the water to form waves which move slowly forward, and get larger. Although the wave shape moves forward, each particle of water moves round in circles and does not change its average position. The height of a wave depends on three factors: how hard the wind is blowing, how long the wind has been blowing, and the *fetch*. The word fetch means the length of the stretch of open water over which the wind is blowing.

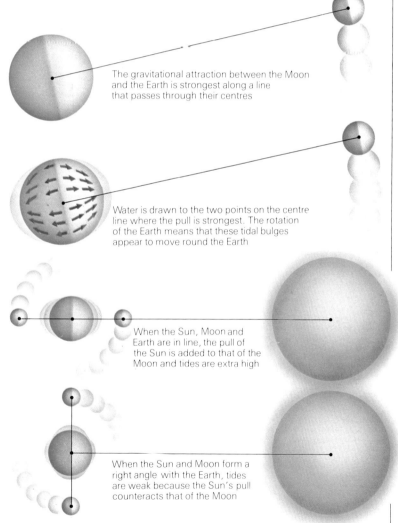

The gravitational attraction between the Moon and the Earth is strongest along a line that passes through their centres

Water is drawn to the two points on the centre line where the pull is strongest. The rotation of the Earth means that these tidal bulges appear to move round the Earth

When the Sun, Moon and Earth are in line, the pull of the Sun is added to that of the Moon and tides are extra high

When the Sun and Moon form a right angle with the Earth, tides are weak because the Sun's pull counteracts that of the Moon

Metamorphic rocks

The third major group of rocks are the *metamorphic* rocks. These are called metamorphic because the prefix 'meta' indicates change and this is exactly what metamorphic rocks are – changed. They are derived from existing rocks within the Earth's crust by heat, pressure and chemically active fluids.

There are two main groups of metamorphic rocks and to understand these two types you should remember that any rocks, whether they are sediments, igneous rocks, or other metamorphics, will respond to any environment which is markedly different from that in which they were formed.

Contact metamorphism

When it is first pushed up through the crust any igneous intrusion is very hot and the bigger the body of rock, the more heat there is. This heat causes the existing rocks around the intrusion to *recrystallize*. The more heat there is and the more hot fluids there are associated with the intrusion, the thicker is the band of rocks round the intrusion that changes. The band of metamorphosed rocks is known as the *metamorphic aureole* and this type of metamorphism is called *contact metamorphism*. The Dartmoor granite mentioned earlier has quite a wide metamorphic aureole.

Regional metamorphism

Sometimes large areas of the Earth's crust undergo a major period of heaving and movement. These movements may subject the rocks to tremendous pressures which, even at quite low temperatures, would be enough to cause many rocks to change their crystallography. But, in addition to the pressure, Earth movements often release a good deal of heat from greater depths. The rocks then are subjected to great heat and pressure and change to a form which is more stable in these extreme conditions. This type of metamorphism is called *regional metamorphism* and is often characterized by rocks that have a *platy* or *foliated* texture. A slate (the same kind that was commonly used to roof houses) is a good example of a regionally metamorphosed rock although perhaps a more dramatic example is called a *schist* where the laminations glisten with flat crystals of the mineral called mica.

Above : A marble quarry in Italy. Marble is metamorphosed limestone.

Below : A typical metamorphic rock – a schist from N.W. Scotland.

ROCK FORMATION AND CHANGE

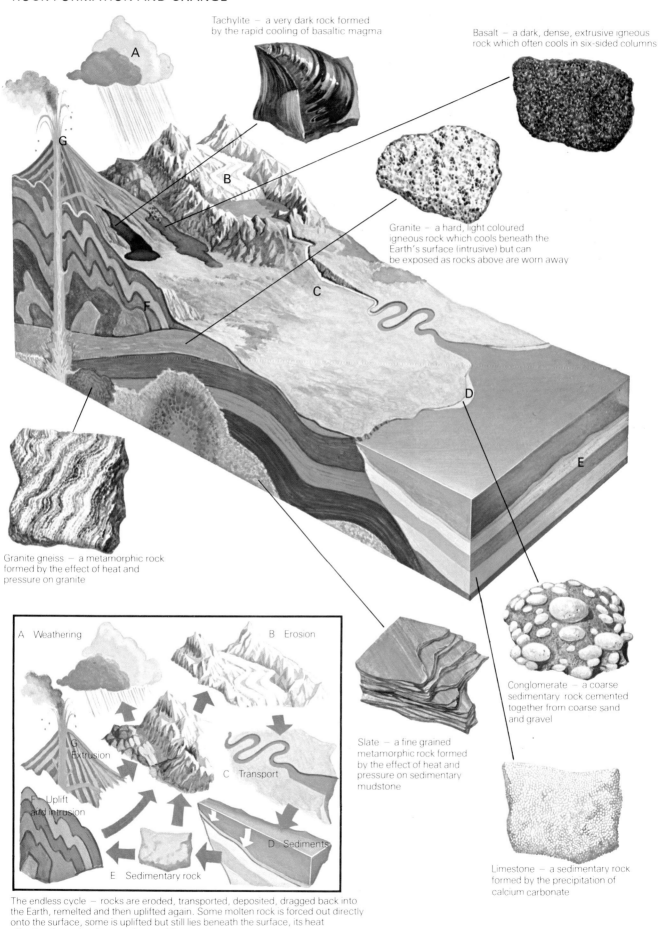

Tachylite – a very dark rock formed by the rapid cooling of basaltic magma

Basalt – a dark, dense, extrusive igneous rock which often cools in six-sided columns

Granite – a hard, light coloured igneous rock which cools beneath the Earth's surface (intrusive) but can be exposed as rocks above are worn away

Granite gneiss – a metamorphic rock formed by the effect of heat and pressure on granite

A Weathering
B Erosion
G Extrusion
C Transport
F Uplift and intrusion
D Sediments
E Sedimentary rock

Slate – a fine grained metamorphic rock formed by the effect of heat and pressure on sedimentary mudstone

Conglomerate – a coarse sedimentary rock cemented together from coarse sand and gravel

Limestone – a sedimentary rock formed by the precipitation of calcium carbonate

The endless cycle – rocks are eroded, transported, deposited, dragged back into the Earth, remelted and then uplifted again. Some molten rock is forced out directly onto the surface, some is uplifted but still lies beneath the surface, its heat affecting the rocks above and around it.

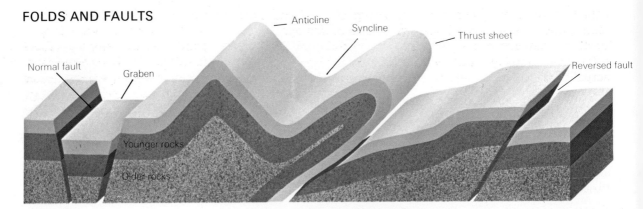

Normal fault — Graben — Anticline — Syncline — Thrust sheet — Reversed fault

Younger rocks

Older rocks

Rocks on the move

Rocks can bend or even break. The Earth's crust is soft compared with the powerful forces locked within it. These forces are able to bend and break solid rocks into extraordinary shapes, often by compression. Hold a piece of paper in your two hands and then push your hands together. The piece of paper will form into one or more folds – this is more or less what can happen to rocks.

Different sorts of folds in rocks are given different names to describe them. A ridge-shaped fold is called an *antiform* and if the rocks that were laid down first are still in the same relative position, that is, if the oldest rocks are in the centre of the fold, it is called an *anticline*. A trough-shaped fold is called a *synform* and if it has the youngest rocks in the centre of the fold it is called a *syncline*. If the rocks have been folded so much that the synclines and anticlines are almost piled on top of one another, the folds are referred to as *recumbent* folds. During periods of intense crustal movement called *orogenies*, beds of rock can be transported

Folded rocks at Lulworth Cove, Dorset, England.

great distances by folding, in huge structures called *nappes*. These nappes may be seen today as mountain ranges such as the Alps. The Alps were formed when Italy ploughed into the underside of Europe. If the rock layers of the Alps were to be flattened out, Italy would be another 100 kilometres (60 miles) to the south.

Sometimes the rocks are unable to take up the Earth movements by folding and the rocks break. Like folds, these *faults* are given different names to describe them. Usually the plane along which the rocks have broken is at an angle to the beds. If the plane slopes towards the down-faulted block of rock, the fault is described as *normal* but if it slopes towards the upfaulted block, it is a *reversed* fault. Normal faults are thought to result from tension, and reversed faults from compression. When a chunk of rock is bounded by two faults and is faulted downwards it is called a *graben* and if a similar chunk is moved upwards it is called a *horst*.

All this folding and faulting of the Earth's crustal rocks

usually takes place over very long periods but sometimes Earth movements occur comparatively quickly and we actually notice their effects. We notice these effects as *earthquakes*. Earthquakes are the shockwaves that spread out in all directions from the source when rocks are suddenly and violently disturbed. Sometimes earthquakes can be of a catastrophic level and cause a great deal of damage.

One of the most destructive features associated with earthquakes are the huge ocean waves that are sometimes caused. These are often incorrectly called tidal waves whereas they should properly be known as *tsunamis*. Submarine earthquakes and volcanoes, send out ripples across the sea similar to the ripples created by throwing a stone into a pond. These ripples travel fairly harmlessly across oceans, but on entering shallow water they pile up and create huge waves which crash onto the shore. The tsunamis caused after the eruption of Krakatoa in 1883 drowned over 30 000 people and threw ocean-going vessels up onto the land.

THE SAN ANDREAS FAULT

In the year 1906 the Californian city of San Francisco was shaken and wrecked by an earthquake. The earthquake was the result of movement along the San Andreas fault which runs for almost 1300 kilometres (800 miles) along the west coast of America. It seemed as though the whole floor of the Pacific Ocean was shifted northwards by a distance of about 6 metres (20 feet). This apparently small lateral movement of rock was enough to kill as many as 500 people and cause $500 000 worth of damage. A great deal of the damage was, however, caused not by the earthquake itself, but by the fires that raged as gas mains were severed. Indeed, you will find that some history books still refer to the disaster as the Great Fire of San Francisco. But this is partly because the authorities were unwilling to admit that building a city along a fault line is a dangerous thing to do.

It is very likely that the San Andreas fault may move again. And the longer it remains without moving the more severe may be the earthquake when it does. It has even been suggested that it would be a good idea to try to make the fault move to relieve the tension that is surely building up. The American army has been experimenting with pumping huge volumes of water into fault zones to see if water will act as a lubricant to enable the fault movement to be controlled.

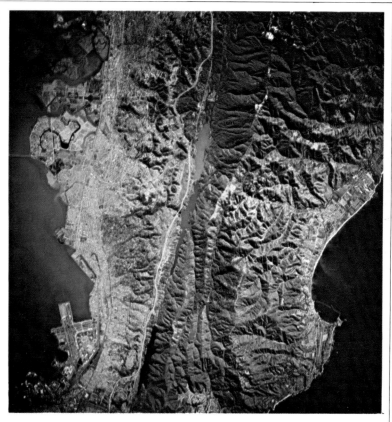

Above: An aerial view of the San Andreas fault area near Palo Alto, California.

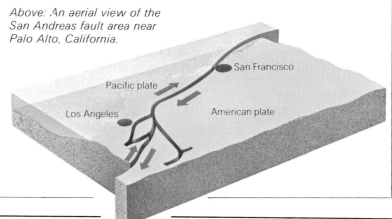

200 million years ago   100 million years ago   50 million years ago

Continental drift

Have you ever noticed, when looking at a map of the world, that the east coast of South America and the west coast of Africa look as though they might fit together, rather like two pieces of a giant jigsaw puzzle? If you have you are not alone. In 1965 the English scientist Sir Edward Bullard used a computer to test the fit of the two continents and found that at an ocean depth of 2000 metres (6000 feet) the match was very close indeed.

It seems too remarkable to be possible, but there is a lot of evidence to suggest that Africa was once joined to South America. For example, there is a belt of ancient rocks along the east coast of Brazil which corresponds with the rocks across the South Atlantic in West Africa.

There is further evidence that existing land masses were once linked. The remnant of a 400 to 500 million year old mountain chain has been found running down the eastern part of Greenland, western Scandinavia, and through north-west Scotland and Ireland, into western Canada, eventually finding its way to north-west Africa.

Then there is the evidence from life itself. In various parts of the world today the same animals and plants can be found on land masses separated by, in some cases, thousands of miles of oceans. Did they evolve at the same time in two different places? It seems unlikely. Biologists believe that there must have been land bridges which have now sunk beneath the sea. Also fossils found in sedimentary rocks (fossils are the preserved remains of life forms) have allowed geologists to trace the same plants from South America, to Africa, India, Australia, and Antarctica in rocks perhaps 300 million years old.

The ice that is now confined to the polar regions has not

THE MOVEMENT OF CRUSTAL PLATES

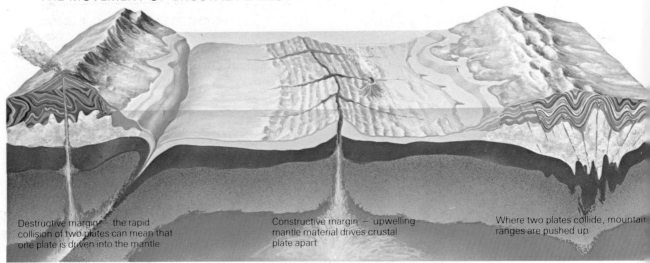

Destructive margin — the rapid collision of two plates can mean that one plate is driven into the mantle

Constructive margin — upwelling mantle material drives crustal plate apart

Where two plates collide, mountain ranges are pushed up

always been so limited in extent. Indeed, during a period of the Earth's history known as the Permocarboniferous age (about 250–350 million years ago) there is evidence from the rocks that there were glaciers covering South America, parts of Africa, India, Australia, as well as Antarctica. On the other hand, in the northern hemisphere, there were deserts. If the continents were distributed as they are today, it is hard to understand how this could be.

So there is considerable evidence to show whole continents moved apart, and naturally many people have tried to discover how and why whole land masses moved.

The theory of plates

Running down the centre of the Atlantic Ocean is a ridge along which volcanic action is common. Scientists have noticed that if the ages of the rocks on either side of the ridge are measured, then they become older as we move away from the ridge. They are fairly sure what this means. The mid-Atlantic Ridge represents the boundary between two huge blocks of crustal material. At this boundary new crust is being created by volcanic material welling up from below and spreading outwards. This process is known as *sea-floor spreading* and the boundary is called a *constructive margin*. But unless the Earth is getting bigger, which it doesn't seem to be, this new crust must go somewhere. Clearly, the Americas and western Europe are slowly being forced apart.

Having established the relevance of faults in the Earth's crust to land movements it is clearly worth looking at the distribution of such faults. The majority of earthquakes and volcanoes occur within two well-defined zones: the first circling the Pacific Ocean and known as the *circum-Pacific ring of fire*, and the second along a belt through the Mediterranean and across Asia. The circum-Pacific ring of fire represents a *destructive margin* where one block or plate of crustal material is actually being

The island of Surtsey 'appeared' off Iceland in the 1960s, formed from material thrown up from below the Earth's crust. Surtsey is located on the mid-Atlantic ridge where two plates appear to be moving apart, allowing molten rock to well up from below.

forced beneath another. It is this movement which results in the earthquakes and volcanic activity that is so destructive in these areas.

From all this information the comparatively new and very exciting theory of *plate tectonics* has been evolved. This theory suggests that the crust and upper mantle of the Earth is broken into a series of plates which move in relation to one another, carrying the continents with them. So far this theory has been able to explain very well most of the things that we know about the behaviour of our planet.

The theory of plate tectonics explains that it is along the plate margins that most of the world's mountain chains are built. In the case of the world's highest mountains the Himalayas, for example, it is believed that they were formed

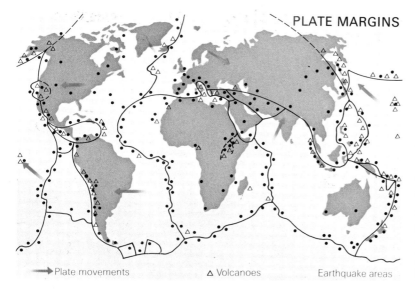

PLATE MARGINS

→ Plate movements   △ Volcanoes   Earthquake areas

Above : Scientists wearing protective clothing carefully explore a volcano — Mount Etna, Italy.

Left : Large waves caused by seismic shock can do a lot of damage.

Below left : Drilling into the Earth's crust for core samples.

Below : Examining core samples in the laboratory.

Opposite above : A seismograph recording data about earthquakes.

Opposite below : Part of a seismogram showing an earthquake in Arkansas, USA.

by the plate which includes the Indian sub-continent drifting towards the main mass of Asia, eventually crashing into it, and throwing up the mountains as the crust crumpled. Continents are still drifting at a rate which, although slow, is measurable in terms of centimetres per year. It is interesting to think that at the present time the Mediterranean Sea is getting smaller while the Red Sea is increasing in size as Africa is swinging around. The Earth is not static – it is constantly changing its face.

Geology and man

Geologists are not only concerned with evolving theories to explain the Earth as a whole and its workings. We depend upon the efforts of these scientists for many of the things that we take for granted today. Have you ever stopped to think why huge buildings or the giant dams and bridges that we are all familiar with very rarely fall down? They would do if their foundations were built into rock that was too weak to support them. Nowadays, before these massive constructions are erected, a careful survey is made of the proposed site by an *engineering geologist* to ensure that it is suitable. In the

past this did not always happen and there were terrible disasters. It is often important to carry out these surveys more than once, for example in winter and in summer, because material such as clay which could seem perfectly sound in dry weather might become soft when wet.

We hear a great deal today about our energy supplies and the possibility of them running out. Admittedly the geologist would not be concerned with the new ideas of generating energy by solar, wind or wave power, but he or she is vital in the search for the more traditional fuels such as coal, oil, or the minerals necessary to produce nuclear power. Most of the large oil companies, coal boards and so on will employ more than one geologist to help them find new

sources of these materials.

In the past geologists would rely on their experience to help them find the raw materials they were looking for but now they have many sophisticated techniques to help them such as the chemical analysis of streams and soils or even the passing of electric currents through rocks. This provides information because rocks vary in their electrical resistance.

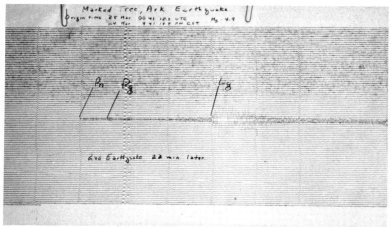

Man and his evolution

When the Earth first formed it must have been far too hot to support any life. Not until it began to cool and form a hard crust could life begin to appear. It is now generally believed that it was about 3500 million years ago that the first simple life forms appeared in the ancient seas. What evidence we have about primitive life forms comes from fossils (the remains of animals or plants embedded in rock), but we can learn very little about the beginning of life on Earth because the first creatures were too small and fragile to have been preserved in the rocks. Exactly how human life as we know it eventually evolved from primitive forms is still something about which we

have much to discover.

One great advance in our understanding came with the publication in 1859 of a book called *On the Origin of Species by Natural Selection*. Its author, the English naturalist Charles Darwin, brought to public attention a theory known as the *theory of evolution*. This theory suggested that all the animals and plants with which we are familiar had their origins in earlier and more primitive life forms and arose as a result of *natural selection*. In other words, those individual plants and animals that for some reason were better suited to their environment survived, to produce offspring with the same characteristics, so that gradually life forms became better adapted to their surroundings. Sometimes a mutation might occur and if this mutation was particularly well suited to the

conditions in which it had to live, a new species might arise.

For a long time, this theory caused outrage among traditional Christians, particularly when it was suggested that people had evolved from the apes. In fact, nowadays it is not generally believed that human beings came directly from apes but rather that modern apes and man had a common ancestor. It is generally agreed that our nearest living relative is the chimpanzee.

Apes and man are, of course, animals. They have backbones so they are *vertebrates*, and as the mothers suckle their young they are known as *mammals*. Further, man, monkeys, apes and animals called lemurs and lorises, are all grouped together and called *primates*. The first primates, small, primitive, lemur-like animals, seem to have been very wide-

Charles Darwin's theory that man and chimpanzees have a common ancestor, met with much disapproval

and anger when first brought to public attention and Darwin's ideas were ridiculed by many people.

THE EVOLUTION OF MAN

Australopithecus robustus (3½-1½ million years ago)

Australopithecus africanus (3½-1½ million years ago)

Ramapithecus (14 million years ago)

Homo habilis (Over 2 million years ago)

Homo erectus (1½ million years ago)

Homo sapiens (100 000 years ago)

spread, their remains being found in rocks some 70 million years old from most parts of the world. From these early primates arose all the species that we know today, from the most primitive tree shrews to modern man, although we cannot trace a direct line from the tree shrew to the first known form of man. There have been various branches along the path of evolution, some of which have been successful and others not.

There is fossil evidence of various man-like apes followed by ape-like men which have come and gone with time. As more and more evidence comes to light, man's ancestry seems to recede further and further into the distant past so that it is perhaps three million years since the first man-like apes appeared.

The first human-like creature seems to have lived about two million years ago and is usually given the name *Homo habilis*. This species certainly used tools and probably walked upright, although not in such an efficient way as modern man. There is a great deal of scientific controversy associated with all the discoveries of fossil men and some authorities argue that *Homo habilis* is simply a regional variation of *Australopithecus africanus*, a species which seems to have lived in southern Africa about three million years ago. They were hairy and ape-like but they ate meat and probably used primitive tools and lived in caves.

In the past when primitive men walked the Earth, the places they chose to live

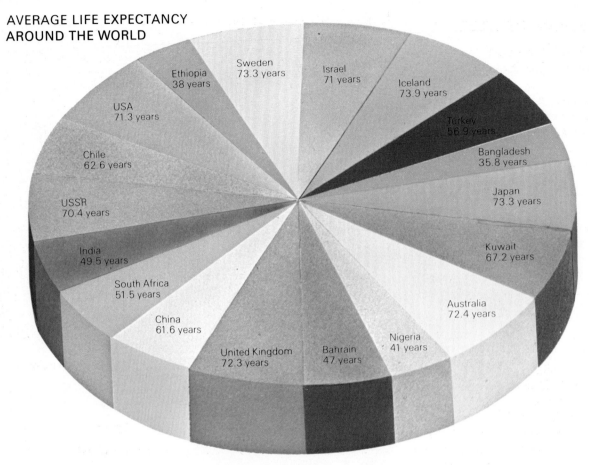

Sweden 73.3 years
Ethiopia 38 years
USA 71.3 years
Chile 62.6 years
USSR 70.4 years
India 49.5 years
South Africa 51.5 years
China 61.6 years
United Kingdom 72.3 years
Bahrain 47 years
Nigeria 41 years
Australia 72.4 years
Kuwait 67.2 years
Japan 73.3 years
Bangladesh 35.8 years
Turkey 56.9 years
Iceland 73.9 years
Israel 71 years

depended entirely on their basic needs for such things as shelter, food, clothing and defence. So these people chose areas where they could find food, (and later, as farming developed, where they could grow crops), where there were materials to build shelters, where the climate was mild, and where there were sites which could be defended against enemies. In this way the early pattern of settlement was established.

Today, modern man does not need to take into account all these considerations. We still live in towns and cities which were founded because of their position close to good farming land, or their position on a navigable river, but we do not have to choose such sites for new towns. Our modern communications and transport systems have changed our dependence on our immediate surroundings.

Human beings today

Human beings have been very successful animals in terms of numbers. In 1970 it was estimated that the total population of the world was about 3660 million, or four times the number of people living less than 200 years earlier in 1800. By now the population of the world has grown to more than 4000 million and it has been estimated by *demographers* (people who study population growth) that by the year 2000 there could be more than 6000 million human beings for the planet Earth and its resources to support. It is, however, very difficult to predict how the population will change in years to come because it is influenced by so many things. For example, a world war temporarily reduces population but then there is evidence that afterwards the growth actually accelerates. In some parts of the world, infant deaths were once very common. With the coming of modern medicine, more babies survive and if people continue to have large numbers of children the population will grow at an alarming rate. On the other hand, in places like the United Kingdom, it seems that the birth rate is falling.

Races of man

Certain distinct 'types' of people can be recognized in various parts of the world. These types of people are generally referred to as *races* although the word race can be a confusing one because it is used in different ways by different people. For example, we often speak of the human race although, in fact, we constitute a *species*. In biology, a race is roughly equivalent to a subspecies or a geographical variation of the species, and members of one race would be able to breed with members of another race and produce fertile young. Referring to man, however, the term race has a slightly different meaning. It is used to suggest that individuals of a given race probably had common ancestors and are also broadly similar in such features as skin colour, build, and shapes of head and face. We should remember, though, that any races that we might recognize have been determined by interbreeding of various groups and now probably only represent extremes of a broad spectrum of different people, one group grading gradually into the next. Accepting these reservations, we can recognize three main divisions.

There are the *caucasians* who have pale skin, are medium to tall in height, have blond or brown wavy to straight hair, and have narrow to medium-broad faces. Then there are the *mongoloid* peoples; they have yellowish skins, are relatively short, have black, straight hair, and broad faces. The third main division is the *negroid* race with brown or black skin, great variations in height, dark, curly hair, and broad to narrow faces.

In many parts of the world today, it is possible to see all three types, but originally caucasians would be found in Europe, western Asia and North Africa, mongoloids in eastern Asia and the Americas, and negroids in most of Africa. In fact, this distribution of people would have been roughly correct until the 15th century when Christopher Columbus and others began the great age of discovery.

Since the 15th century when new lands were revealed to European explorers, there have been great movements of mankind in search of new trading routes and new homes. As groups of people have moved from place to place there has been inter-breeding and a mixing of the races.

Different racial groups have different physical characteristics:

Above : Mongoloid

Below left : Negroid

Below right : Caucasoid

The world today

The land masses of the world are usually divided into seven continents: Europe, North America, South America, Africa, Asia, Australasia, and Antarctica. In earlier times when communications between different parts of the world were much more difficult than they are today, peoples and countries tended to be completely divided from one another by physical barriers such as seas, mountain ranges, rivers and deserts. Today, these geographical barriers mean little for the modern traveller, who can be jetted across the skies of the world in a matter of hours, and for many people, trade and communication with those on opposite sides of the globe are a rapid and essential part of everyday life.

The barriers of the modern world are much more complex, and are based to a large extent on the political divisions and unities that exist between countries.

Political systems

Many people regard the world today as divided up into four (sometimes three) great units in terms of racial similarities, political ideologies, and economic status. These units are referred to as the first, second, third and fourth worlds. The first two worlds are also sometimes referred to respectively as the Western and Eastern blocs and these two groupings represent the main centres of military might and trading power. Among the Western bloc countries are the USA, Australia, Britain, and those of Western Europe, whereas the Eastern bloc includes the USSR, and its satellite countries.

It is probably useful to think of the countries outside the Western and Eastern blocs as comprising a third *and* a fourth world; the third world being the remaining rich (and therefore powerful) states of the Middle East, peopled mainly by the Arab nations,

A world map showing the seven continents. In order of size they are: Asia, Africa, North America, South America, Antarctica, Europe and Australasia.

and the fourth world being all the developing countries, many of which are to be found in parts of Asia, Africa and Latin America.

The Western system of politics and government is often referred to as *capitalism* although the individual governmental systems vary considerably from state to state. The Eastern bloc countries on the other hand, dominated by the Soviet Union, are usually thought of as *socialist* or *communist* states. In general terms, in a capitalist society a person works for money with which he is able to purchase and own privately whatever goods he wants and can afford. In a socialist country work is done for the well-being of the state and all goods are owned communally.

The difference in political beliefs between the Western and the Eastern bloc countries has created the term 'Iron Curtain'. This is certainly not a real curtain made of iron, but it does, in effect, divide one side from another like a curtain, and along much of its length it is defended by the military equipment of the respective armed forces. The Iron Curtain is more significant than most national borders. Along the Western border there is West Germany, Austria and Italy, and along the Eastern border, East Germany, Czechoslovakia, Hungary and Yugoslavia. But these countries are only those that are physically in contact along the border. More important is the fact that the Iron Curtain represents the two separate ways of political thinking of the East and West.

Below : The May Day parade in Moscow celebrates Russian economic, technical and military achievements.

Bottom right : The Houses of Parliament in London. The British parliament is sometimes referred to as the 'Mother of Parliaments', because other countries have based their constitutions on the British model.

Right : A section of the Berlin Wall, which divides East and West Berlin. The concrete and barbed wire wall was erected in 1961 and is patrolled by armed guards along its length.

Centre right : American election campaigns are lively, but expensive. Candidates can spend a great deal of time and money on getting their message across to the electorate.

Arctic Ocean

Reykjavik
ICELAND

Arctic Circle

Faeroe Is.

Atlantic Ocean

Shetland Is

Orkney Is.

NORWAY

FINLAND

Oslo

Helsinki

SCOTLAND

Edinburgh

North Sea

Stockholm

SWEDEN

Nth.
IRELAND
Belfast

Dublin

IRELAND
(EIRE)

DENMARK

Baltic Sea

Copenhagen

U S

WALES

ENGLAND

Amsterdam

Elbe

Hague

London

NETHERLANDS

Berlin

Vistula

Warsaw

POLAND

Brussels

Rhine

BELGIUM

Bonn

GERMANY
(EAST)

LUXEMBOURG

Paris

Loire

GERMANY
(WEST)

Prague

CZECHOSLOVAKIA

C A R P A T H I A N   M T S.

Dniester

FRANCE

Vienna

Bern

SWITZERLAND

AUSTRIA

Budapest

HUNGARY

Bay of Biscay

Rhone

ROMANIA

PYRENEES

Po

A P E N N I N E

Belgrade

Bucharest

Danube

PORTUGAL

Ebro

ITALY

M T S.

Adriatic Sea

YUGOSLAVIA

BULGARIA

Lisbon

Madrid

Corsica

Rome

Sofia

Guadiana

Tirana

ALBANIA

Aegean Sea

S P A I N

Sardinia

GREECE

Gibraltar

Sicily

Athens

Crete

Mediterranean Sea

0   750 km
0   500 miles

Europe

Europe is bounded by the Atlantic ocean to the west, the Arctic ocean to the north and the Mediterranean sea to the south. The total land area is 10 354 588 square kilometres (3 997 929 square miles). Many geographers consider Europe to be part of Asia, to which it is connected in the east. The major land areas of Europe are the central plains, stretching from the mid west to the Urals in the east, the northern mountains of Finland and Scandinavia and the southern mountains, which include the Alps, Caucasus and Pyrenees. Mont Blanc, at 4807 metres (15 781 feet) is Europe's highest mountain. Most of Europe was once covered by forest, but land clearance for farming has meant that only the cooler north of the continent still retains any significant areas of natural forest. Northernmost Europe has very cold winters, often with heavy snow falls, and cool summers. Central Europe has warm summers and cool winters, and southern Europe has hot summers with mild winters.

Most of Europe lies in a temperate zone and that, together with the fertile soils, mean that crops and livestock rearing are possible almost everywhere. Europe is also blessed with huge quantities of raw materials such as coal and iron ore. The fast expansion of industrialization – the Industrial Revolution of the 18th century – added still further to Europe's already considerable military and trading power at that time. At the

beginning of the 20th century it was still the most powerful continent in the world.

A long history, much of it spent at war with neighbours and with other continents, has resulted in the small continent of Europe being divided into many countries. Throughout history, its influence has been immense, and from Europe the spread of western civilization has reached all parts of the world.

Two world wars – 1914 to

Above : Duisberg, Germany. Industry and agriculture live side by side.

Below : Rome, capital of Italy, from St. Peter's.

1918 and 1939 to 1945 – resulted in new divisions and alliances. The most important of these was the political formation of Western and Eastern Europe, the former allied strongly to the USA and the latter to the USSR.

Since the last world war, strong trading powers such as Japan and the USA have made it more and more difficult for many of the countries of Europe to compete alone in world markets. To try and overcome this, many countries have joined together in trading alliances, the most important being the European Economic Community (EEC). This is a union between Great Britain, Eire, France, the Netherlands, West Germany, Italy, Belgium, Luxembourg, Denmark and Greece. Many other nations are also associate members of the EEC.

In addition to these trade links, the build up of military power in the USSR and the Eastern bloc countries has resulted in the joining together of the military forces of the Western powers to form the North Atlantic Treaty Organization (NATO).

Below : Rotterdam in the Netherlands has the world's largest artificial harbour and (under the name Europoort) is a leading container port with access to the North Sea.

Above : Steel works in Wales. The United Kingdom is the fifth largest steel producing country in the world. This important British industry is challenged by foreign competition.

Countries of Europe

If *politically*, Europe is divided into two zones, *geographically*, we can divide Europe into four distinctive zones. Northern Europe consists of Norway, Sweden, Denmark (together called Scandinavia) and Finland. Sometimes Iceland is also included as part of Scandinavia. Western Europe is made up of France, Belgium, the

Netherlands, Luxembourg, Switzerland, Austria and Germany. The British Isles – the largest island group in Europe – is usually considered to be part of western Europe. Eastern Europe comprises Poland, Czechoslovakia, Hungary, Romania, Bulgaria and Yugoslavia. Southern Europe consists of Portugal, Spain, Monaco, Italy, Albania, Greece and Malta.

Generally speaking, the countries of northern and southern Europe have a form of government similar to those of the western European countries.

Economy and produce

Despite the growth in the trading power of Japan and the United States of America, Europe still dominates the world in the output of manufactured products, which range from textiles to heavy engineering goods.

Europe has had plenty of time in which to develop its skills as the centre of manufacturing. Coal, and metals such as iron, were mined from very early times. Well over one third of the world's coal production still comes from Europe, with extensive fields being found on the southern edge of the central plain. In addition to coal, there are large deposits of iron ore, lead, zinc, bauxite and mercury. Recently, large deposits of natural gas and oil have been discovered in the North Sea.

For countries such as Great Britain, in whose territorial waters these discoveries have been made, they will be of great help in reducing the cost of importing energy sources from other countries.

Despite this great industrial power, Europe is still a highly developed farming continent. In fact, it has the most highly efficient and intensive agricultural methods in the world. Farming is particularly important in the central and southern parts of Europe where such crops as wheat, rye, oats, barley and potatoes are grown. Cattle are grazed on the lush green pastures, and from cattle come beef and dairy products.

Europe was once heavily forested, although most of the land has now been cleared for agricultural use. Finland, Sweden and Norway all export significant amounts of forest products. Northern Europe produces quantities of dairy products, as well as huge amounts of timber.

The southern countries are particularly important for citrus fruits, and for many, especially those bordering the Mediterranean, tourism is also an important industry.

Left above: Vineyards in France. Wine is an important industry in much of Europe, the main producers being France, Italy and Spain. Portugal, Algeria and West Germany also export wine.

Left below: Prague, capital of Czechoslovakia, is situated on the River Vltava (a tributary of the Elbe).

Left: Britain's ship-building industry has declined in recent years, in the face of competition from new, modernized yards in West Germany, Sweden and Japan.

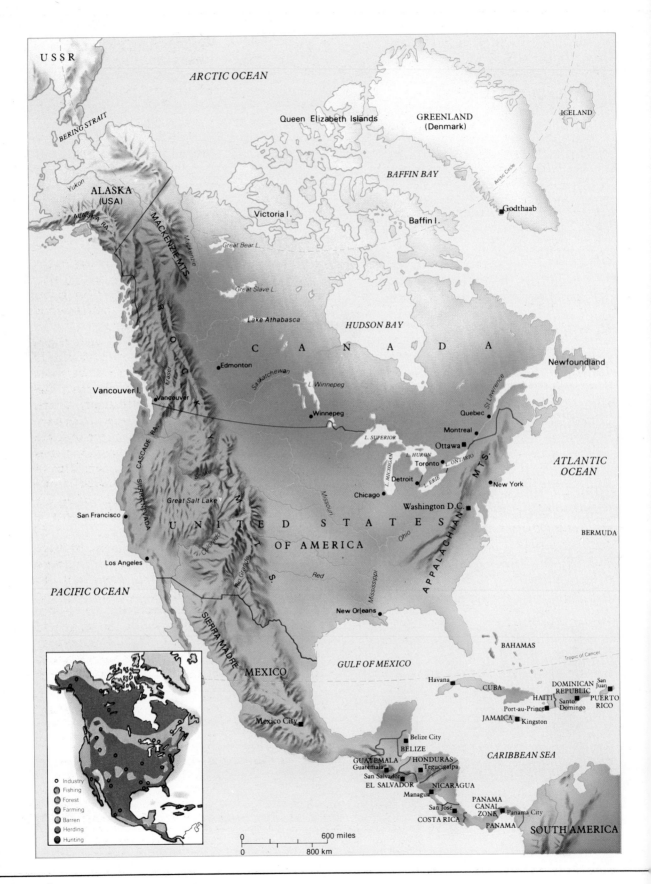

USSR

ARCTIC OCEAN

BERING STRAIT

GREENLAND
(Denmark)

ICELAND

Queen Elizabeth Islands

BAFFIN BAY

ALASKA
(USA)

Yukon

ALASKA RA.

MACKENZIE MTS.

Mackenzie

Victoria I.

Baffin I.

Arctic Circle

■Godthaab

Great Bear L.

Great Slave L.

R   O   C   K   Y

Lake Athabasca

HUDSON BAY

C   A   N   A   D   A

Newfoundland

•Edmonton

Saskatchewan

L. Winnepeg

Vancouver I.

•Vancouver

•Winnepeg

St. Lawrence

Quebec•

Montreal•

L. SUPERIOR

Ottawa■

CASCADE RA.

L. MICHIGAN

L. HURON

Toronto•

L. ONTARIO

ATLANTIC
OCEAN

SIERRA NEVADA

Snake

Detroit•

L. ERIE

APPALACHIAN MTS.

■New York

San Francisco•

Great Salt Lake

Chicago•

Washington D.C.■

M

Missouri

U   N   I   T   E   D   S   T   A   T   E   S

BERMUDA

Colorado

OF AMERICA

Ohio

Los Angeles•

T

Red

S.

Mississippi

Red Grande

PACIFIC OCEAN

SIERRA MADRE

New Orleans■

BAHAMAS

Tropic of Cancer

MEXICO

GULF OF MEXICO

Havana■

CUBA

DOMINICAN
REPUBLIC

San
Juan

HAITI■

Port-au-Prince■

Santo
Domingo

PUERTO
RICO

JAMAICA

Kingston•

Mexico City•

Belize City

BELIZE

CARIBBEAN SEA

GUATEMALA

Guatemala•

San Salvador•

HONDURAS

Tegucigalpa•

EL SALVADOR

NICARAGUA

Managua■

PANAMA
CANAL
ZONE

San José•

■Panama City

COSTA RICA

PANAMA

SOUTH AMERICA

Inset map legend:
- ○ Industry
- ● Fishing
- ● Forest
- ● Farming
- ● Barren
- ● Herding
- ● Hunting

0   600 miles

0   800 km

Left : Chicago – the third-largest American city is situated near the southern end of Lake Michigan.

North America

North America is the third largest continent, covering some 24 248 400 square kilometres (9 362 400 square miles). It extends from the Arctic Circle to the Tropic of Cancer. In the south the narrow land chain of Central America links North and South America. In the north the frozen waters of the Arctic Ocean contain a great many islands. The most important of these is Greenland (an overseas territory of Denmark), which is the world's largest island. In the extreme north-west only 90 kilometres (56 miles) of sea (the Bering Strait) separates North America from Asia.

A great mountain chain dominates the western side of North America, the largest part of this being the Rocky Mountains range, which runs from Alaska into northern Mexico. Two large countries occupy most of North America: the United States of America and Canada. The USA is slightly smaller than Canada but has a much larger population.

The United States of America

There are more than 210 million people living in the USA, but it is such a big country that there are only about 22 people for every square kilometre (a little over a third of a square mile) of land, compared with 241 in the United Kingdom or 319 in Holland. These people come from a very wide range of races and backgrounds.

The American Indians (or Red Indians) were the first settlers; their ancestors arrived from Asia about 20 000 years ago. When Europeans arrived, the Red Indians were driven from their lands. Many of the tribes still survive but in very reduced numbers, having lost a good deal of their original identity and culture.

European settlement began on the east coast of America in the 16th century, but was most rapid from 1850 onwards. The east coast settlements which formed the original 13 states were of British origin and are represented by the 13 stripes on the American flag. The 13 colonies rebelled against the British in 1775 and set up the United States of America a year later.

European settlers brought negroes from Africa to work as slaves on their land. In the 1860s a war was fought in America between the States of the Union in the north and the States of the Confederacy in the south. One of the causes of the war was that the north

THE NEW WORLD

In the year 1492, Christopher Columbus, the Italian navigator in the service of Spain, sailed across the Atlantic Ocean and discovered the western islands of the Americas. He believed that he had sailed right round the world and reached India, so the islands became known as the West Indies. Actually, it is now believed that America was discovered by sailors long before Columbus set foot on the soil of the New World (as it was called). It is thought, for example, that the Scandinavian explorer, Leif Eriksson, landed in Canada perhaps more than 400 years earlier. But it was from the 15th century onwards that North America began to develop into what it is today.

America is the wealthiest country in the world, having enormous natural resources including vast forests, fine agricultural land and a great deal of mineral wealth. It is a highly industrialized country too, and has a huge trading network with the rest of the world.

Above: Wheatfields in Minnesota, USA. Agriculture is important in the central states of America.

Right: The Golden Gate Bridge in San Francisco crosses the city's excellent natural harbour.

Below: The Mississippi in flood. Much has been done to strengthen its banks because the river floods good farm land.

wished to see slavery abolished, and their victory meant that all slaves were freed. Today, 10 per cent of the population of the United States is black. Since the Civil War the Union has grown steadily and now comprises 50 states, each of which is represented by a star on the national flag.

America is the wealthiest country in the world, having enormous natural resources including vast forests, fine agricultural land and a great deal of mineral wealth. It is a highly industrialized country too, and has a huge trading network with the rest of the world.

Western USA

Western USA contains the Rocky Mountains and many other ranges, including several areas of high plateaux, and basins surrounded by mountains. Most of the west is arid and is sparsely populated, except where irrigation is possible and where there are important mineral deposits. West of the Sierra Nevada and Cascades, where there are fertile lowlands and the climate is wetter, farming and forestry are important.

The west of America also includes the isolated 49th and 50th states, Alaska and Hawaii. Alaska has become important, and wealthy since 1970 when its vast oil deposits began to be developed.

Central USA

The river Mississippi flows through the central states of America, and is joined by its large tributaries: the Missouri, Ohio and Tennessee rivers.

Above : Up-to-date Eskimos in N.W. Territory, Canada.

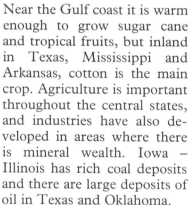

Left : Timber and its products are important in Canada.

Near the Gulf coast it is warm enough to grow sugar cane and tropical fruits, but inland in Texas, Mississippi and Arkansas, cotton is the main crop. Agriculture is important throughout the central states, and industries have also developed in areas where there is mineral wealth. Iowa – Illinois has rich coal deposits and there are large deposits of oil in Texas and Oklahoma.

Eastern USA

Eastern USA includes the Appalachian Mountains and the Atlantic coastal plain. The lowland area is narrow in New England but becomes much wider in Georgia and Florida. The coastal plain is heavily populated: Boston, New York, Philadelphia and Baltimore are all ports and large industrial centres. The large urban population creates a demand for dairy products and vegetables. Inland in Pennsylvania there are rich coal deposits and the

steel industry is important. The capital of the USA, Washington, is near the east coast. It was specially located near the dividing line between the North and South at the time of the Civil War, in an attempt to satisfy both sides.

Canada

Canada is divided into 11 provinces ranging from Prince Edward Island which covers 5700 square kilometres (2200 square miles) to North West Territory and Yukon which occupies 3 778 000 square kilometres (1 460 000 square miles). Transcontinental railways help to link these provinces.

The three Atlantic provinces are quite small and sparsely populated, but are important for some fruit farming, timber products and coal. The Province of Newfoundland includes Labrador which contains large deposits of iron ore.

Ontario and Quebec are both well-populated in the south, near the USA, but are virtually empty in the north. The Great Lakes and St. Lawrence are used for imports and exports, except in winter when this seaway freezes up. Many industries and some mixed farming are found near the Great Lakes.

The three prairie provinces contain grassland in the south, but are forested in the north. The Prairies are well farmed for cereals but also contain large oil, gas, coal and potash deposits.

British Columbia is west of the Rockies and, although very mountainous, it is a wealthy state with some good farming, vast forests and many mineral deposits. The ports never freeze up in winter and the west coast has average January temperatures above freezing point, because onshore winds are warmed by the North Pacific current.

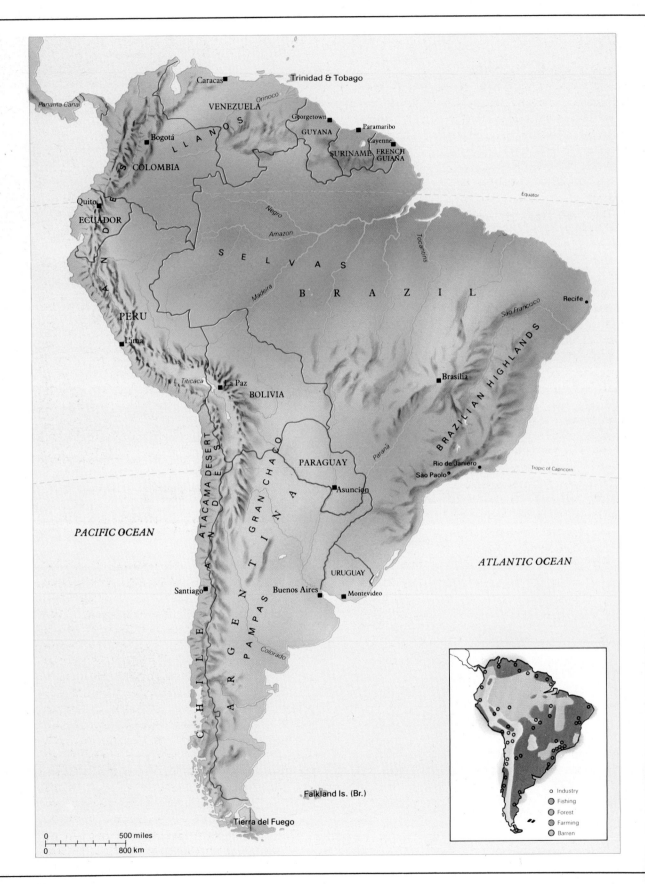

Caracas

Trinidad & Tobago

Panama Canal

VENEZUELA

Orinoco

Georgetown

Bogotá

GUYANA

Paramaribo

COLOMBIA

Cayenne

SURINAME

FRENCH
GUIANA

Quito

Equator

ECUADOR

Negro

A
N
D
E
S

Amazon

S E L V A S

Tocantins

PERU

B R A Z I L

Madeira

Recife

São Francisco

L I A N O S

Lima

L. Titicaca

La Paz

Brasilia

BOLIVIA

B
R
A
Z
I
L
I
A
N

H
I
G
H
L
A
N
D
S

PARAGUAY

Paraná

Rio de Janiero

Tropic of Capricorn

São Paolo

Asunción

A
T
A
C
A
M
A

D
E
S
E
R
T

PACIFIC OCEAN

A
N
D
E
S

G
R
A
N

C
H
A
C
O

A
R
G
E
N
T
I
N
A

ATLANTIC OCEAN

URUGUAY

C
H
I
L
E

P
A
M
P
A
S

Santiago

Buenos Aires

Montevideo

Colorado

Falkland Is. (Br.)

Tierra del Fuego

0   500 miles

0   800 km

Industry

Fishing

Forest

Farming

Barren

West Indies

The West Indies are a chain of islands extending in a 4000 kilometre (2500 mile) arc. The West Indies enclose the Caribbean Sea – to the north lies the Gulf of Mexico and to the east the Atlantic Ocean. Most West Indians are descendants of black Africans, brought to the Islands to work as slaves for European plantation owners, but there are also many people of mixed origin. By far the largest of the West Indian islands are Cuba, Hispaniola (divided into Haiti and the Dominican Republic), Jamaica and Puerto Rico.

The West Indies are noted for their warm climate, and for their ample, often seasonal, rainfall. They produce sugar and bananas which are important exports. Some of the islands, particularly Jamaica, are densely populated because Europeans brought so many people from Africa to work as slaves. This has meant that many people have emigrated to look for work. Tourism is now important on some islands.

Central America

Central America is the narrow, winding strip of land connecting the continental land masses of North and South America. This region includes southern Mexico, Guatemala, Belize, Honduras, El Salvador, Nicaragua, Costa Rica and Panama. Two major Indian civilizations had developed in Central America before the arrival of the Spaniards in the 16th century – the Aztec, near Mexico City, and the Mayan in Yucatan. Indians have intermarried with Europeans throughout Central America and more than half the people are now *mestizos*, or crossbreeds. There are some rich mineral deposits in Central America, but farming is still the largest employer of labour, and most countries have few industries. The recent discovery and development of oil deposits in Mexico, however, will certainly bring new wealth to this area.

Above right : Pueblo of the Taos Indians, New Mexico.

Right : Brasilia – capital of Brazil since 1960.

South America

The first people to inhabit South America probably came from Siberia, moving into North America and then spreading southwards across Panama and into South America. Today, it is obvious from the language and culture of most of South America that the most dominant influence has been that of Spain and Portugal. In fact, the Spanish *conquistadores* succeeded in taking most of Central America and a good deal of South America in the first 50 years of the 16th century. Most of Latin America became independent from Spain and

THE CARIBBEAN

Florida

Atlantic Ocean

Andros Is.
Bahama Islands

Cuba

Jamaica

Haiti
Dominican Rep.

Virgin Islands
Leeward Islands
St. Kitts-Nevis
Puerto Rico
Antigua
Guadeloupe

Dominica
Martinique
St. Lucia
St. Vincent
Barbados

Caribbean Sea

Grenada
Tobago
Trinidad

Windward Islands

Venezuela

Above : A ferry along the route of the Trans-Amazonian highway.

Above right : The Andes are important for their mineral deposits.

Portugal in the 19th century.

South America is a very mountainous region with the Andes running the whole length of the western side of of the continent. Much of South America's 18 000 000 square kilometres (7 000 000 square miles), is tropical, because the wide part of the continent is in the north. The tropical lowland areas are sparsely populated and most people live in the elevated tropics or in the more temperate southern parts.

The economy of South America is in the process of changing from being primarily agricultural to being more highly industrialized. South American countries have always relied on producing food-stuffs and raw materials for export, but now these raw materials are increasingly being used at home. One result of the growth of new industries has been the movement of people away from the countryside to the cities.

South America has considerable mineral wealth – mostly in the Andes and the highlands of Guiana and Brazil. In the Chilean Andes there are huge copper mines and large deposits of sodium nitrate. In Bolivia and Peru there are important deposits of tungsten, vanadium, lead, zinc, tin and silver. Bauxite occurs in huge quantities in the highlands of Guiana and Brazil.

At one time South American industries suffered from the scarcity of coal deposits in the continent, but now the discovery and development of oil and natural gas resources means energy is available for industrial development. Venezuela is the biggest oil producer in South America and has earned a great deal of foreign currency from its oil deposits. Brazil, Argentina and Chile have now established heavy industries including oil refineries, steel mills and smelting plants for processing iron, copper and bauxite ores. Light industries are spreading to most parts of South America, making use of local materials.

Northern South America

This area includes French Guiana, Surinam, Guyana, Venezuela, Colombia, Ecuador, Peru and Bolivia, as well as much of Brazil. It consists of the Amazon and Orinoco lowlands and narrow coastal plains. The countries in this area are thinly populated and still industrially underdeveloped, but they have important mineral resources. The agriculture is mostly poor subsistence farming with maize and potatoes being the main food crops in the mountainous areas, with manioc in the tropical lowlands.

Brazil, or the United States of Brazil as it is correctly called, is the largest of the countries that make up South America, covering nearly half the continent. The Amazon Basin occupies almost one half of the country, and is covered by tropical forest which is sparsely inhabited. There are few roads and the many rivers and streams which flow into the Amazon are the 'highways' of the Indian tribes who live there. The tribes mostly depend on hunting and fishing, but some also practise a kind of shifting agriculture known as 'slash and burn'. Small areas of jungle are cleared, used for two or three years for crops, and then abandoned.

The Brazilian Plateau is quite densely populated in the south-east, but is sparsely populated in the interior. Coffee, cotton, tobacco and sugar are important crops, and there are iron and many other mineral deposits. This part of Brazil has several hydro-electric power stations. Altogether, Brazil produces nearly a half of the continent's hydro-electric power.

Below: Coffee plantations near Sao Paulo, Brazil.

Above: Gauchos driving cattle in Argentina.

Southern South America

Argentina, Uruguay, Chile, Paraguay and Southern Brazil contain the temperate lands of South America. The Andes run parallel to the west coast, but between the mountains and the Pacific are stretches of desert in northern Chile, a Mediterranean type region in Central Chile, and a mild wet forested area in Southern Chile. East of the Andes are the grasslands of the Pampas, the Chaco scrub forest of Paraguay and northern Argentina and semi-arid, poor grassland regions west and south of the Pampas. The Pampas region covers more than half of Uruguay and much of Argentina. Sheep and cattle are reared in large numbers, and wheat, maize and flax are grown. Large quantities of surplus food and wool are available to be exported.

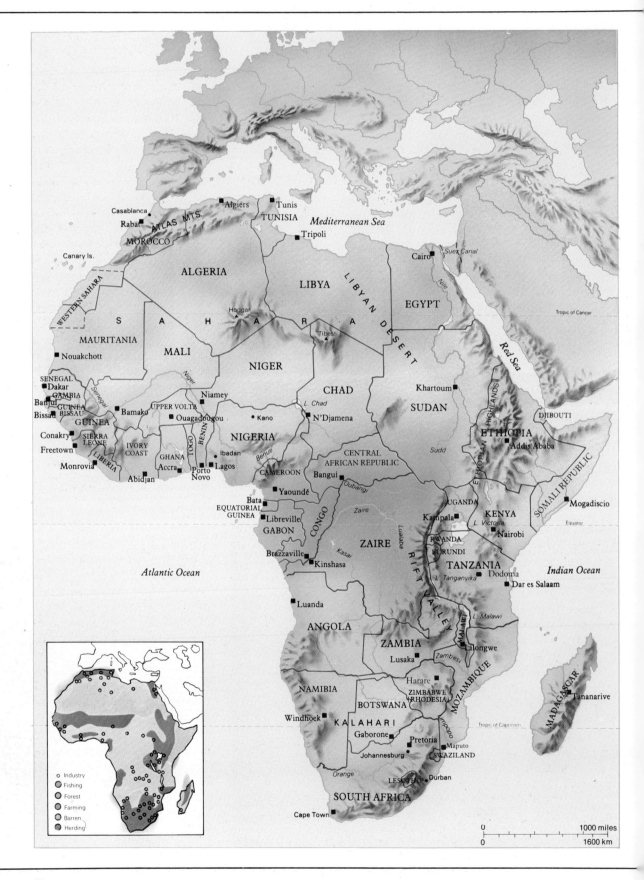

Casablanca
Rabat ATLAS MTS.
MOROCCO
Algiers
Tunis
TUNISIA
Mediterranean Sea
Tripoli

Cairo
Suez Canal
Nile

Canary Is.
WESTERN SAHARA
ALGERIA
LIBYA
LIBYAN DESERT
EGYPT
Tropic of Cancer

S   A   H   A   R   A
MAURITANIA
Nouakchott
MALI
Hoggar
Tibesti
Red Sea

NIGER
SENEGAL
Dakar
GAMBIA
Banjul
Bissau
GUINEA
BISSAU
GUINEA
Conakry
SIERRA
LEONE
Freetown
LIBERIA
Monrovia
Niger
Senegal
Bamako
UPPER VOLTA
Niamey
Ouagadougou
Kano
CHAD
L. Chad
N'Djamena
NIGERIA
Khartoum
SUDAN
DJIBOUTI
ETHIOPIA
Addis Ababa
ETHIOPIAN HIGHLANDS

IVORY
COAST
GHANA
Accra
TOGO
BENIN
Porto
Novo
Ibadan
Lagos
Benue
CAMEROON
CENTRAL
AFRICAN REPUBLIC
Bangui
Yaoundé
Oubangi
Sudd
SOMALI REPUBLIC
Abidjan
Bata
EQUATORIAL
GUINEA
Libreville
GABON
CONGO
Zaire
Kasai
ZAIRE
UGANDA
Kampala
L. Victoria
KENYA
Nairobi
Mogadiscio
Equator
RWANDA
BURUNDI
Lualaba
Brazzaville
Kinshasa
RIFT VALLEY
TANZANIA
Dodoma
Dar es Salaam
L. Tanganyika
Indian Ocean

Atlantic Ocean
Luanda
ANGOLA
L. Malawi
ZAMBIA
Lusaka
MALAWI
Lilongwe
Zambesi
MOZAMBIQUE

NAMIBIA
Harare
ZIMBABWE
(RHODESIA)
MADAGASCAR
Tananarive

BOTSWANA
Windhoek
KALAHARI
Gaborone
Pretoria
Maputo
SWAZILAND
Johannesburg
Tropic of Capricorn
Orange
Limpopo
LESOTHO
Durban

SOUTH AFRICA
Cape Town

○ Industry
○ Fishing
○ Forest
○ Farming
○ Barren
○ Herding

0   1000 miles
0   1600 km

Africa

The huge continent of Africa (30 230 000 square kilometres or 12 000 000 square miles in area) was once known as the Dark Continent, because until the 19th century little of its interior was known to people from the rest of the world.

Africa is a continent which had important early civilizations. Indeed, many scientists believe that man first developed in Africa. One important empire that existed 5000 years ago was the Benin Empire, in what is now Nigeria.

Various parts of Africa were invaded and colonized first by Roman and then Arab empires, and more recently other parts of Africa were controlled by European countries, chiefly Britain, France, Belgium, Italy and Spain. In the 16th century a cruel slave trade existed, with Arab, British and other colonial traders capturing natives to sell to landowners in the New World, who had at that time too few people to work the vast areas of land they owned. In this century, independence from European rule has been granted to one country after another.

Most of Africa's countries are still developing, and farming and health programmes are urgently needed. Many wealthier governments give aid to the developing countries, partly in the hope that they will become future customers and allies. In 1963, many African states joined together to form the Organization of African Unity, an organization which pledges itself to a policy which includes the respect for the sovereignty of member states and the promotion of mutual co-operation.

Regions of Africa

Africa today is a continent where extremes of poverty and wealth are often found side by side. Diseases such as malaria and sleeping sickness can cause huge areas of otherwise suitable land to be denied to man or his livestock. Africa is peopled mainly by negroes south of the Sahara, and by Arabs and Berbers north of the Sahara. The people north of the Sahara – the so-called non-black Africans – have much in common with groups of Asian origin. Despite Africa's size, much of the land is unusable because it is desert or diseases abound and, compared to Europe where more than a quarter of the land is arable, it is poorly farmed. Less than an eighth of Africa is used to grow its main crops of millet, maize, wheat and other cereals, oilseeds, cotton, and pulses. There are also very large areas of equatorial forest and tropical woodland although these are now being cut down at an alarming rate, firstly to provide timber and then new land for the ever-growing population of the developing countries. Most of the people of Africa are still living an agricultural or pastoral way of life. Africa is nevertheless a continent rich in culture, and its art, music and sculpture have much influence in the world. Despite the fact that much of Africa is developing, there are of course areas of great modernization, especially in the wealthier countries like South Africa and Nigeria.

An aerial view of Port Harcourt, in south-eastern Nigeria. Much export traffic, including coal, passes through the port, and there is an important oil refinery.

Northern Africa

This includes the Sahara and the northern lands. The Sahara, an area of shifting sands and extremes of hot days and freezing nights, covers an area of 9 065 000 square kilometres (3 500 000 square miles). The monotony of this inhospitable area is broken here and there by oases.

The population of Northern Africa is generally sparse, with nomadic tribes of herdsmen, and farmers growing crops such as ground nuts, fruit and cotton wherever conditions allow. Egypt is densely populated along the fertile Nile valley. Libya and Algeria are important for petroleum and natural gas respectively.

West Africa

West Africa stretches from the coast of Senegal across to Cameroon, and includes 13 countries. The coastal region is humid, with tropical rain forest and swamps. Inland, the forest thins out, and grassland occurs. Towards the north the grassland turns to sparse scrub. Cocoa is the main crop near the coast, but palm oil, yams, cotton, millet and nuts are also important.

West Africa's richest country is Nigeria, which has oil reserves in the Niger delta. It is one of the world's main oil producers. Inland, there are tin and coal mines.

Liberia was created as a settlement for freed slaves in 1822.

Central Africa

Central Africa mainly lies in the basin of the River Zaire, and is surrounded by mountain ranges such as the Adamawa in the north, the Ruwenzori in the east, and the Bie plateau of Angola. It is a humid area with dense forests.

Like much of black Africa, the countries of Central Africa are developing, but are still poor. The main crops are ground nuts, coffee, cotton, rubber, palm oil and maize. Several countries have minerals such as iron ore, copper, zinc, manganese, lead and coal.

East Africa

East Africa stretches from the Sudan in the west, down to Tanzania, and across to the east coast. It is a mountainous region, and includes Africa's highest peak, Mount Kilimanjaro (5899 metres or 19 321 feet). Lake Victoria is surrounded by a huge plateau which itself is crossed by the Great Rift Valley. The climate on Kenya and Tanzania's coasts is hot and humid, forming rain forests, whilst that of northern Sudan and Somalia is desert. The high plateau region consists mainly of savannah grassland. Crops in-

Opposite left : Burning off natural gas from oil wells in Libya.

Opposite right : Tropical forest in the Congo in torrential rain.

Opposite below : On the banks of the River Niger, Mali.

Below : Tourism is a growing industry in parts of Africa.

Bottom : Johannesburg is the industrial and commercial centre of South Africa.

clude cotton, coffee, tea, maize and coconuts. Cattle, sheep and goats are also reared. Tanzania has deposits of gold, diamonds and lead, and Zambia is rich in copper. Kenya has a thriving tourist industry and includes several important wild game parks. Most of Africa's large wild game now lives in protected reserves.

Southern Africa

This region is basically a series of plateaux bordered by mountains in the east. Deserts on the west coast (in Namibia) change to forests on the east coast. There are grasslands in the north and south. As in other parts of Africa, farming is important, and in addition to cattle, crops such as maize and tobacco are grown, especially in Zimbabwe (Rhodesia). Mozambique produces sugar and cotton. Southern Africa is rich in minerals, and diamonds are found in Namibia and South Africa, and coal and copper in Zimbabwe (Rhodesia). South Africa also produces cereals, citrus fruits, iron and coal.

South Africa is unique among African countries in that it is ruled by the minority white population. South Africa practises a policy known as *apartheid* – which results in separate development for black and white people. Apartheid is an issue about which people in many parts of the world feel very strongly, and it is to be hoped that a system of government will evolve which enables all people to help determine their country's future.

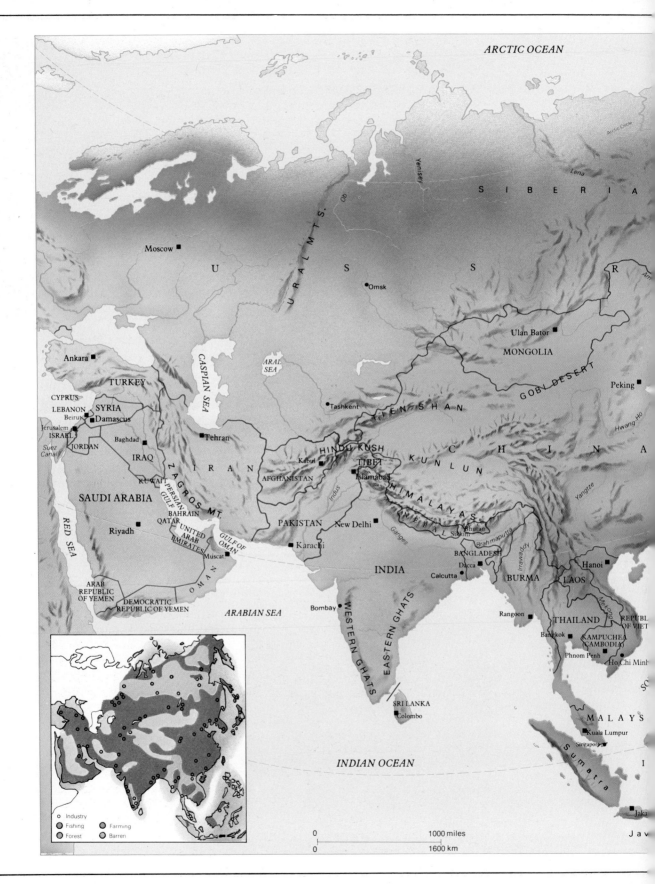

ARCTIC OCEAN

Arctic Circle

S I B E R I A

Yenisey

Lena

Ob

Moscow ■

U   S   S   R

●Omsk

Ulan Bator ■

MONGOLIA

G O B I   D E S E R T

Ankara ■

Peking ■

CASPIAN SEA

ARAL SEA

TURKEY

●Tashkent

T I E N   S H A N

Hwang Ho

CYPRUS

LEBANON   SYRIA

Beirut ●   ■Damascus

HINDU KUSH

K U N L U N

C H I N A

Jerusalem

ISRAEL   Baghdad ■

Tehran

Kabul ●

TIBET

Yangtze

Suez
Canal   JORDAN

IRAQ

I R A N

Islamabad

AFGHANISTAN

H I M A L A Y A S

KUWAIT

Z A G R O S   M T.

SAUDI ARABIA

PERSIAN GULF

BAHRAIN

QATAR

New Delhi

Indus

PAKISTAN

N E P A L

Bhutan

Sikkim

Brahmaputra

RED SEA

Riyadh ●

UNITED
ARAB
EMIRATES

GULF OF OMAN

Ganges

BANGLADESH

Dacca ●

Irrawaddy

Hanoi ■

Muscat ■

Karachi ●

OMAN

INDIA

Calcutta ●

BURMA

LAOS

ARAB
REPUBLIC
OF YEMEN

DEMOCRATIC
REPUBLIC OF YEMEN

ARABIAN SEA

Bombay ●

W E S T E R N   G H A T S

E A S T E R N   G H A T S

Rangoon ●

THAILAND

Mekong

REPUBL
OF VIET

Bangkok ■

KAMPUCHEA
(CAMBODIA)

Phnom Penh ●

Ho Chi Minh ●

SRI LANKA

Colombo ●

M A L A Y S

INDIAN OCEAN

Kuala Lumpur ■

S u m a t r a

Singapore ●

I

Jaka ■

J a v

○ Industry

◐ Fishing   ◐ Farming

◐ Forest   ◐ Barren

| 0 | | 1000 miles |
| 0 | | 1600 km |

56

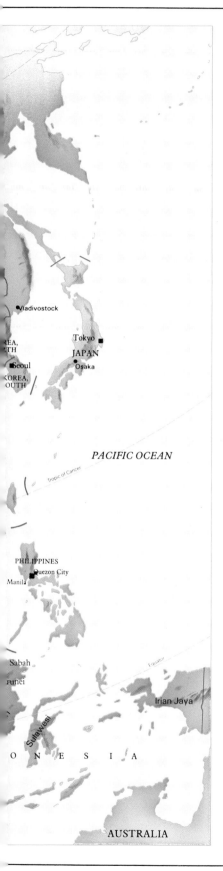

Asia

Asia is the largest continent; it makes up one third of the world's land mass (44 339 377 square kilometres, 17 119 528 square miles) and is home for more than half of the world's population.

It is a continent of widely differing climatic conditions, extending as it does from the Arctic to the Equator, and stretching half way around the world. Its people differ widely too, with Caucasoids in the West and in the Indian sub-continent, Arabs in the Middle East, and Mongoloids, including the Chinese, Japanese, Koreans and Siberians.

The earliest known civilization in Asia emerged about 6000 years ago and the Chinese civilization is now the oldest in existence.

With so many countries, different religions and climatic conditions, Asia's political and economic status is very complex. The USSR forms the Eastern bloc, and although there are many other communist countries in Asia, such as China, Afghanistan, and much of the Far East, their methods and ideas vary greatly. In fact the gulf between Russian and Chinese communism is possibly as great as between the ideals of Russia and the West.

The USSR

The Union of Soviet Socialist Republics (USSR) is the largest country in the world, with a population of 250 million. It lies partly in Europe and partly in Asia and forms

St. Basil's Cathedral in Red Square, Moscow.

Asia's northern boundary.

The Republic came into being in 1917 following the October revolution by the Russian Bolshevik Party, led by the writer, Nikolai Lenin.

Over the past 60 years the USSR has developed rapidly from a feudal dictatorship to one of the two (the other is the USA) most powerful nations in the world.

Western Russia is the most highly developed area and contains most of the largest cities including the capital, Moscow. The country is divided into 15 areas called union republics.

The USSR is fortunate in having the greatest reserves of fossil fuels of any nation in the world. So it has less need than other countries such as the USA to pursue a nuclear energy programme. Western Russia is heavily industrialized but still produces most of its own food, with huge planned agricultural programmes, which have involved in one case, the diverting of the river Volga to provide irrigation for the grain fields. Forests have also been planted to act as windbreaks to protect the soils from erosion.

Much of Eastern Russia lies within the Arctic Circle and here vegetation is sparse and people few. Further south, the steppelands grow immense quantities of wheat. However, the climate is extreme, very hot in summer and freezing in winter.

South West Asia

This area includes Saudi Arabia, Yemen, Oman, Iran, United Arab Emirates, Qatar, Bahrain, Kuwait, Iraq, Jordan, Syria, Lebanon, Israel and Turkey.

The Arabian states are bounded by the Red Sea, the Arabian Sea, the Persian Gulf and the Gulf of Oman. The land is mostly covered by dry, sand deserts and until recent years these countries were extremely poor. With the discovery of vast oil reserves beneath the desert, the situation has changed, and the Middle East has become very important in world economics. The four main oil producers are Saudi Arabia, Iran, Kuwait and Iraq.

Turkey, without the advantage of great oil reserves, and with a more hospitable climate is mainly an agricultural country, although it is also the world's largest chromium producer and has extensive coal mines.

Israel was set up as a Jewish state in 1948, surrounded by Arab countries which have always opposed its establish-ment. Four Arab-Israeli wars have taken place in the past 25 years. But despite this turmoil, Israel has employed advanced farming techniques and irrigation systems to make the land fertile, and cereals and citrus fruits are widely grown.

The Indian sub-continent

This area includes India, Afghanistan, Nepal, Pakistan and Bangladesh. It is very mountainous with the Himalayas and the Hindu Kush in

Above : In the now wealthy oil states, old and new ways of life are in sharp contrast.

Below : Tea plantation in India.

the north, and the Ghats running down the east and west coasts of India. Highly fertile plains are to be found in the south. The area has wet and dry seasons, with annual monsoons, but rainfall varies greatly from desert conditions in north-west India and heavy rainfall in Assam.

India, the main country in this area, is rich in mineral deposits, but farming is the chief occupation of the people. The country supports a staggering population of 600 million and most of the people follow the Hindu faith.

India is a country of great contrasts in its peoples, its climates and in its landscape. It ranges from the Himalayas in the north with the world's highest mountain peaks, to the lowland belt of Indo-Ganges, to the volcanic plateau of the Deccan Traps, and the forested areas of the coast. The climate conditions vary from arid to monsoon.

For countries like India with little or no industrial development, primitive agricultural methods and few resources either in terms of natural resources or trained people, it is hard to envisage a prosperous future. Naturally, some inhabitants of these underdeveloped countries are very bitter that they have such a small share of the world's wealth that many people actually starve to death, or live in very deprived conditions. Richer nations have made contributions to help these fourth world countries but much more needs to be done if these countries are to develop and become reasonably self-sufficient.

Central and East Asia

China, Mongolia, North and South Korea, Taiwan and Japan form Central and East Asia.

China, with the largest population in the world, 700 million, is a vast land stretching from its Russian borders to the Pacific Ocean.

China was a feudal country until 1911 and was gripped by civil war from then until 1949 when the Peoples' Republic of China came into being. China, then led by the Chairman of the Chinese communist party, Mao Tse-Tung from 1949 until his death in 1976, has grown in prosperity and power. Today it is a nuclear power of considerable strength. Although the country is communist, there are considerable ideological differences between China and the USSR, and these have led to conflict along their extensive border.

When the Communists took over in China in 1949, exiles fled to the small island of Taiwan, which became known as Nationalist China. Here they have prospered, growing crops, ship-building and mining for coal, gold and sulphur.

Japan is made up of four islands off the east coast of Asia, and was virtually isolated from the western world until just over 100 years ago. It is now quite 'westernized' and has, in this relatively short time, become the world's third most productive nation, after the USA and USSR.

Japan is a highly industrialized nation, and now leads the world in ship-building, the production of optical equipment, electronics, textiles and fertilizers.

It is also the world's major fishing nation. Fishing is a very important industry in Japan, employing over 500 000 people.

South East Asia

This area includes many nations including Thailand, Burma, Malaysia, Singapore, Laos, and the Socialist Republic of Vietnam.

The climate in this corner of Asia is monsoonal with high temperatures. The heat and wet cause the area to have vast areas of jungle and the monsoonal forests contain sandalwood, teak and bamboo. Population densities vary a great deal according to the richness of the soil.

Top right : Japan – staff exercises in a camera factory.

Above right : Ship-building yard, Nagasaki, Japan.

Right : Factory buildings in Shenyang, China.

Below : Singapore harbour.

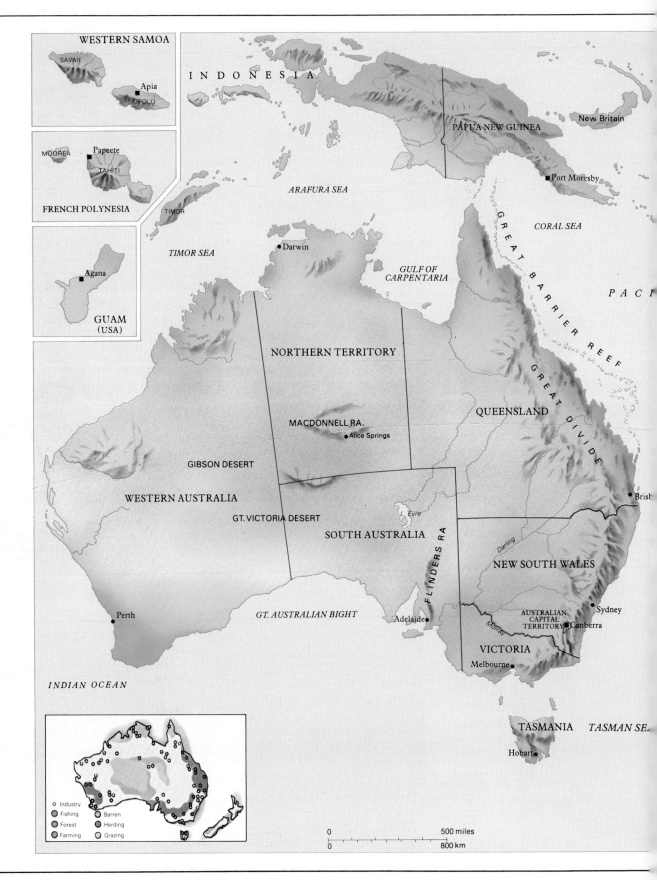

WESTERN SAMOA

SAVAII

Apia
UPOLU

MOOREA

Papeete
TAHITI

FRENCH POLYNESIA

TIMOR

Agana

GUAM
(USA)

INDONESIA

ARAFURA SEA

TIMOR SEA

Darwin

GULF OF
CARPENTARIA

PAPUA NEW GUINEA

New Britain

Port Moresby

CORAL SEA

GREAT BARRIER REEF

PACI

NORTHERN TERRITORY

MACDONNELL RA.

Alice Springs

GIBSON DESERT

QUEENSLAND

GREAT DIVIDE

WESTERN AUSTRALIA

GT. VICTORIA DESERT

L. Eyre

SOUTH AUSTRALIA

FLINDERS RA.

Brisb

Darling

NEW SOUTH WALES

Perth

GT. AUSTRALIAN BIGHT

Adelaide

Murray

AUSTRALIAN
CAPITAL
TERRITORY

Canberra

Sydney

VICTORIA

Melbourne

INDIAN OCEAN

TASMANIA

TASMAN SE.

Hobart

Industry
Fishing   Barren
Forest   Herding
Farming   Grazing

0   500 miles
0   800 km

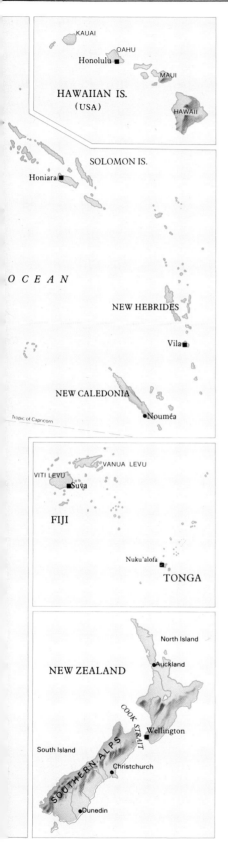

Australasia

The area known as Australasia comprises Australia, New Zealand and the many, tiny islands of the South Pacific. New Zealand and Australia have adopted an essentially western way of life, which is not surprising since they have been settled by emigrants from the west, particularly those from Britain.

Before the arrival of the Europeans in the 1700s, the only inhabitants were the Aborigines in Australia, the Maoris in New Zealand and the Polynesians in the South Pacific islands.

Because of its isolation, Britain established a penal settlement in Australia in 1788, free settlers moving in a few years later. The discovery of gold in Australia and New Zealand increased settlement and by early this century both countries had become independent.

Australia

Australia is a huge island of more than 7·5 million square kilometres (about 3 million square miles) but about two-thirds of its area is desert, known as the Western Plateau, and is barely habitable. Most of the white settlers have established their homes around the coastal region and in the centre are only a few remaining Aborigines in scattered communities living a very harsh existence. Despite its vast area, the population of Australia is only about 13 million. Almost a quarter of the people live in the capital

city of the state of New South Wales, Sydney. The administrative capital is the much smaller city of Canberra.

The country is divided into six states: Western Australia, South Australia, Queensland, New South Wales, Victoria and Tasmania, and the Northern Territory.

A wealthy country, Australia's economy is divided between agriculture and industry. Agriculture is mainly concentrated in the southern coastal areas which are most densely populated and where the rainfall is reliable. Australia leads the world in sheep raising, exporting large quantities of wool and mutton.

The country is also rich in mineral reserves including uranium, gold, silver, lead,

Above: Palm Valley near Alice Springs in central Australia.

Below: A small mining settlement.

Above : Aborigines were the original inhabitants of Australia, settling there about 12 000 years ago.

zinc, coal and iron. These are found in the harsher northern areas.

Australia's isolation from other land masses has had a considerable effect on animal life. Animals peculiar to this southern continent include marsupials, such as the kangaroo, which carry their young in pouches and monotreme mammals that lay eggs – like the duck-billed platypus.

New Zealand

New Zealand lies about 1930 kilometres (1200 miles) southeast of Australia. It consists of two islands; North Island which has a mountainous core containing active volcanoes and geysers surrounded by fertile lowlands, and South Island which has rich grass-

land areas and forests.

New Zealand is very sparsely populated and its rich agricultural land could support far more people than its present population of three million.

The British first settled in South Island, but gradually the population in North Island has overtaken that of the South because conditions for rearing cattle are more suitable there. Most agricultural produce was sold to Europe but gradually New Zealand has widened her markets to include other countries such as Japan.

Like Australia, New Zealand is a wealthy country with small deposits of gold and coal, as well as oil reserves. Hydro-electric and geothermal power is produced. However its economy is based on agriculture, especially cattle and sheep.

The Pacific Islands

More than 30 000 small islands are scattered over thousands of miles of the South Pacific Ocean. Most islands in this region are tropical, the rain being heaviest on the volcanic islands, which have tropical forest and fertile plains.

The original inhabitants are the Melanesians, who live on islands to the north and northeast of Australia including Fiji, the British Solomon Islands and Papua New Guinea; the Micronesians, who live on the tiny scattered islands of the central Pacific Ocean, including the Gilbert Islands; and Polynesians who live on the Hawaiian Islands, Tonga, Samoa and many smaller island groups.

Centre : Sydney Harbour Bridge and the Sydney Opera House. Sydney is the capital of New South Wales.

Above : The Wairakei geothermal power project in North Island, New Zealand. The heat produced from beneath a volcanic plateau is being tapped.

Right : A native of Papua New Guinea in ritual costume. Once administered by Australia, Papua New Guinea is now a fully independent state.

The Polar Regions

There are two huge areas surrounding the North and South Poles that are only sparsely inhabited and, as yet, are of limited importance politically and economically. In the north the region is called the Arctic and the southern area is called the Antarctic or Antarctica and is a continent in its own right.

The Arctic is bounded in the south by the Arctic Circle which is 23°28′ from the North Pole. A great deal of the North Frigid Zone, as it is called, consists of the Arctic Ocean, but there are areas of land including the North-west Territories of Canada, Alaska (one of the states of the USA), Greenland (the largest island in the world and a territory of Denmark) and large parts of northern Russia, Asia, and Europe.

The people that we typically associate with the frozen North are the Eskimos who spread from Siberia through to Greenland and Alaska. They are remarkably well adapted to their life in these extreme conditions and are well-known for the houses they used to build of blocks of frozen snow known as igloos. Their traditional way of life of hunting sea mammals is fast changing, however, although they are becoming more aware of their own culture and are fighting to preserve it.

It is interesting to note that there was once a northern equivalent to the penguin to be found in the Arctic. It was called the great auk and, like the penguins, could not fly.

The continent of Antarctica is almost 9 million square kilometres (5 million square miles) in area, and most of it is enclosed by ice all the year round. The famous explorer, Captain Cook, tried to find the 'Unknown Continent' in the 1700s but it was not until 1820 that it was finally discovered and by the beginning of the 20th century a good deal of it had been explored. Much more was found out about the continent, however, in 1957 and 1958 by the English explorer and scientist Vivian Fuchs and his team. The Antarctic region is now important because of the reserves of oil which are concealed beneath the ice.

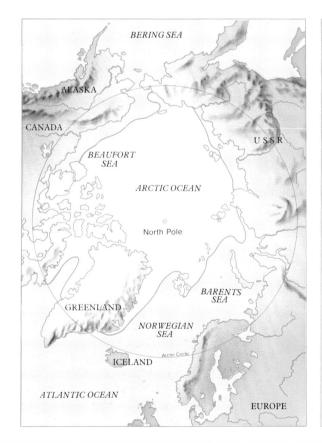

SPACESHIP EARTH

In this section we have tried to show you how our planet evolved, what it is like, and who are the people that live on it. Once, people thought that the Earth was flat and if you came to the edge you could fall off. Now we know it is a sphere or, more exactly, an oblate spheroid 'floating' in space. It is rather like a giant space capsule only instead of having a few passengers on board, it has thousands of millions. The idea of the Earth being like a spaceship was first put forward by an American statesman, the late Adlai Stevenson. And it was also suggested that every astronaut on Spaceship Earth should follow the rules of its operating manual. The Earth is so big and accommodating that we do not easily notice the harm that we are doing to our spaceship by being careless, but on a tiny, real, spaceship it would soon be noticed. For example, when astronauts go into space, they are only able to take a limited amount of food and fuel with them and if they use it up too quickly they would not survive. Similarly, the Earth can only grow so much food and there are finite amounts of fuels to be had, but we go on increasing our population and finding more ways to consume energy. A space capsule only has a limited amount of air, too, so astronauts would not waste it, but every day we cut down forests which oxygenate the atmosphere and burn fossil fuels that use up oxygen. We need to try harder to look after our spaceship even if it is so big and has so many failsafe systems that we haven't yet noticed its rapid deterioration.

Above: These people in India have been driven to find a temporary 'home' in some unused sewage pipes.

Below: Poverty is not confined to the industrially under-developed nations. New York's Harlem, has poor housing and overcrowding problems.

Science and Technology

Contents

Space exploration

Over the past three centuries, man has learned more about himself and the planet on which he lives than at any other period in his history. And in the last 20 years he has begun to understand the Universe, of which our planet, Earth, forms a tiny part.

Our galaxy

You can form an idea of the insignificance of our planet by going outside on a clear night and looking up into the sky. When your eyes have become adjusted to the darkness, you will be able to see vast numbers of stars. Even with the naked eye it is possible to see several thousand stars in the galaxy which includes our own Solar System, and with the aid of a big astronomical telescope this increases to 50 million.

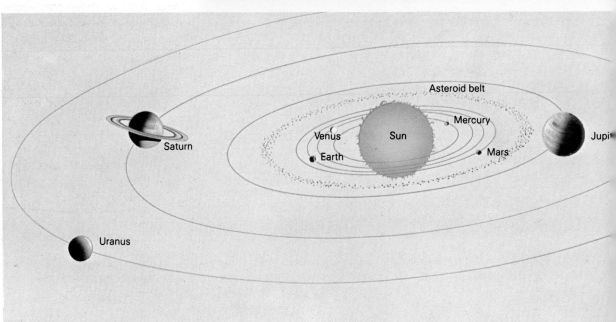

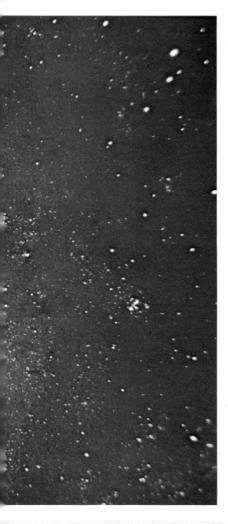

The Sun, which gives our planet its light and warmth, is our nearest star, and many of the tiny pinpoints of light you can see in the night sky are other solar systems, similar to our own, with groups of planets circling round them.

No one really knows how many stars there are in the Universe, but astronomers calculate that there must be about 100 000 million of them in our own galaxy, and in the Universe as a whole there may be as many as 10 000 million *galaxies*! On this gigantic scale the Earth is about as significant as a single grain of sand on a beach, which illustrates just how immense is the task of exploring even the merest fraction of outer space.

Before examining the efforts man has so far made in exploring the areas in the immediate vicinity of Earth, it is important to understand the problems he has to overcome. First, there is the question of the immense distances in-

volved. Even in our own Solar System these are very large. The Moon, our nearest neighbour in space, is 400 000 kilometres (250 000 miles) away, while the Sun's distance from us is about 150 million kilometres (93 million miles). The whole Solar System, measured from the Sun itself to the outermost planet of Pluto, stretches a distance of nearly 6000 million kilometres (3666 million miles).

The second, and equally important problem is that once outside the Earth's atmosphere, human beings cannot survive unless they are totally enclosed in a capsule, or a space suit, which contains an atmosphere similar to the one they experience on Earth.

The third problem is the difficulty of leaving the Earth and then travelling at a speed fast enough to cover the vast distances in a reasonable length of time. The American *Apollo* space capsules which carried men to the Moon took about three days to make the single journey, travelling at an average speed of a few thousand kilometres an hour, while the unmanned space probes to the outer planets took several months to complete their journeys. If astronauts were to attempt to travel to Barnard's Star, one of our nearest star systems, in spacecraft designed with our present scientific knowledge, the journey would take about 30 000 years!

Above left: The galaxy in Triangulum photographed through a 5 metre (200 inch) telescope.

Left: Our own solar system, showing the orbits and relative positions of the planets.

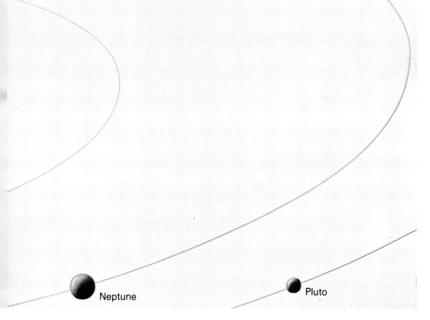

Neptune

Pluto

Satellites in space

The first man-made objects to be hurled into space were comparatively small, weighing only a few kilograms, and performed no useful scientific experiments. They were the Russian *Sputnik* (1957) and the United States of America's *Explorer 1*, which followed it into Earth orbit less than a year later. Nevertheless, they served as proof that man had the means to place objects in the sky, outside the Earth's atmosphere – and to keep them there.

The early space capsules were really artificial satellites, and simply orbited the Earth. The basic method of launching a satellite is to place it on the 'nose' of a launcher rocket capable of reaching a speed of about 28 000 kph (17 500 mph), and then to release it. The speed – known as the *orbital velocity* – is sufficient to counteract the pull of Earth's gravity, and because there is no friction beyond the atmos-

phere, the satellite will continue to circle the Earth. In fact, some of the early satellites were orbiting in the thin outer fringes of our atmosphere, and as their speed slowly decreased, their orbits *decayed* and they re-entered the dense layers of the atmosphere where they were burned up by the intense heat generated by the friction.

There are now a considerable number of artificial satellites at distances varying between several hundred and several thousand kilometres above the surface of the Earth. These satellites have become highly sophisticated, and many of them perform important functions. The weather satellites *Tiros* and *Nimbus*, for example, take a steady stream of photographs of cloud formations over the Earth and transmit them back. These enable meteorologists to forecast the movements of storms and hurricanes, and help them in general weather forecasting.

Astronomers also have a

number of satellites supplying them with information. Orbiting solar observatories, or OSO satellites, make continuous observations of the Sun. Sunspots – huge areas of cooler gases on the Sun's surface – can be studied, and any changes in their activity detected at once. Sensitive instruments in other satellites report back differences in the pressure and temperature of the upper atmosphere.

Above : A Nimbus weather satellite.

Below : Explorer (left) and Sputnik (right), two of the first satellites in Earth orbit.

Some satellites such as *Telstar* and *Early Bird*, were placed in what are called *synchronous* orbits. This means that once in position, they remain over the same spot on the Earth's surface keeping pace with the speed of its rotation. These satellites are used for communication purposes. Powerful transmitters on Earth beam up radio and television programmes, and telephone calls, which the

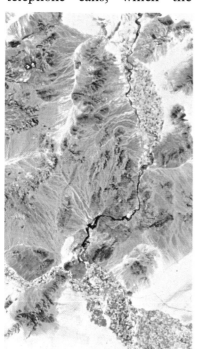

satellites then relay to receiving stations thousands of kilometres away.

One exceptionally useful function performed by a group of satellites put into orbit by the United States of America enables ships with suitable equipment to pinpoint their position at sea with much greater speed and accuracy than conventional methods allow. The system employs five 'man-made moons' which circle the Earth in slightly elliptical orbits at heights of between 850 and 1200 kilometres (450 and 650 nautical miles). Each one completes its high-speed journey round the earth in 107.5 minutes, and each one sends out a radio signal which is picked up by a special aerial on board ship. The data from the signals are fed into a computer, and in less than a minute the ship's navigating officer will have a 'fix' accurate to within 122 metres (400 feet). Because of the speed at which the satellites are circling the Earth, it is

possible for a position 'fix' to be taken every 90 minutes day and night, irrespective of weather conditions. A clear view of either the Sun or the stars is essential when a navigating officer has to use a sextant to help him find his ship's position.

The United States hopes to have a much improved satellite navigation system in operation by 1984. Called the Navsat Global Positioning System it will employ a total of 24 satellites in circular orbits 20 000 kilometres (12 000 miles) out in space, and its users will be able to fix the position not only of ships, but also of aircraft, and even ground vehicles such as tanks.

Left : A picture taken from an Earth Resource Satellite (ERS), which can give information about minerals, crops, pollution on the Earth's surface.

Below : This diagram shows how satellites in synchronous orbit can relay communications throughout the world.

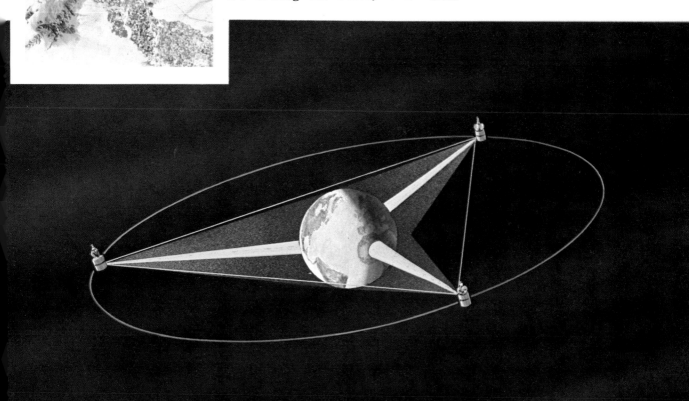

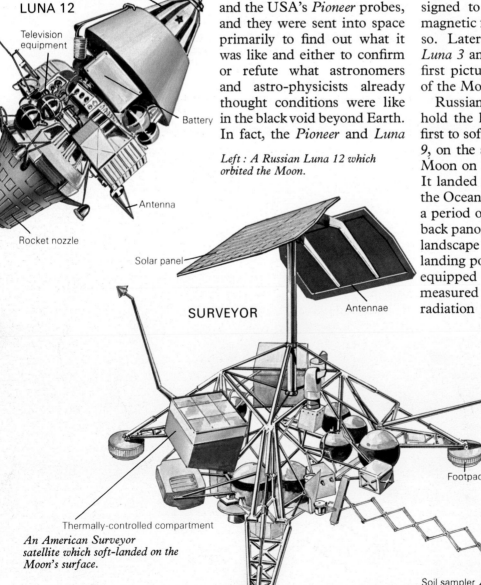

Radio antenna

Solar paddles

Heat sink

Payload of scientific instruments

Solar paddles

PIONEER

Above : American Pioneer satellite used to investigate the environment between the orbits of Earth and Venus.

Instrument compartment

LUNA 12

Television equipment

Battery

Antenna

Rocket nozzle

Solar panel

SURVEYOR

Antennae

Thermally-controlled compartment

An American Surveyor satellite which soft-landed on the Moon's surface.

Footpad

Soil sampler and digging scoop

Unmanned space probes

Although men have actually left this planet and set foot on the Moon, the first objects to escape from its gravity and strike out into the unknown depths of space were unmanned space probes which were sent to survey and photograph the surface of Earth's only natural satellite.

The first unmanned spacecraft were the Russian *Luna* and the USA's *Pioneer* probes, and they were sent into space primarily to find out what it was like and either to confirm or refute what astronomers and astro-physicists already thought conditions were like in the black void beyond Earth. In fact, the *Pioneer* and *Luna*

Left : A Russian Luna 12 which orbited the Moon.

probes radioed back data which proved that outer space is not a total vacuum devoid of all matter, but that there are about 10 hydrogen atoms in every cubic centimetre (164 hydrogen atoms in one cubic inch). This is infinitely less than the number of gas molecules in the atmosphere we all breathe at sea level.

Russia's *Luna 1* was the first probe to burst its way out of the Earth's gravitational pull when it was launched on January 2, 1959. It was designed to detect the Moon's magnetic field, but failed to do so. Later Russian probes – *Luna 3* and *Zond 3* – took the first pictures of the dark side of the Moon.

Russian space scientists also hold the honour of being the first to soft-land a probe, *Luna 9*, on the actual surface of the Moon on 3rd February, 1966. It landed in an area known as the Ocean of Storms, and over a period of three days radioed back panoramic pictures of the landscape surrounding its landing point. *Luna 9* was also equipped with sensors which measured temperature and radiation levels, but perhaps the most important fact to emerge from this first landing was that contrary to many long-held theories, its surface was hard, and quite capable of taking the weight of any future spacecraft. Previously, many scientists had thought that the Moon had a soft, powdery crust into which a spacecraft might sink. The confirmed hardness of the surface was a vital piece of information for any future planned landing of a manned craft.

The American Moon probe programme involved two highly developed robot spacecraft which they named *Surveyor* and *Ranger*. Their purpose was to obtain information about conditions on the Moon and contribute as much as possible to planned lunar landings which the Americans hoped to

achieve before the end of the 1960s. After several early failures with *Ranger* probes, the United States finally succeeded. Three of them returned the incredible total of 12,954 pictures of the surface before crashing into it. The pictures they sent back to the eagerly watching scientists were much better than any ever obtained by conventional telescopes.

It was vital to the American lunar landing programme, however, to soft-land a space probe on the Moon's surface just as the Russians had done earlier. Between 1966 and 1968, five out of seven *Surveyor* unmanned spacecraft landed successfully, and four of them settled gently in locations where it was intended the first manned landings should be made.

Above : How the Moon looked to the Apollo astronauts as they approached it from Earth.

Below : Thousands of pictures were taken of the Moon's surface before a landing was undertaken. This picture is of the far side of the Moon.

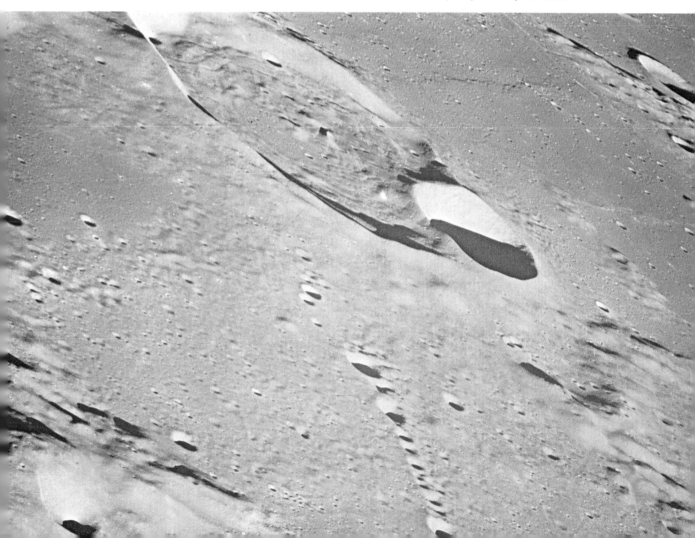

The Moonscape

Photographs transmitted back by the *Surveyors* were spectacular, and people all over the world saw clearly for the first time the awesome, yet beautiful, mountains and craters of the Moon. The high definition cameras could be controlled by radio instructions sent out from Earth. They could be swung round, and have their focus altered so that they could pick out objects as tiny as 1 mm (0.04 in) in diameter. They also had a device for sampling the lunar soil.

In addition to the soft-landing probes the Americans also launched lunar *Orbiter* spacecraft to 'fly' round the Moon, taking hundreds of photographs which were later assembled into a giant 'mosaic' forming the first really detailed map of its rugged surface. It was from such a map that a final landing site in the Sea of Tranquillity was chosen. The stage was now set for man's greatest adventure yet – an attempt to leave our planet and set foot on another world. How they achieved this technological miracle we shall learn about later.

One group of space scientists believe that unmanned spacecraft can supply us with all the information we need about the planets in our Solar System without taking the risks of sending astronauts into such a hostile environment. Unmanned spacecraft are also cheaper to build, because they do not need to be large enough to carry human beings with all their vital life support systems.

In any case, a round trip to some of the outer planets of our Solar System would take many months, and in some cases, even years. This would subject the astronauts to great physical and psychological pressure, and there is always the risk of a space accident which could result in a tragic loss of life, so let us take a look at what can be achieved by one of these long-range space probes.

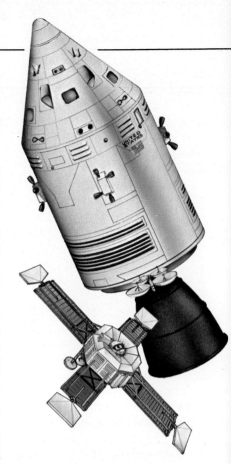

Above : This illustration shows the relative sizes of manned and unmanned spacecraft. The upper one is a manned Apollo capsule, the lower one is a Mariner used for a Mars fly-by.

Below : A photo-mosaic of the Moon's surface.

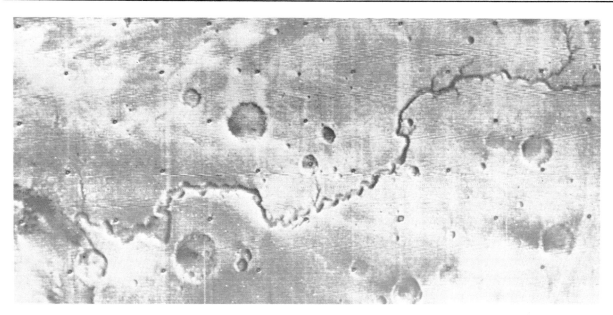

Mariner looks at Mars

Of all the planets which circle the Sun, the one which has always excited the greatest interest amongst writers of science fiction is Mars. Known as the Red Planet because of its red appearance, even when viewed with the naked eye, it has also commanded the close attention of astronomers over the centuries. At certain times, what appear to be *canals* appear on the surface of Mars, and this is one of the phenomena which has caused speculation about the possibility of intelligent life there. Now, of course, we know a great deal about the mysterious planet which, after the Moon, is our nearest neighbour in space. All this new knowledge has been gained from the *Mariner* series of space probes which were blasted off from the United States of America's space centre at Cape Kennedy in Florida.

The first successful probe was *Mariner 4*, which flew past Mars on July 14, 1965, coming within 9600 kilometres (6000 miles) of its surface. The 21 pictures it transmitted back to Earth came as a shock to astronomers. The surface of the planet did not resemble that of Earth; it was heavily pitted with craters similar to those found on the Moon!

Two further *Mariner* probes were despatched in July and August, 1969, and between them they sent back a total of 198 photographs taken with television cameras, some of them from a height of 3200 kilometres (2000 miles). The high resolution telephoto lenses revealed that the area near Mars' South Pole is rugged, with huge craters and mountains, while the equatorial regions are smoother. Disappointingly perhaps, the *Mariner* pictures did not record any canals, nor did they reveal any signs of cities or other structures indicating the presence of intelligent beings.

Above : A picture of a 400 km long valley on Mars, taken from an orbiting satellite.

Below : Viking photograph of Mars taken from 321 869 km (200 000 miles).

Problems of space travel

Perhaps at this point it would be useful to pause for a moment and examine the immense problems that have to be overcome by space scientists when they launch probes to the planets. First of all, it must be remembered that our Solar System, and indeed the whole of the Universe, is in a constant state of movement.

Our Sun is revolving on its axis as are all the planets, but they are not all revolving at the same speed. In addition to this movement, each planet, (together with any moons it may have moving round it) is itself swinging through space round the Sun in a gigantic elliptical orbit. Furthermore, these orbits are not all on the same plane, so when a rocket bearing the space probe is fired from Earth, it has to be aimed at where the target planet is going to be when the probe arrives several months later!

There is one further complication – the Earth is also spinning like a top and is itself swinging round the Sun in its own orbit. So trying to reach a planet with a robot spacecraft, is rather like trying to shoot at a spinning cricket-ball thrown in from the boundary while you are sitting on a mobile roundabout!

How is it done? The movements of the planets are known and their orbits can be accurately predicted from astronomical observations. With the help of computers, complex calculations have to be made so that radioed instructions can be sent to the space probe to alter its direction

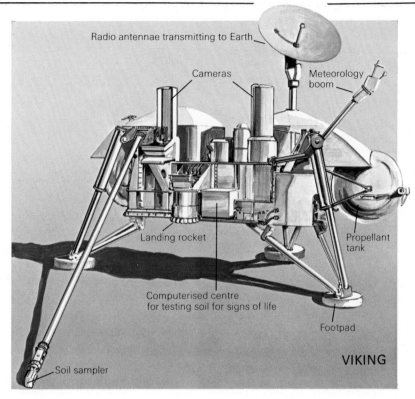

Radio antennae transmitting to Earth

Cameras

Meteorology boom

Landing rocket

Propellant tank

Computerised centre for testing soil for signs of life

Footpad

Soil sampler

VIKING

slightly as it hurtles on towards its target.

Any spacecraft, robot or manned, is first put into Earth orbit before it finally fires its rocket engines to raise its speed to what is called 'escape velocity', around 40 250 kph (25 000 mph). The moment at which this escape firing takes place is critical and is calculated to within fractions of a second.

Although the information sent back by the *Mariner* probes was extensive, what astronomers and scientists on Earth needed was positive knowledge of conditions on the planet which they could obtain only from a spacecraft designed to land on the surface of Mars. This incredible technological triumph was achieved by the USA on 20th July, 1976 when they successfully soft-landed a probe they called *Viking* on the Chryse Plain of Mars.

Barely six weeks later, on 3rd September, *Viking II* landed in the Utopia Plain region.

The remarkable colour pictures sent back were televised, and published in newspapers and magazines; they revealed a reddish brown rock-strewn area. Unfortunately the highly complex robot-controlled experiment devised to analyze a portion of the planet's soil in the hope of discovering life, was not completely successful.

However, a great deal is now known about conditions on Mars, and it seems to be a rather inhospitable place – certainly not suitable for human occupation. From the data sent back by both the *Viking* landers, added to the information obtained by the orbiting *Mariner* probes, scientists have built up what must be a remarkably accurate picture of its climate and terrain.

Apart from being cold and dry, with temperatures ranging between minus 84°C (minus 120°F) at night to minus 30°C (minus 22°F) at midday, the mainly carbon dioxide atmosphere on Mars is subject to sudden fierce wind storms which rage with hurricane velocity, often over almost the whole surface of the planet. Some astronomers now believe that the features on the surface once thought to be 'canals' are really whirling columns of dust whipped to a frenzy by winds of 241 kph (150 mph) and more.

Despite the mass of information resulting from space probes to Mars, American scientists still need to know what it looks like 'over the horizon' from where the *Viking* landers took their pictures. And, of course, they still want to resolve the question of whether there is any form of life on the planet. In the hope

Opposite page : An American Viking Lander spacecraft.
Below : A Russian space-flight control centre.

Above : A photograph taken by the Viking's camera showing the surface of Mars. The arm on the right is a soil sampler.

of providing the answers to these questions, the National Aeronautics and Space Administration (NASA) are planning to send another *Viking* space probe to Mars. If all goes according to plan, *Viking III* will take off some time in 1984, and it will probably have a small battery-powered, wheeled vehicle attached to it which will be able to travel short distances across the surface in response to instructions radioed from Earth – a truly remarkable technological achievement.

The planets in the solar system drawn to the same scale to show their relative size.

Visiting the planets

The planets Mercury, Venus, Mars and Earth are known to astronomers as the inner planets of the Solar System, while Jupiter, Saturn, Uranus, Neptune and Pluto are known as the outer planets. Towards the end of the summer of 1977, NASA space scientists launched two spacecraft which they named *Voyager I* and *Voyager II*. These two robot probes are truly on a journey to infinity. After leaving Earth they rendezvoused with Jupiter and Saturn, bringing us the first close-up photo-

graphs of these planets and their moons. They are now leaving the Solar System.

Saturn is one of the most beautiful objects to be seen in the sky, and one of the most unusual because of the extensive system of rings that surround it. These shining rings puzzled astronomers for years, but now they are known to be made up of millions of separate particles of solid matter, which revolve round Saturn like tiny moons. Saturn, the sun's second largest planet with a diameter of 119 000 kilometres (74 000 miles), also has at least 17 moons of different sizes moving round it.

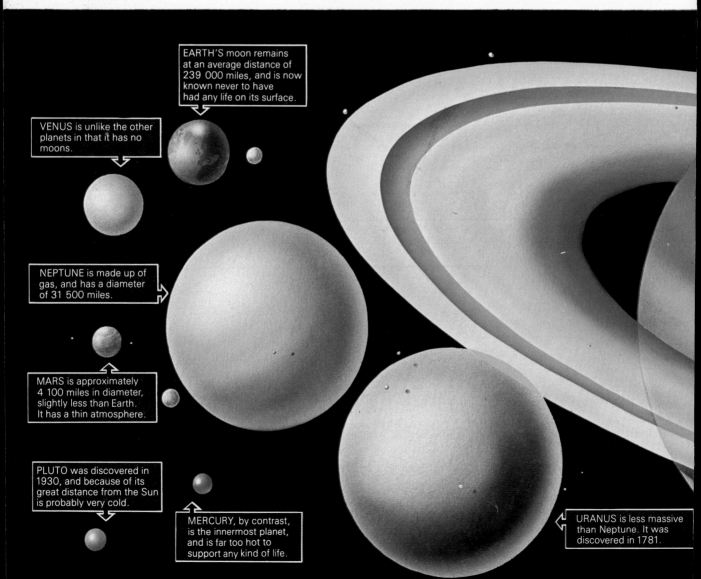

EARTH'S moon remains at an average distance of 239 000 miles, and is now known never to have had any life on its surface.

VENUS is unlike the other planets in that it has no moons.

NEPTUNE is made up of gas, and has a diameter of 31 500 miles.

MARS is approximately 4 100 miles in diameter, slightly less than Earth. It has a thin atmosphere.

PLUTO was discovered in 1930, and because of its great distance from the Sun is probably very cold.

MERCURY, by contrast, is the innermost planet, and is far too hot to support any kind of life.

URANUS is less massive than Neptune. It was discovered in 1781.

JUPITER is the largest planet with an equatorial diameter of 88 700 miles.

SATURN with its spectacular rings is next in size with a diameter of 75 100 miles.

The Apollo programme

Despite the information space scientists have acquired from the many remotely controlled space probes, it seems that man will never let go of his ambition to venture into space himself. His first successful attempt at space travel was, of course, the historic landing on our own Moon.

It was in 1961, that John F. Kennedy, then President of the United States of America, gave the 'go-ahead' for his country to make the maximum effort to put a man on the Moon 'before the end of the decade'. In fact, the first true 'Men on the Moon' landed on its Sea of Tranquillity on 21st July, 1969. They were Americans Neil Armstrong and Buzz Aldrin. A third astronaut, Michael Collins, remained aboard the command module which continued to orbit the Moon for the entire *Apollo 11* mission.

Above : An American astronaut salutes the Stars and Stripes as he stands on the surface of the Moon.

Below : Astronaut David Scott prepares to spacewalk from Apollo 9.

The Moon landing

It was *Apollo 11* (eleven) that carried Armstrong, Aldrin and Collins to the Moon. Earlier *Apollo* spacecraft had been used to carry out orbiting missions round the Earth, a trip round the Moon and back without actually landing, and practice 'docking' flights with a tiny spacecraft known as the lunar module (LM). It was the lunar module that made the final touch-down, and it was from its cramped cabin that Neil Armstrong climbed cautiously to descend the metal ladder leading to the dusty surface.

His words as he made the last little jump on to the lunar surface will remain forever in the history of space exploration: 'That's one small step for a man. One giant leap for Mankind.'

The sequence of events that had to take place before the astronauts could step out on to the airless and barren surface of the Moon was both lengthy and complicated. The power unit which initially hurled the three men into Earth orbit was a three-stage *Saturn V* rocket weighing over 3000 tonnes at take-off. The first stage used kerosene and liquid oxygen as its fuel and lifted the entire rocket with the *Apollo* space capsule on its nose, to a height of 50 kilometres (31 miles) above the Earth. This stage was then discarded, while the two lighter stages were boosted to a height of 160 kilometres (99 miles) by the firing of the second stage rocket. The third stage was not used until the astronauts were ready to hurl themselves out of Earth orbit towards the Moon. Stages two and three burned oxygen and hydrogen.

The moment of firing the final stage of the rocket had to be precisely calculated in order to accelerate the spacecraft into a trajectory which would enable it to arrive at a point in space where the Moon would be at the appointed time.

On the way to the Moon the astronauts in the command service module (CSM) had to be detached from the third stage of the *Saturn* rocket, and then turn round in space to link up with the lunar module which would finally take two of them down to the Moon's surface.

When *Apollo 11* was about

Right : A Saturn V rocket takes off from Cape Kennedy, Florida, USA.

80 000 kilometres (43 000 nautical miles) out in space and moving at just over 9646 kilometres (6000 statute miles) per hour, its crew set controls that would revolve the spacecraft slowly about its own axis, rather like a chicken on a spit. Unless this was done the side facing the sun would overheat, and cause a possible explosion of the fuel tanks.

The speed of the spacecraft gradually lessened until it reached the point between Earth and Moon where the gravity of the two bodies was equal. From then, the pull of the Moon's gravity (which we know affects our tides even down here on Earth) began to accelerate it to a speed which eventually placed it in an orbit round the Moon itself. Now began a critical phase of the mission. The two astronauts selected to make the actual landing – Buzz Aldrin and Neil Armstrong – entered the lunar module and prepared to separate it from the command module orbiting the Moon.

The lunar module – called a Lem for short – had to fire its retro-rockets again at a precise moment, so that it would slow down out of orbit, and land at the predetermined spot on the Moon. In fact, although the descent of the Lem was largely computer-controlled, when it was about 600 metres (2000 feet) above the surface, Neil Armstrong realised that the automatic guidance system was going to carry it into a crater with fairly large boulders, so he immediately switched to manual control. With his fuel almost exhausted he steered away from the large crater where the uneven ground might have tipped the Lem over on landing. The actual touchdown was made with barely 60 seconds of landing fuel left!

After donning their space suits and life support 'backpacks' – a task that took them over six hours – Aldrin and Armstrong de-pressurized the

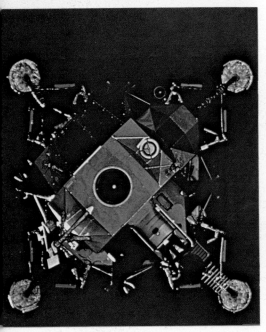

cabin of the Lem and prepared to step on to the surface of the Moon.

After a day of taking photographs, gathering precious samples of Moon rock and dust, and laying out a few simple experiments such as a seismometer to measure moonquakes, and a reflector to catch laser beams from Earth, the two men returned to the Lem to get some sleep.

The rocket engine of the Lem did not, of course, have to be anything like as powerful as the mighty *Saturn V*, because, apart from having to lift the comparatively lightweight Lem, the gravity to be overcome was only one sixth that on Earth – a fact that had enabled the two astronauts to enjoy themselves when they skipped and jumped in their bulky spacesuits.

Armstrong and Aldrin spent some 22 hours on the Moon before blasting themselves back into orbit where they rejoined Michael Collins, who had been orbiting the Moon waiting for them to link up. Once all three were back together inside the command module, and the air-lock secured, the Lem was released to be left behind, and ultimately crash down on to the lifeless globe below them.

Apollo 11 splashed down into the Pacific Ocean on 24th July – just 10 seconds behind its predicted time after a voyage lasting 195 hours 18 minutes, and within a mile of its target point. All that was after a round trip of 800 000 kilometres (500 000 miles)!

The Americans continued with their *Apollo* programme, and with *Apollo 12* they landed two more men on the Moon on 19th November, 1969. The *Apollo 13* flight almost ended in disaster when an oxygen tank exploded at a distance of 320 000 kilometres (200 000 miles) from Earth. The three crew members, James Lovell, Fred Haise and Jack Swigert, obeying urgently radioed instructions from the space centre at Houston in Texas, used vital power and oxygen supplies in the Lem to bring them back to Earth.

The last mission to the Moon was *Apollo 17* and included a scientist, Harrison 'Jack' Schmitt who was a trained geologist. The lunar module crew, one of whom was Schmitt, not only landed on the Moon, but also took with them a lunar rover vehicle which enabled them to travel several kilometres away from the Lem and thus explore and bring back rock samples from a much wider area.

Opposite top : Buzz Aldrin walking on the moon's surface.

Opposite bottom, left to right :
Lunar Module (LEM) in orbit round the Moon.
The Command Module orbiting the Moon.
LEM tilting as it prepares for a landing.
Returned astronauts waiting to be picked up.

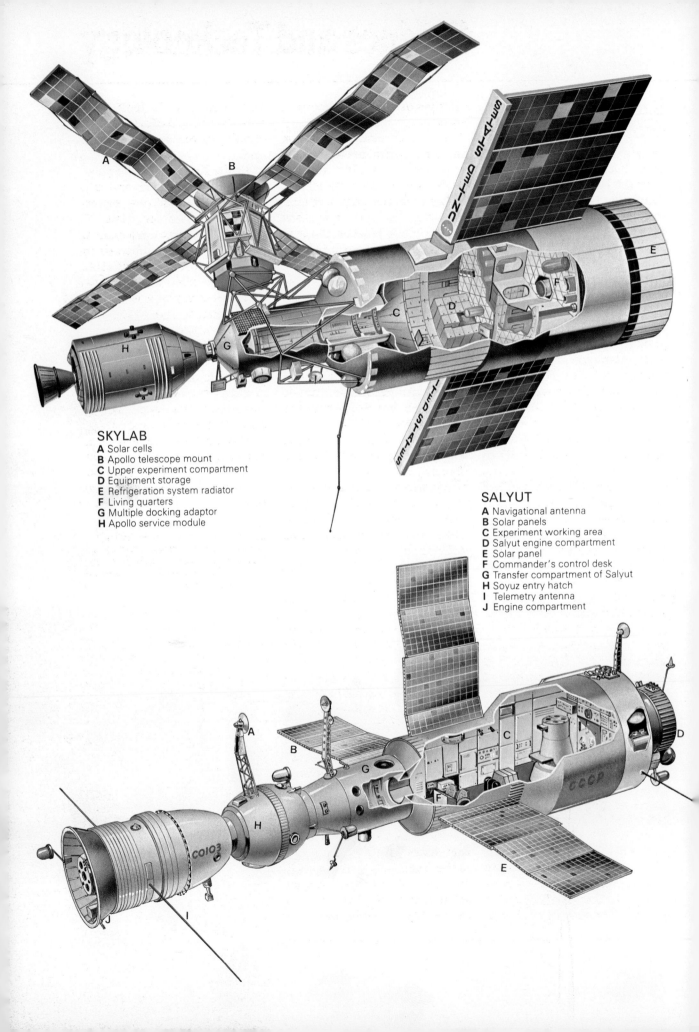

SKYLAB
A Solar cells
B Apollo telescope mount
C Upper experiment compartment
D Equipment storage
E Refrigeration system radiator
F Living quarters
G Multiple docking adaptor
H Apollo service module

SALYUT
A Navigational antenna
B Solar panels
C Experiment working area
D Salyut engine compartment
E Solar panel
F Commander's control desk
G Transfer compartment of Salyut
H Soyuz entry hatch
I Telemetry antenna
J Engine compartment

Salyut and Skylab projects

Of all the spacecraft which have been placed in Earth orbit the largest have been the Russian *Salyut-1* and the American *Skylab*. The Russians placed *Salyut-1* in orbit nearly 200 kilometres (124 miles) above the Earth on 19th April, 1971. Several weeks later, on 7th June, three Russian cosmonauts – as they call their spacemen – were blasted into orbit in a *Soyuz* capsule to dock with the *Salyut*, and occupy it. The three men, Commander Dobrovolski, and his comrades, Vladislav Volkov and Viktor Patsayev, spent nearly 23 days in the 100 cubic metres (3531 cubic feet) of living quarters provided in the space station. The main object of the experiment was to continue research into the effects of a prolonged stay in the weightless conditions of space.

The reports they sent back indicated that man need suffer no ill-effects from prolonged weightlessness. Unfortunately, however, shortly after the three men re-entered the *Soyuz* spacecraft that had remained 'docked' with the *Salyut*, and started their re-entry into the atmosphere, a faulty valve allowed their air to escape and the three men died.

During their stay on board the space station the men carried out a number of biological experiments. Shortly before the flight started a container of drosophila flies was taken aboard the *Soyuz*. These tiny insects multiply very rapidly, enabling scientists to study the effects of weightlessness on several generations of drosophila born in space.

The cosmonauts undertook similar experiments with frogs' eggs. Five days after arriving in the *Salyut* space station the eggs had turned into tadpoles, and one of the crew then 'froze' them at that stage in their evolution because biologists in Russia wanted to study how their balancing organs had developed in zero gravity. The balancing organs in the human ear work in a similar way.

The seeds of several species of plants, including cabbages and leeks, germinated while they were in space, and the cosmonauts took photographs at regular intervals to record the plant growth. All the material connected with these experiments was found inside the *Soyuz* capsule together with the bodies of the cosmonauts, so their tragic deaths had not been in vain.

Salyut-1 was not visited again, and eventually on 11th October, 1971, after six months in orbit, it was decelerated by remote control from Earth and burned up in the lower layers of the atmosphere.

The United States of America launched their *Skylab* satellite in 1973, as part of a series of three-man space flights up to an orbiting workshop. The laboratory, or workshop, was actually the modified third stage of a *Saturn V* rocket. It could accommodate three men and a great deal of special equipment for a large number of experiments, many of them similar to those carried out by the ill-fated *Salyut* cosmonauts. *Skylab* was 6.6 metres (21.6 feet) in diameter,

and 11 metres (36 feet) long, with facilities for docking an *Apollo* space capsule at one end.

At the launch on 14th May, *Skylab* was damaged, and as a result one of its solar panels failed to open out, but 11 days later three astronauts, blasted into orbit aboard an *Apollo* spacecraft, were able to enter the orbiting laboratory, and after carrying out repairs they remained aboard it for 28 days.

Two further crews came up at different times to take over the work in the 'lab', remaining in it for 59 days and 84 days respectively – a space record. As a result of all the knowledge gained from these long stays in space, space stations with as many as 12 people aboard may be orbiting the Earth in the 1980s.

Below : While on board the orbiting laboratories the astronauts carried out a number of experiments, including a study of their own bodies' reactions to space environment.

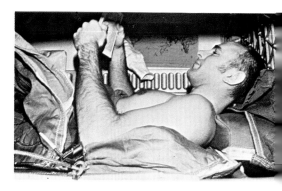

Spacelab

An exciting development of the *Skylab* project is the *Spacelab*, a much more sophisticated scientific workshop which is carried into space not by a large rocket like the *Saturn V*, but by the *Space Shuttle*.

The *Space Shuttle*'s first flight into orbit took place on 12th April, 1981. It resembles an extremely large aircraft. It is designed to take off like a rocket, fly in orbit like a spacecraft, and then return to Earth like a conventional aircraft by gliding through the air to land on a normal runway. The great advantage of using this type of vehicle is that it can be used over and over again, thus saving the millions of dollars needed to make spacecraft like the *Apollo* that can be used only once.

Spacelab is designed to fit into the large cargo hold of the *Space Shuttle* which will place it in a suitable orbit. Once a set of experiments are completed, the *Space Shuttle* can reload it into its cargo hold and return to Earth.

On board the *Spacelab*, and inside its pressurized working areas, up to four non-astronaut scientists will be able to conduct a wide variety of experiments. Looking into the not too distant future, it is more than likely that *Spacelab* will form the basic unit of a larger space habitat, assembled from interlocking modules brought up piecemeal by the *Space Shuttle*.

SPACE SHUTTLE

Arm to launch and recover satellite

Computerised navigational controls

Flight deck

Accommodation compartment

Temperature control panel

Bay to hold Spacelab

Payload bay doors

Main rocket engines

Instrument to undertake geological surveys of Earth

Device using laser beams to sound the atmosphere

pressurised laboratory

SPACELAB

Tunnel linking Spacelab with Orbiter cabin

Space telescope

One NASA project which astronomers are awaiting with excited anticipation is a forthcoming space telescope whose unequalled capabilities will allow observers to make a new search of the Universe, and even look at the interiors of stars.

Astronomers have been using both optical and reflecting telescopes to explore the heavens for centuries. Apart from the limitations of the telescopes themselves, their observations have always been impaired by the layer of atmosphere surrounding the Earth which distorts the light coming through from space.

For some years now it has been possible to send small astronomical observatories into space where they are well clear of the Earth's atmosphere. These have been of great value, but have also been limited by available technology, and by fairly short operational lives. Now, a magnificent 2.4 metre (8 feet) diameter space telescope able to accommodate up to five different astronomical instruments, will allow observations to be made far deeper into space, and with far greater clarity than has ever before been possible, even by large Earth based telescopes like the giant 5.08 metre (200 inch) mirror reflecting telescope at Mount Palomar in California.

Optical telescopes used by astronomers fall into two categories – refracting telescopes and reflecting telescopes. The first kind use a convex lens as the 'objective' together with a smaller convex lens for the eyepiece, while reflecting telescopes use a concave mirror of large diameter for 'gathering' light from the star or planet being observed.

Sir Isaac Newton, the British astronomer and physicist (1642–1727), was the first man to employ a concave mirror for the objective of a telescope, because he was not satisfied with the colour defects which occur with large lenses.

The Royal Observatory has a reflecting telescope named

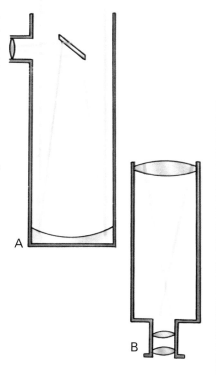

Top right : Sir Isaac Newton's early reflecting telescope.

Right : A proposed orbiting space telescope.

Above : (A) – Newton's reflecting telescope uses a large concave mirror which brings parallel beams of light to a point. Photographs can be taken when a camera is attached. The refracting telescope (B) uses a lens instead of a mirror to focus the object.

after Sir Isaac Newton sited in La Palma, in the Canary Islands. It has a mirror 2.5 metres (98 inches) in diameter. The Mount Palomar Observatory with its 5.08 metre (200 inch) mirror is the largest in the world, and it can make stars appear a million times brighter than they can be seen by the naked eye.

Although optical telescopes are excellent instruments for astronomers to use in their study of the stars, they are limited in their ability to penetrate the outermost depths of the Universe. However, for some years now an entirely new 'tool' has come into use, known as the 'radio telescope'.

The fact that stars and other bodies in space emit radio waves was discovered in 1931, and radio telescopes listen to the stars instead of looking at them. With their giant 'listening' dish aerials radio telescopes are able to probe into areas of the universe beyond the range of optical telescopes, and astronomers have discovered strange objects called 'quasars' and 'pulsars'. Quasars emit enormous quantities of energy as radio waves, while pulsars transmit their radiation in short regular bursts, or pulses.

Strangest of all the 'objects' discovered by radio astronomers are the black holes in space. The 'holes' themselves cannot actually be detected; it is the unusual behaviour of certain other phenomena that has suggested there is *something* nearby where there appears to be absolutely nothing!

A British space satellite, launched by the Americans from Cape Kennedy and known as UK-5 sent back information about X-rays coming from sources far out in interstellar space. These made astronomers believe that the so-called black holes may be one result of the death of a star when it has finally collapsed and shrunk to an incredibly high density. One effect of its collapse is to make its gravitational pull so strong that none of the radio emissions by which we normally identify a star is able to escape – not even light waves!

The evidence of this is that when certain stars flare up and throw out particles, the particles suddenly increase speed giving off large quantities of X-rays. This acceleration scientists believe, indicates the presence of an unseen but incredibly powerful inward-drawing force – a black hole.

Above : The giant 5 metre (200 inch) reflecting telescope on Mount Palomar in California, USA.

Below : This huge dish aerial radio telescope is sited at Effelsberg in Germany.

UFOs

Throughout the past few centuries there have been recorded reports of space vehicles which have visited our Earth from an alien planet. In more recent years, these reports of Unidentified Flying Objects (UFOs) have attracted a great deal of public interest.

The reports of UFOs seem to increase over periods of a year or two, and then die down again. Many of the people who claim to have seen them are skilled observers of the air, such as airline pilots. The number of reports runs into thousands, and they come from many parts of the world. There are also a number of supposedly authentic photographs of these spacecraft which have earned themselves the nickname of 'flying saucers' because of their flat, disc-like shape.

So persistent have been these 'sightings' that during the 1960s, the USA set up the National Investigations Committee on Aerial Phenomena to investigate them. Nearly 11 000 reports were analysed and after eliminating sightings which could be explained away as normal phenomena, such as meteorites, high altitude weather balloons, and even robot satellites re-entering the atmosphere, they came to the conclusion that UFOs were genuine. They could not, however, explain what they were or from where they came.

Good photographs of UFOs are rare and difficult to authenticate. These two are from the USA.

The United States Air Force, on the other hand, also carried out an evaluation of UFO sightings, and concluded that *all* but a very few of the thousands of sightings could be logically explained away, or traced to some natural source, and the few unexplained ones were only unexplained because the evidence was insufficient to draw any definite conclusion.

Well, are UFOs spaceships from a distant planet, and are they under the control of extra-terrestial beings who are keeping our Earth under surveillance? It can only be said that the case for UFOs remains as yet unproven. One thing *is* certain, man is as curious and determined to find the answer to the problem of UFOs as he is to unravel all the other unsolved mysteries of our Universe.

Fuel Science

At some point in his history primitive man learned how to make a fire. No one is quite sure when this happened, but the occasion marked an important stage in his development, because for the first time he began to use *fuel*. The first fuel man used would, in all probability, have been wood, but as the centuries went by he discovered that other substances would burn such as coal and oil.

Legend has it that coal was discovered in China about 3000 years ago. An iron smelter is supposed to have dug a pit and lit a fire of wood in it to melt some iron ore when, to his surprise, he noticed that the sides of the pit were glowing red, and were even hotter than the wood fire. What he had inadvertently done was light his fire on an outcrop of coal.

Whether or not this story is true, coal did not come into widespread use as an energy fuel until much more recent times, and Britain was one of the first countries to use it on a large scale. Coal was the substance that fuelled Britain's great Industrial Revolution of the 18th and 19th centuries, and it is still the fuel that generates most of the electricity used in Britain today.

When considering various fuels available to man, it is best to think of them as sources of *energy*. Without these sources of energy, the modern world with all its vast factories, its electricity generating plants, and all its different forms of transport, would grind to a halt.

Above : This beautiful Greek Urn illustrates the importance of fire to early civilisations.

Below : Before the invention of modern machinery coal-mining was largely dependent on manpower.

Coal – the major source of energy

Early man had no source of energy apart from his own muscles, and later, the work of domesticated animals, but once he found ways of converting fuels, such as coal, into energy, his life was transformed. In spite of new, alternative energy sources, coal is still civilization's main standby fuel. Modern methods of mining and, perhaps more important, modern methods of actually burning it, mean that coal is still a cheap, economical source of energy.

Britain has one of the world's largest reserve deposits of coal, and consequently some of the most modern mining techniques: coal cutting machines operated by compressed air; hydraulic jacking systems for supporting the 'roof' of galleries from which the coal has been removed; and long mechanical conveyor belts to help bring the coal to

the surface. At some pits the conveyor system brings an endless moving river of coal direct to waiting trains, ready to transport it to power stations. There, it is used to fire boilers producing steam to drive turbine generators.

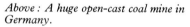

Above : A huge open-cast coal mine in Germany.

Below : A power-operated coal cutter at work in a Staffordshire mine in England.

The most modern pit power stations are to be found in the USA, Poland and at Longannet in Scotland. In these, the mines are linked directly to the fuel bunkers in the power stations themselves. At Longannet five separate mines are linked underground by an 8-kilometre (5-mile) long 'roadway', and a 'mix' of different coals is controlled by computer so that the correct blend for power station boilers is maintained.

What is often not realised about coal technology is the number of useful and varied 'by-products'. Coke and other smokeless fuels are produced by heating coal in special ovens. Gas is given off by the coal, and when this is cooled a

BY-PRODUCTS OF COAL

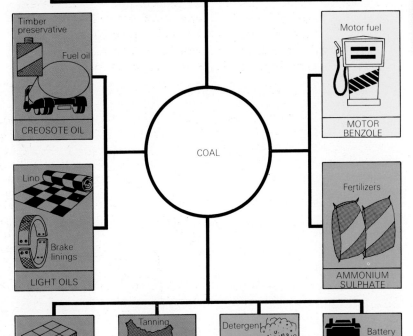

ANTHRACINE OIL — Road Tar, Fruit tree sprays, Dyes

PITCH — Road Tar, Roof felt, Rust preventative

XYLENE TOLUENE — TNT, Paints, Saccharine, Printing inks

BENZINE — DDT, Nylon

CREOSOTE OIL — Timber preservative, Fuel oil

MOTOR BENZOLE — Motor fuel

LIGHT OILS — Lino, Brake linings

AMMONIUM SULPHATE — Fertilizers

COAL

NAPHTHALENE OIL — Firelighters, Plastics

CARBOLIC OIL — Tanning, Adhesives, Aspirin, Disinfectant

LIQUID AMMONIA — Detergent, Soap, Explosives, Ammonia

SULPHURIC ACID — Battery electrolyte, Galvanizing

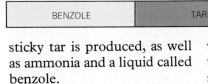

BENZOLE	TAR	AMMONIA

Above : An off-shore oil rig.

than the original oil!

Because the world's reserves of oil are running out, coal scientists and technologists are working on methods of extracting petrol from coal. Laboratory experiments have discovered a method of producing 227 litres (50 gallons) of petrol, plus 364 litres (80 gallons) of other oil fractions from 1 tonne (1 ton) of coal. This development alone will ensure the continuing importance of one of man's earliest sources of energy.

The need for new energy sources

The story of man's search for sources of energy has been one of brilliant success, but now the outlook is not so certain, and the rate at which the Earth's supplies of energy-producing fuels is being used is causing deep concern.

Man's principal energy supplies are unable to reproduce themselves. Coal and oil, known as fossil fuels, took about 250 000 000 years to form, and although new oil and coal are being formed in parts of the Earth, this happens very

sticky tar is produced, as well as ammonia and a liquid called benzole.

When the tar is put through a distilling process a number of different oils are produced. These include light oil, naphthalene oil, carbolic oil, wash oil, anthracene oils and pitch. These oils, in turn, produce different chemicals which are used in the production of many useful substances, such as antiseptics, disinfectants, dyes, fertilizers, plastics, mothballs, wood preservatives, paints and road-making tars. Benzole is used in the manufacture of nylon, plastics, photographic materials, and even in the making of perfumes, which smell much nicer slowly. The coal and oil now being extracted at an extremely fast rate are not being replaced, and estimates arrived at by scientists suggest that oil will become very expensive and hard to find by the end of the 20th century – and that is only a few years away!

The world's coal reserves overall are believed to be sufficient to last about 100 years, although some countries have supplies to last longer than that. So, even coal has a foreseeable end, and unless man can find some alternative sources of energy he may well have to go back to sleeping in cold caves, and doing without machines.

Nuclear power

Alternative energy sources must be found and developed. At present we have plenty of these, but unfortunately they can provide only a small fraction of the world's enormous energy needs. One of the best-known alternatives is nuclear power. Nuclear fuels, such as uranium-235 and plutonium, can be made to undergo an energy release called 'fission', a process that produces heat. Scientists have found a way to control this complicated release of atomic energy so that when a cooling flow of liquid or gas is passed over the hot nuclear fuel, the heat can be used to raise the temperature of water to the level of steam. This can then be used to drive conventional steam turbines connected to dynamos, and electricity is generated.

One great advantage of nuclear fuels is that they are used up very gradually. One tonne (1 ton) of uranium-235 will generate as much heat as 3 000 000 tonnes of coal. There are, however, disadvantages to using nuclear power stations. They are extremely complicated and expensive to build, and there is the problem of disposing of the dangerous radio-active waste which is left behind after most types of nuclear fuel have been used.

Although nuclear reactors have been used successfully in ships and submarines, it is difficult to make them small and light enough to operate small vehicles such as cars and aircraft, which are at present powered by oil-based fuel. In addition to this, there is always the danger of an escape of harmful radio-active material in the event of a crash. So it would seem that although there will be an increasing amount of electricity generated by nuclear power stations, man will have to look elsewhere to satisfy his need for energy.

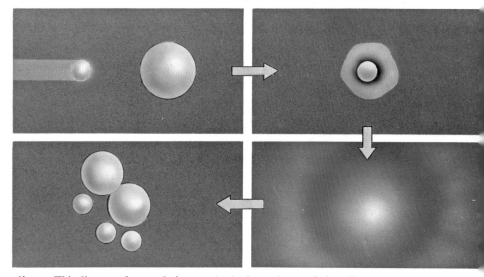

Above: This diagram shows a fission reaction. A fast moving neutron collides with the nucleus of a uranium-235 atom, the nucleus becomes distorted on impact. This stress breaks it in two, releasing energy in the form of an explosion. Two lighter nuclei and three free neutrons result from the explosion.

Below: A nuclear power station in America.

Solar energy

One other source of energy that is receiving increasing attention in many countries where the climate is suitable, is that original source of all energy on Earth – the Sun. A great deal of experimental work has been carried out, particularly in the USA, on capturing the Sun's rays and turning their heat into a controllable form of power.

The interior of the Sun is like a hydrogen bomb of enormous size, where hydrogen is changed into another gas called helium. As this change takes place, some matter is converted into energy which radiates out into space. Some of this energy reaches the surface of the Earth in the form of heat – as anyone can discover for themselves when they lie on the beach on a hot summer's day.

In fact, the amount of energy coming from the sun can be measured, and expressed in watts – the units of electric power. The amount falling on just 1 square kilometre (0.3861 square miles) of the Earth's surface is about 4000 megawatts – more than enough to light and heat a small town. The problem is harnessing this enormous and almost inexhaustible source of energy.

At a solar research establishment in the French Pyrenees, a huge parabolic mirror with 9000 facets collects the Sun's rays and focuses them onto the central part of a furnace. Here again, the heat produced can be used to produce steam to drive turbogenerators. In America, an enormous solar furnace is being built in a desert area where several hundred dish-shaped mirrors are arranged in straight rows all facing the Sun. A computer controls their movement and keeps them aligned as the Sun moves across the sky, so that they always receive the maximum radiation. A tower-mounted boiler receives the concentrated reflections from the mirrors.

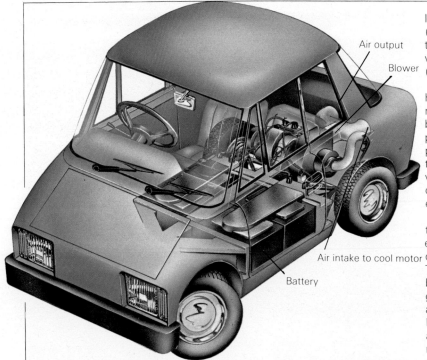

Air output

Blower

Air intake to cool motor

Battery

BATTERY POWERED

Electric cars are often thought to be a new development in the world of transport, but the first world land speed record was set by a battery-powered car as long ago as 1898. By the early 1900s there were hundreds of electric cars and trucks on the roads of New York, Paris and London.

However, no electric car of the day could compete with the petrol engine for speed, acceleration and, most important of all – range. The best of the electrics could manage little more than 96 kilometres (60 miles) before its battery had to be recharged, and its top speed would be little more than 48 kph (30 mph).

The day is not far distant, however, when the electric car may come into its own once more, because after the year 2000, petrol-powered vehicles will probably be on the decline due to the approaching exhaustion of the world's oil supplies, which in any case, will become increasingly expensive.

Leaving aside the problem of their comparatively short range, electric cars have many advantages over their petrol driven cousins. They are much easier to drive, because there is no need for a gearbox, and only a brake and accelerator pedal are necessary. No fuel is actually burned so there are no exhaust gases and therefore no pollution – a tremendous advantage in congested cities. They are ideal for the short range work of milk floats, fork-lift trucks, postal delivery trucks, and some small delivery vehicles. For vehicles such as a small town car, battery recharging could be a problem, although one or two leading manufacturers of motor

Above : A solar-powered boiler developed by Professor G. Francia, an Italian scientist.

Solar heat can also be used on individual buildings as small as a single house, not to generate electricity, but simply to heat water for domestic use. Extraction of low-grade heat from the Sun's rays does not require complicated equipment. A solar collector panel has a darkened absorber (backed with insulating material to reduce heat loss) through which a heat-exchanger fluid, usually either air or water, is circulated. The panel is covered with glass or transparent plastic material, which transmits the visible light energy from the Sun, but does not pass the infra-red, or any heat energy re-radiated from the absorber.

Use of the Sun's energy in this form contributes to the sum total of our energy requirements by reducing the need to use some other power source to heat the domestic water supply. But again there are drawbacks in using solar energy in this way. The house heater panels which collect the heat are large, and have a high installation cost, and of course in the temperate zones of the world, they would only work to full efficiency during the summer months. Unhappily, those parts of the world where the sun shines almost continuously during daylight hours are largely desert where electricity requirements are lower, and central heating is not needed anyway.

cars have produced prototypes like the Commuta car, built by Ford, a handy little two-seater with four standard 12-volt lead-acid batteries supplying power to two electric motors each of 5 bhp. The motors are air-cooled and the warm air from them can be used for heating the interior of the car.

It would seem that with our present knowledge, using lead-acid batteries, small town cars will be useful for short-range work, but longer-range vehicles will have to await the development of some new source of electric power, such as solar energy.

Below: The battery-powered Ford Commuta Car.

Below : A French designed solar furnace.

Wind and waves

Another source of natural energy – and one of the oldest known in the world – is wind power. Sailing ships and windmills have for centuries harnessed the ever-moving atmosphere.

NASA, the American space agency, has developed a horizontal axis windmill with blades 37.5 metres (41 yards) in diameter. On a day with a good stiff breeze blowing, it has a maximum output of 100 kilowatts, and should have an average output of between 30 and 35 kilowatts. Although it is only experimental, and much larger ones could be built, the amount of electricity generated is very small.

There is an enormous amount of power contained in the oceans of the world, not only because of their constant movement in the way of waves and tides, but because water itself contains one of the most abundant fuels on the Earth – hydrogen. The hydrogen, of course, would have to be extracted, but this can be done, and when it is liquified it becomes an extremely powerful fuel – as the astronauts who rode the giant *Saturn V* rockets know only too well.

Many scientists are of the opinion that hydrogen will be the most important fuel of the early part of the 21st century. It is a fuel that can be used in engines similar to those which burn petrol and oil today. It also has one great advantage. When it is burned it merely produces water, and no polluting gases.

Aircraft engineers with an eye to a future without the

Above : Wind powers the sailing clipper Sussex.

Left : A modern wind-driven experimental electricity generator.

Above, opposite page : An artist's impression of a hydrogen powered airliner.

Right : A hydro-electric power station.

Below : The turbine hall of a Drax coal-fired power station in England.

oil-based fuels used today to power jet engines, consider that after the year 2010, more and more aircraft will have to use liquid hydrogen (LH_2) in their place. Liquid hydrogen condenses to a thin bluish liquid, but in order to accomplish this change from gas to liquid, it has to be cooled to the incredibly low temperature of minus 253°C (minus 423°F) – not much above absolute zero! This makes it a highly volatile fuel and dangerous to handle. One tiny drop on the skin would cause a severe burn, even though it would vanish into its gaseous state in a split second.

If the problem of storing in specially insulated tanks could be solved, the aircraft designers think it would be possible to make smaller and more efficient engines. However, there is a snag in using LH_2 as an aircraft fuel. It has what is called a 'low density', which means that a tonne of it would take up much more space than the same weight of kerosene, and this would necessitate large storage tanks somewhere in the design of the plane. Designers, however, think this problem could be overcome, and two American aircraft companies – Lockheed and Boeing – have already considered ways in which some of their larger passenger planes might be adapted to the use of liquid hydrogen fuel.

Apart from yielding hydrogen, water can be used in other ways to help generate electricity. One of these, hydroelectric power, has been used for many years by the simple technique of holding back the waters of a river by means of a dam and controlling its flow near the foot of the artificial barrier where the pressure is greatest. The water flows over the blades of a turbine/generator and thus produces electricity. Hydro-electric power stations are efficient and economical, but can be built only in those parts of the world where there is a suitable geographic combination of mountains and rivers.

Experiments are being conducted off the coasts of Britain to see if there is a feasible way in which the wave movements of the sea can be turned into electricity. Various floating rafts have been tried, but the studies are far from complete. Harnessing the tides to provide a form of hydro-electric power is also under consideration and one such tidal generating station is already in operation in a river estuary on France's Atlantic coast. The incoming tide is trapped in an artificial 'harbour' and its outward flow controlled through water-driven turbines.

Will man solve the energy problem? It is too soon to be sure, but man is an ingenious and resourceful creature, particularly when his existence is threatened, and the odds are very much in favour of him finding a way out of the difficulties that loom ahead. In the meantime, however, one thing is essential – we must all conserve the fast dwindling fossil fuels and use them more sparingly, or we are heading for the catastrophe of a world without power.

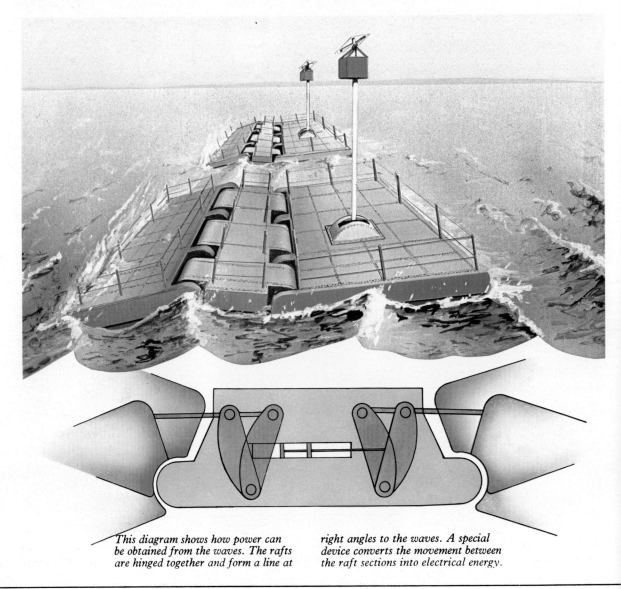

This diagram shows how power can be obtained from the waves. The rafts are hinged together and form a line at right angles to the waves. A special device converts the movement between the raft sections into electrical energy.

Lasers

If you shine a torch outside in the darkness you can see a beam of light coming from it and striking objects within the range of its power. Although the beam is concentrated by the curved reflector of the torch, you can see that much of the light is scattered around the general direction in which it is being pointed.

Ordinary light is made up of a mixture of waves of different lengths travelling in many directions. The waves overlap in places, but generally they are out of step with each other, and this is why they become scattered from a source such as a battery-powered torch.

In July, 1960, an American scientist named Theodore H. Maiman, working in a laboratory near Malibu Beach in California, produced a beam of light that was so narrow and concentrated that it could be used to cut a hole no larger than the dot over the letter 'i'. It is called a 'laser', a word which is formed by the initial letters of the rather long phrase describing how it is formed – Light Amplification by Stimulated Emission of Radiation.

The important difference between a beam of ordinary light and a laser beam is that in a laser the light waves are not only of the same length, but they are also all of the same frequency and move in step (phase) with each other. Because they are in phase their energy is combined and concentrated, there is no scatter at all, and they all arrive at a given point at the same instant. This gives them an intensity

millions of times greater than any other kind of artificial light.

There are several types of laser, and one of the simpler kinds uses a crystal, such as a ruby. The diagrams overleaf will help to show what happens when a light source is shone on to the ruby and 'excites' the atoms of which it is made. As the light source strikes them the electrons jump a fraction farther away from the nucleus of each atom. When they jump back they emit light, and the trick is to cause as many electrons as possible to jump back at the same instant to create Stimulated Emission. When enough electrons have jumped back

to their normal position, the light they produce is reflected up and down the crystal by the silvered ends.

Because the light emitted by the laser is all in waves of the same length, it comes out as an incredibly pure colour – red in the case of a ruby crystal – and is known as *monochromatic coherent light*. If the original light source is shone on to the ruby in pulses lasting a fraction of a second, this boosts the power of the beam enormously. So great is the peak power of a pulsed laser that it can develop temperatures double

Below: A coiled laser tube used in an aircraft factory in the United States of America.

those on the surface of the Sun in a fraction of a second.

Lasers have many uses which are of great benefit in both the medical and industrial fields. A laser beam can be used to drill tiny holes in diamonds, and to cut through steel and even harder metals such as tantalum. It can even be used by surgeons to carry out delicate operations on the human eye.

Some idea of the immense power in a laser beam can be grasped when you realise that scientists directed one at a mirror left behind on the Moon by the American astronauts. The light was reflected back, and by measuring the time it took to make the double journey of 800 000 kilometres (500 000 miles) they were able to calculate the distance to within an accuracy of 33 centimetres (13 inches). And that is something well beyond the reach of a battery-powered torch!

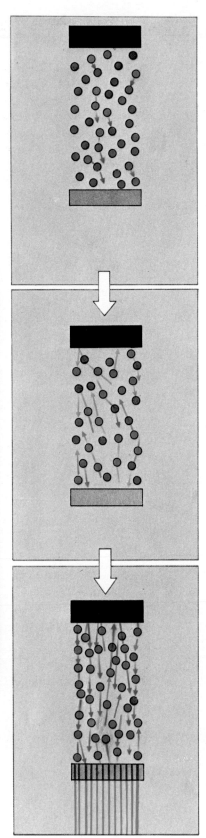

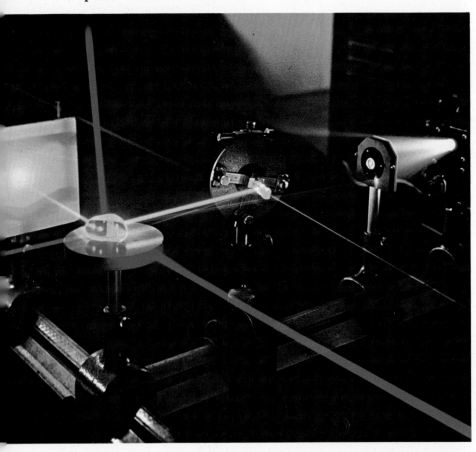

Above : A ruby laser in action in a laboratory.

Right : The ruby (coloured red) is struck by a light source, causing the electrons to jump. The light they produce is reflected up and down the crystal by silvered ends, until eventually the light emitted emerges in waves of the same length.

Communication

The ability that man has to communicate with his fellows has helped him to progress from being a primitive cave-dwelling primate to his present highly civilized state. Once language developed, men were able to exchange thoughts and ideas, and perhaps most important of all, they were able to co-operate in improving their living conditions. The written word came after the spoken word, and enabled people to record their thoughts and their discoveries for future generations to study.

Early man must have been fairly isolated and the amount of information passing from one group to another would have been sparse. Even with the development of printing in Europe in the 15th century and the production of books that followed, communication was limited to the educated minority. It was not until the invention of radio in 1896 that communication on a wider scale became possible – and this was later enhanced by the arrival of television in 1929. Nor must we forget the tremendous contribution made by the invention of the telephone in 1876.

Although telephone and radio communication between countries has been available for many years, radio transmitters and telephone cables have limitations. Laying telephone cables is a fairly slow and laborious process, and over long distances there is the problem of linkage through exchanges between towns and then between countries. Transmission of voices over a long distance by means of underground cable, or overhead telephone wires also requires 'booster' stations at various intervals along the chosen route.

Left : The Peterborough Psalter, a beautifully Illuminated Manuscript done entirely by hand.

Below : Some early radio and television receivers.

Radio waves

Radio transmissions are also subject to interference of various kinds. Radio waves travel outwards in straight lines from the transmitting aerial and do not follow the curvature of the Earth. When Guglielmo Marconi sent the first radio signal across the north Atlantic he was able to do so only because of an electrical reflecting layer in the upper atmosphere, which bounced the radio waves back to Earth.

This part of the upper atmosphere is known as the ionosphere and is made up of several layers of ionized gases with this reflecting property. One of these regions is called the Appleton layer, or F-region, and lies between 150 and 400 kilometres (93 and 250 miles) above the Earth. Beneath this is the Heaviside-Kennelly or E-region, which is about 90 to 150 kilometres (56 to 93 miles) above the Earth. Long radio waves are reflected by the Heaviside-Kennelly layer and short wave transmissions bounce back from the Appleton layer. Very short waves, called VHF (Very High Frequency), and Ultra High Frequency, or UHF waves, are not affected by these reflecting layers and pass through them into space – a lucky phenomenon for astronauts in spaceships, and for unmanned orbiting satellites.

The ionosphere can be affected by sunspot activity and by magnetic storms; both these cause the height and densities of the layers to change. As a result radio programmes from overseas sometimes fade away as you are listening to them. All these difficulties have now been largely overcome by the use of communication satellites placed into orbit. Some, like the *Early Bird*, are put into stationary orbits as much as 35 000 kilometres (21 700 miles) out in space.

These stationary, or *synchronous*, orbits mean that the satellites are whirling around the Earth once every 24 hours and travelling in the same direction as the Earth's natural rotation – thus they remain continuously above the same spot on its surface.

There are now a number of these communication satellites in orbit around the Earth, and they are permanently available for re-transmitting television programmes from one region of the Earth to another. Huge dish aerials are used to transmit and receive the signals, and delicate machinery keeps them aimed at the correct point in space. The satellites are powered by solar cells which top up their batteries

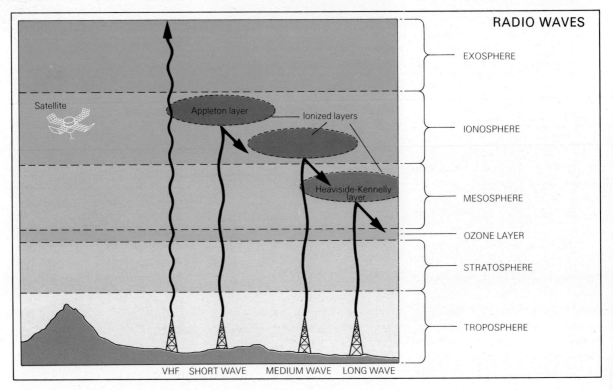

RADIO WAVES

EXOSPHERE

IONOSPHERE

MESOSPHERE

OZONE LAYER

STRATOSPHERE

TROPOSPHERE

Satellite

Appleton layer

Ionized layers

Heaviside-Kennelly layer

VHF   SHORT WAVE   MEDIUM WAVE   LONG WAVE

Telstar

The largest satellite communications station in Europe is at Goonhilly Downs in England. This station took part in the first transatlantic television transmission made via an artificial satellite – *Telstar*. Communications satellites, like many others, have a limited life of about five years. New ones, usually with a greater capacity for carrying more two-way transmissions, have to be launched at regular intervals to keep the system fully operational.

Above : The American 'Early Bird' Satellite, the first communications satellite to be launched into Earth orbit.

Left : The screen of a home television set displaying information known as CEEFAX.

Opposite page : Diagram to show how radio waves of varying lengths are affected by the atmosphere. Short, medium and long waves bounce off ionized layers, while very high frequency and ultra high frequency waves pass through the atmosphere and out into space.

Instant fact-finding

In today's busy world there is an increasing need for up-to-date information on news, sport, financial matters and travel.

One new method of communication which will meet this need will probably be in almost every Western household before the end of the 20th century. It is a system of transmitting facts of all kinds onto the screen of your television set – rather like the page of a magazine. The system, a British invention called CEEFAX, has been in operation since 1973.

A simple way of understanding how this system works is to regard it as a visual news and information service that allows a viewer to 'see facts' written in words and figures on the television screen. A special adaptor has to be built into the television set, then the viewer uses a hand-sized control unit, similar to a small battery-operated calculator and punches a series of codes which enable him to select the information he requires from the service.

Normally, the ordinary picture programme is blacked out while the information is displayed, but there is one selector button on the hand control unit which will superimpose a newsflash – a brief description of the latest news about some important event of the day.

In fact, the information which can be communicated by such systems is almost limitless, and you can get it all without leaving your home!

Above : An early print of a Bell telephone being used.

Telephone link-up

Alexander Graham Bell, the Scots inventor of the telephone, contributed a great deal to the world of communication. It was on March 11, 1876, in a hotel in Boston, USA, where he was carrying out experiments with his early telephone apparatus, that he spoke the words: 'Mr Watson, come here; I want you'. Perhaps equally deserving of a place in the history books is the man who heard those words – the first ever successfully transmitted in speech by wire – Thomas A. Watson, who was Bell's assistant.

Bell's idea was soon taken up in both Britain and North America. The first telephone exchange was provided in New Haven, USA in 1877. Today, of course, there are millions of homes and offices with telephones, and the improvements on Bell's original idea have made communication by word of mouth both simple and immediate.

Development of the telephone system was, of course, a gradual process, and depended not only on the spread of overhead wires and underground cables, but on the building of telephone 'exchanges' where each subscriber call could be connected to other numbers he wished to call. Early 'exchanges' were all manually operated, and then, in March 1912, Britain opened its first public automatic telephone exchange at Epsom in Surrey.

Electronic systems

The automatic exchange, working in conjunction with the telephone dial, brought a tremendous acceleration in connections between subscribers, but now new electronic systems are being used. A 'family' of electronic exchanges will revolutionize telephonic communication.

Telephones using this system do not have dials, but push-button switches which are quicker in operation. Other advantages are less line noise and distortion of speech, greater reliability and ease of maintenance. Customers will also have a better and more flexible service. For example, it will enable subscribers to use a simple code for calling numbers they use frequently instead of having to 'dial' the number in full. Users will also be able to 'hold' an incoming call, and then make an outgoing call over the same phone if they need to make a quick inquiry. The equipment is also able to give a 'call waiting' signal to tell two people already talking that someone else is trying to contact one of them. It will also enable a number of people to talk to each other on a 'conference' call.

Above: A modern electronic telephone exchange.

Below: The British Post Office Telecommunications Cable Ship Alert.

Computers

When a scientist is tackling a problem of research which involves making observations and recording what he observes, it is normally quite impossible for him to proceed unless he has some means of measuring his results.

Making calculations is a time-consuming process, and over the centuries men have tried to find ways of calculating quickly. One of the earliest ideas for speeding up simple arithmetic was the *abacus*, which consisted of a frame with coloured beads that could be moved along parallel rods.

In some countries in the Far East the abacus is still used today, and experts can make calculations on it at great speed. Although the abacus could be described as a form of 'computer' it is certainly a far cry from the modern electronic computers which are in widespread use today.

Charles Babbage, a British mathematician, invented a machine in 1812, which he called a 'difference engine'. Babbage was given a grant of £17000 by the government to build this machine which he started in 1823. The mechanical construction was so delicate that he had to train workmen and design special tools to build the gears required. Babbage's machine was intended to work in decimal numbers, but unhappily, because of a dispute the machine was never completed and was abandoned in 1842.

Despite this setback, however, Babbage went on to produce many improved designs, and his last model, called an 'analytical engine', employed many of the principles of mechanical calculators which were applied in the

Opposite top : Charles Babbage's amazing 'difference engine' (left) and his 'analytical engine' (right).

Opposite bottom : By contrast, a number of silicon chips are compared with a postage stamp for size.

Below : IBM portable desk computers in use.

Bottom left : Complicated wiring behind a panel in a computer.

Bottom right : Reels of memory tape in a big computer.

1940s. Today, of course, computers employ electrical circuits using the amazingly tiny silicon chips, and transistors. They work using the binary system rather than the decimal system of mathematics. Binary numbers need only two symbols, '0' and '1'. When counting in binary you start with '1' for one. Two is expressed as '10', and you call it one-oh, not ten. Three is written as '11', four as '100', five as '101', six as '110', seven as '111', and so on. A new digit is added at two, four, eight, 16 etc., whereas in the decimal system they are added at ten, hundred, thousand, and so on.

In a modern computer when the electric current is *not* flowing, the effect is represented as the binary number '0', while a current flowing is represented by '1', so that any number can be converted into a series of electric pulses.

One great asset of a computer is its 'memory'. Information previously fed into the memory can be called up by the operator at the press of a button. A central processing unit, or CPU, contains electronic circuits for adding, subtracting, multiplying, dividing, and other calculations such as square roots.

Computers have not only removed the drudgery from long, tedious calculations but they have transformed many areas of commerce such as insurance and banking, by their ability to make calculations in minutes that would take years to complete. If man is destined to visit the stars, the complex calculations involved with astral navigation would be impossible without miniaturized computers like those already used by astronauts in the Soyuz and Apollo spacecraft.

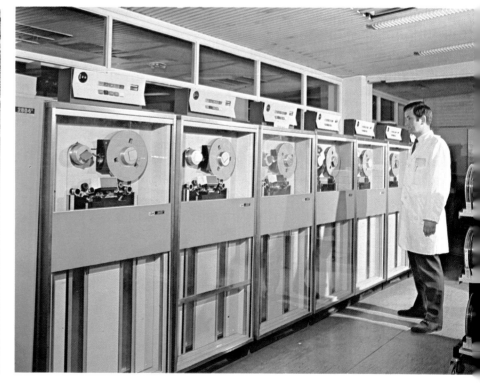

Printing

The spoken word, although always important in the exchange of ideas and information, has the disadvantage of being temporary. Any information exchanged only lasts as long as the memories of the two people holding the conversation, and as we all know, memories can be short! When man learned to write, he was able to store his knowledge and experience, so that it could be passed on after his death. But writing is a slow, laborious business, and it was not until the arrival of printing that knowledge could be both stored and passed on to an ever increasing number of people.

The earliest surviving printed book was produced in China in AD 868, and it was made by carving letters or designs in relief on blocks of wood, which could be inked and stamped or 'printed' on sheets of paper.

Printing today is very different; it uses *movable types*, a process that was invented by the German Johann Gutenberg. In about 1456, Gutenberg and his associates Fust and Schoeffer printed the first copy of the Bible, a task that took several years.

The Gutenberg Bible has 280 pages containing more than $3\frac{1}{4}$ million separate letters, or movable types, and it has been calculated that if it had been printed on engraved wooden blocks following the earlier Chinese method, it would have taken 10 engravers 10 years to complete.

William Caxton, England's first printer, learned the trade

Above: A page from the Gutenberg Bible which can be seen in the British Museum.

Above: Egyptian hieroglyphs, or picture writing, on an ancient papyrus.

Left: An old print showing a screw-press, taken from the Book of English Trades, 1821.

at Cologne in Germany. After his training, he set up a press at Westminster, London, in 1476. In Caxton's day printing presses were crude wooden structures in which a 'platen' was screwed down to press a moist sheet of paper against an inked 'forme' of type. Some years later, hand presses were invented, which were operated by a lever. Rotary presses with cylinders (originally powered by steam engines) were first used in Britain about 1814.

In all these early printing processes the letters or 'type' had to be positioned or set by hand, and typesetters, called *compositors*, worked this way until almost the end of the 19th century. Although compositors became extremely skilled at their trade, and could select and put together a line of type by hand very quickly, it was nevertheless a tedious job. Many attempts were made by engineers to replace this laborious method by a mechanical

one. After a number of failures, an extremely ingenious machine called a *Linotype* was produced and patented in 1884 by Ottmar Mergenthaler.

Linotype

A Linotype machine creates lines of metal type which can be used for direct printing. The operator sits at a keyboard, similar to a typewriter, and 'types' out the words after having set controls on the machine to govern the width of each line.

Molten metal, contained in a reservoir, is kept in a liquid state by heaters. As the opera-

tor presses each letter-key a hard metal matrix with the letter engraved on it drops into position. When the whole line of words and the spaces between them has been completed, the operator presses another key which forces the wedge shaped 'spacers' between the words until the line is spaced out to fill the measure selected.

The hot metal is now forced into a mould, one side of which is formed by the row of letters or matrices. When the mould is full, the metal is cooled so that it solidifies, and by pressing a lever the operator causes

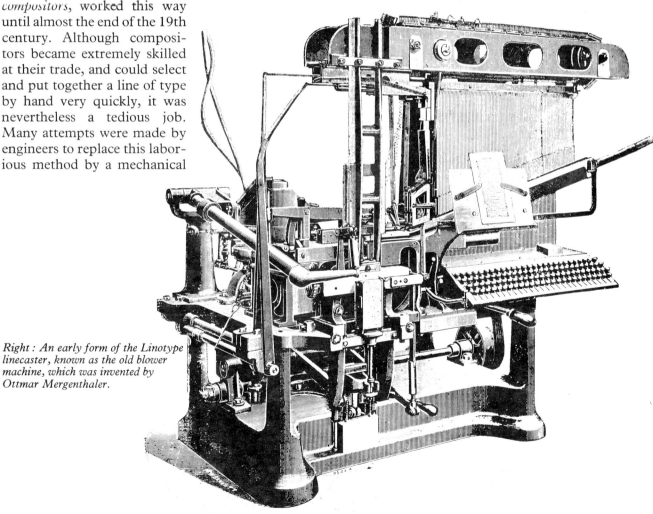

Right : An early form of the Linotype linecaster, known as the old blower machine, which was invented by Ottmar Mergenthaler.

the machine to deliver the whole line of type, called a *slug*, into a tray or *galley*.

The matrices can be used over and over again, and even the metal used to mould the lines of type can be melted down and re-used.

Monotype

Another mechanical typesetting machine is the Monotype. Unlike the Linotype which produces solid bars or 'slugs' of metal each with a whole line of words on its face, Monotype machines cast each individual letter separately. One of the advantages of this system is that the movable type can be hand-corrected letter by letter, instead of having to re-set a whole line as would have to be done on a Linotype. Both these type-making machines are used for producing the text for newspapers and many books.

Computer setting

In recent years new technology has brought great changes to the printing world, and many of these are due to the use of the computer in printing.

Typesetting systems using a computer to assist them can produce printed *copy* in a much shorter time than conventional methods allow. As you will already know from an earlier section in this book, computers are sophisticated counting machines with an electronic 'memory' from which information can be drawn at a high speed. Computers that work with a typesetting machine are usually specially designed for the job they have to do. The memory part of the computer is fed, or *programmed*, with

Colour printing is a skilled and complicated process. No. 7 is a colour photograph printed in four colours. The original transparency is photographed a number of times in order to separate the colours which are then printed progressively, one on top of the other.

1. Cyan
2. Yellow
3. Cyan and yellow
4. Magenta
5. Cyan, yellow and magenta
6. Black
7. Cyan, yellow, magenta and black.

1

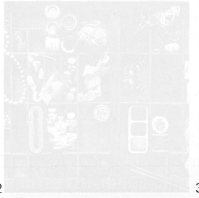
2

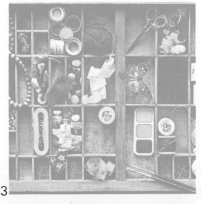
3

4

5

6

7

codes. One code, for example, will tell the computer about selecting the size and style of type, while another will instruct it about the length of lines. It is even possible to feed into the memory banks instructions on words that have to be hyphenated, and where to break words which will not quite fit at the end of a line. The operator working at the keyboard can also carry out corrections on the computer which produces a *print-out* for him to read.

The advantages of computer-assisted typesetting are that several keyboard operators can work at the same time using only one computer, and because each operator does not have to put in hyphens or *justify* (making each line fit the measure exactly) the copy, they can increase their output.

Computers are playing an ever-increasing role in the newspaper world, and during the next few years methods of producing morning and evening papers will have changed dramatically.

Journalists in the 1980s will be able to tap out 'copy' on a keyboard, and design or 'make-up' their pages on TV screens, including headlines, and even photographs.

ELECTRON MICROSCOPE

Although the principles of optical microscopes have been known since the 17th century, it was not until the early 1800s that optical lenses were sufficiently improved to give scientists an instrument that would enable them to examine minute objects by greatly enlarging their image. Modern light microscopes are widely used but they have almost reached the limits of their optical performance. One reason is the limit imposed by the 'resolving' abilities of glass lenses passing ordinary light. No matter how many times an object may be magnified, if its image is blurred, it will always be so.

Electron microscopes make use of a stream of electrons to 'illuminate' the object to be magnified. The electron stream can be focused by means of an electro-magnetic field, and because electrons travel with a wave motion similar to that of light, but over 100 000 times shorter, it is possible to focus them to much finer limits. The minimum details resolvable under a light microscope would be 0.000025 cm apart, while one of the latest electron microscopes is able to resolve details 10 000 times smaller.

In 1965, *scanning* electron microscopes became available which enable scientists to study tiny objects in three dimensions.

An enormous electron microscope in Japan.

Medical advances

Medicine has been described as an art that makes use of all the sciences. Its purpose is to maintain the body in good health, to relieve pain, mend injury, and help prolong life. Today most of us take our health for granted, and if we are young we probably never think about being ill. Occasionally, of course, we do suffer from some ailment, and we would be very lucky indeed to go through life without being ill at all.

When we are ill, however, we know that we can get expert treatment from our doctors or specialists, and sometimes we may have to go into hospital for more intensive treatment, or for an operation. All this, too, we tend to take for granted, but it is only in the last hundred years that the really dramatic advances have been made in medicine and surgery. People are living longer today than ever before, and although the battle against diseases has not been won completely – and probably never will be – the fight against the organisms

which cause them is more intense than ever.

Cures for disease

Among the principal weapons in this battle are modern drugs called antibiotics. The word antibiotic really means 'against life', and these drugs attack and destroy bacteria and other micro-organisms. Antibacterial drugs are obtained from

Right : The big CIBA factory in Switzerland where drugs are manufactured.

Opposite top : David was born with insufficient immunity to infection. Modern technology has been able to provide him with a safe environment in which to live, namely his 'space suit' and a push cart mounted with a life-support system.

Opposite bottom : One stage in the manufacturing of antibiotics. The workers wear protective clothing to prevent contamination from the drugs.

living organisms, such as moulds or bacteria, and they work by reducing the growth and reproduction of micro-organisms in the body, sometimes even destroying them.

Antibiotics such as penicillin, streptomycin, and aureomycin are used to combat a wide range of illnesses, but they have to be used carefully and selectively, because if they are taken over a long period the bacteria in the body build up resistance to them. Antibiotics are of little or no use against diseases caused by the organisms known as viruses, which are much smaller than bacteria.

Another group of drugs which also kill bacteria and inhibit their rate of growth in much the same way as antibiotics are the sulphonamides. Sulphonamides have been largely replaced by antibiotics, but they are still quite widely used and are effective against certain types of infection.

There are, of course, thousands of other drugs used in the treatment of disease, and it would be impossible to list them all here. Millions of pounds are spent every year by the various drug manufacturing companies on research,

and new medicines are being discovered and tested all the time. New drugs are subjected to exhaustive tests before being given to human patients to make sure they not only do the job for which they are intended, but also to ensure that they do not have any dangerous side-effects.

One of the problems of making drugs effective against disease is finding a way of getting the drug to that part of the body which is diseased. *Drug delivery systems* are being tested in medical research laboratories in Britain and in the United States of America. One way of giving what are called 'targeted drugs' are by means of *liposomes*. These are tiny droplets of oil, invisible to the naked eye, and each made up of several layers, with the

drugs held in between them.

The liposomes are then injected into the bloodstream, and the drugs do not disperse until they reach the organ in the body which requires treatment. Drugs given in this way can be used to treat cancer patients because they go straight to the point where the cancer cells are attacking the body, and their effect is concentrated.

Another remarkable method of giving drugs externally, instead of taking them into the body through the mouth, is also under test. A specially made 'wafer' is impregnated with the prescribed drug and then strapped or stuck on to the skin for a number of hours. The drug is then absorbed slowly and evenly into the bloodstream.

111

Disease prevention

'Prevention is better than cure' is an old saying which holds more true today than ever before, and one of the ways in which modern medicine has made this a reality is by the use of vaccines for immunization. Like many discoveries in medicine the effectiveness of immunization was discovered quite by chance when a surgeon's apprentice named Edward Jenner, a native of Berkeley, Gloucestershire, overheard a milkmaid say, 'I cannot take smallpox, because I have had cowpox'.

Without realising what it meant, the country girl had revealed the basic principle of immunization – that a small dose of the infection can produce immunity (resistance to the disease). After many years of study, Jenner carried out his first experiment in immunization in May, 1796, when he inoculated a boy with cowpox from a cowpox sore on the hand of a dairymaid. After waiting for the boy's arm to heal, Jenner then inoculated him with smallpox viruses, but the boy did not get the disease. This was because the cowpox and smallpox viruses are very similar, and so, as a result of having had cowpox, he was immune to smallpox. The immunization had given him resistance to a disease which had been bringing suffering and death to an average of one million people every year for 800 years. Because of almost universal immunization against smallpox, the disease has been virtually wiped out in the world.

Modern vaccines are prepared in a variety of ways. The preparation may contain germs (bacteria or viruses) which are dead, or still alive but weakened. The germs may be killed by heat or the use of sound waves, or treated with chemicals. Once the vaccine has been introduced into the bloodstream it stimulates the white

An 18th century cartoonist's view of Edward Jenner's vaccination against smallpox. People were injected with a mild form of cowpox, which caused great consternation.

The Cow-Pock — or — the Wonderful Effects of the New Inoculation! — Vide the Publications of ye Anti-Vaccine Society.

blood cells and other parts of the blood to produce 'antibodies'. Although these antibodies tend to disappear after a number of weeks have passed, if the person who has been immunized should become exposed to the disease for which the vaccine has been given, more antibodies are produced and set to work to neutralize the invading bacteria.

Immunization against smallpox is carried out by breaking the surface of the skin and smearing a little of the vaccine on the wound. Other vaccines are introduced into the bloodstream by means of a hypodermic syringe, the injection usually being made into the upper part of the arm, or the leg.

Apart from smallpox, the diseases for which vaccines give either total or partial immunity, include diphtheria, typhoid, tetanus, whooping cough, measles, certain influenza strains, poliomyelitis, cholera, and some allergies like hay fever.

Although a great deal was known about the human body even in the 17th and 18th centuries, it was not until the end of the 18th century that surgery formed an accepted part of the world of medicine. Even then, operations were carried out only when patients were in dire distress and no other course seemed likely to help them, because they usually died later from blood poisoning as a result of the operation.

The man responsible for greatly reducing the suffering resulting from surgery was Joseph Lister, who was born in 1827. Lister was for most of his life a professor of surgery

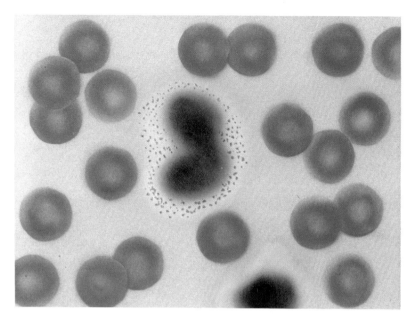

at Edinburgh and Glasgow Universities, and at King's College, London. In the year 1886, he made the discovery that the wound infections following surgery were due to bacteria, and he began to use carbolic acid in an attempt to destroy the bacteria in the air round the operating table.

Clean, sterile operating theatres as we know them were unknown in Lister's day, but he was the first surgeon to realise the importance of antisepsis – the killing of bacteria in and around the incision

Top : Human blood cells greatly magnified. The black blob is a 'leucocyte' with plasma granules.

Above : Smallpox has been eliminated throughout the world by modern methods of immunization.

necessary for the operation, and it was his pioneering work with antiseptics that led to the strict aseptic routines which surround modern operating theatres, where surgical instruments are sterilized before use, and all the theatre staff have to 'scrub up' and wear sterilized gloves and clothing.

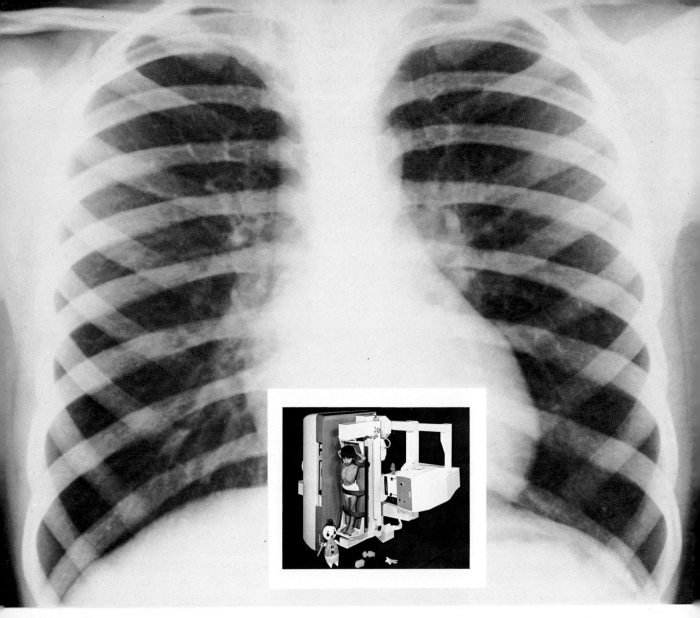

Looking inside the body

The use of X-rays as a means of photographing broken or fractured bones is something many people experience. Being hard tissues, bones show up clearly on an ordinary X-ray photograph, but internal organs of the body which are made up of soft tissues, require special techniques to make them visible. The digestive system can be photographed with X-rays when the patient has eaten a barium meal. The barium restricts the passage of the X-rays through the organs and outlines them as a shadow on the photographic plate. Radio-opaque fluids can also be injected into the blood system when parts of this need to be seen.

X-rays, however, can be dangerous and have to be carefully controlled. Now, a new method of looking inside the body without using X-rays has been developed. It is called an ultrasonic body scanner and makes use of high frequency sound waves which reflect an image of the internal organs. This image can be transposed onto a TV screen and the doctor can actually watch the

Above : An X-Ray picture of the upper part of the body showing the rib cage.

Inset : A modern X-Ray machine, designed to take complete body pictures, especially of children.

image being formed as he moves the scanner over the patient's body.

Scientists are working on revolutionary scanners which make use of a system called Nuclear Magnetic Resonance or NMR. It may be some years before these are perfected, but it is hoped that they will enable doctors to look into the deeper recesses of the body, and even into the living brain.

Spare-part surgery

X-rays and other scanning methods can be used to detect damage to the skeleton other than fractures. Sometimes the joints become damaged, either as a result of an accident, or more often by diseases such as arthritis, or simply by the wearing away of a joint through old age. One of the wonders of modern medicine is spare-part surgery, which enables many of our joints to be replaced by manmade ones of stainless steel alloys, or plastics.

A common joint replacement is that of the hip, but others such as elbows, shoulder and knee joints can also be replaced with artificial ones.

In spare-part surgery, the materials used have to be what is known as *inert*. They must not cause the body's natural defences to reject them, and the materials must not corrode – it would not be very pleasant to end up with a rusty hip joint!

Plastics are widely used in spare-part surgery to replace diseased parts of important blood vessels such as arteries in the legs, and even the aorta in the heart. Soft plastic lenses are now being used to help people with defective eyesight. Contact lenses, as these are called, are virtually unnoticeable, and can even be coloured to enhance the natural colour of the eyes.

Special plastics known as silicones are used for the remodelling or reconstruction of external organs such as ears and noses which may have been damaged, and silicone

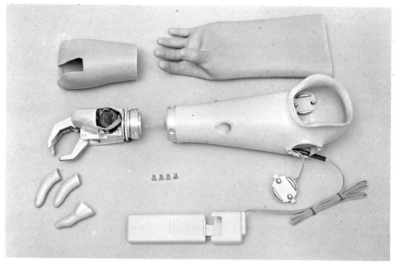

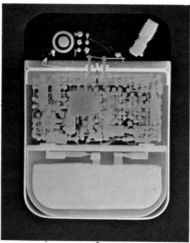

rubber rods can be implanted in the fingers, where they serve as temporary replacements for the tendons.

Perhaps the most remarkable spart-part replacements of all are the artificial heart-valves which consist of a silicone-coated rubber ball fitted inside a small stainless steel cage. Such prostheses, as artificial parts are called, help a heart, which had a defective valve, to operate more efficiently, although they can never equal the performance of normal healthy heart valves. Silicones are a natural lubricant, are water-repellent and pro-

duce hardly any adverse bodily reaction.

Sometimes a heart does not beat or pump in a regular rhythm and has to be helped with a device known as a *cardiac pacemaker*. These produce tiny electrical impulses which help to restore the natural rhythm. The tiny pacemakers are silicone-coated and some, which surgeons implant in a patient's chest, have been fitted with tiny nuclear-powered batteries!

Top : The most complex materials have been used to create this artificial arm which responds to the person's requirements, just as a natural limb.

Above left : An X-Ray picture of a cardiac pacemaker.

Below : A contact lens

Above : Philip Blaiberg, the first man to survive a heart transplant operation leaves a hospital in South Africa.

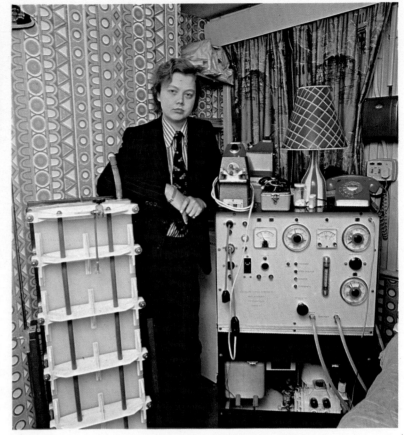

Above : A kidney machine which can be used in a patient's home.

Below : A well-equipped hospital operating theatre.

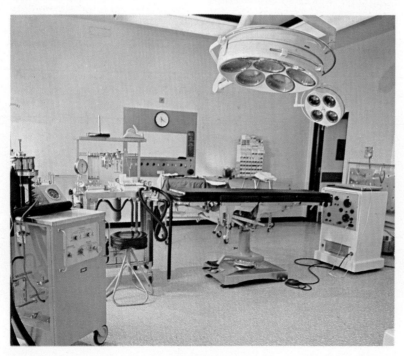

Transplant surgery

In recent years there has been an advance in the technique known as transplant surgery. This means the replacement of a diseased or damaged part of the body by a healthy one from another person. The biggest stumbling block in this area of medicine has been the body itself. Our bodies' natural defences against any 'invader' – the immune system – attempt to destroy the transplanted organ.

Before any transplant surgery is undertaken a number of factors have to be carefully considered. The organ to be transplanted must be healthy, and it must be a good 'match' with the tissues of the *recipient*,

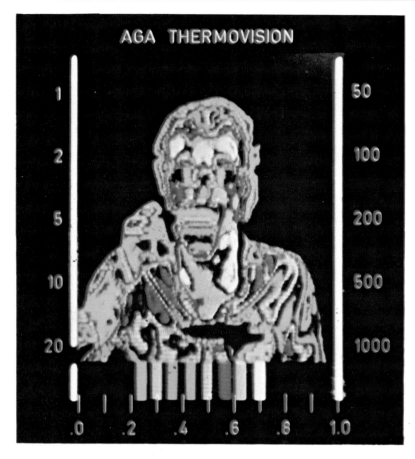

AGA THERMOVISION

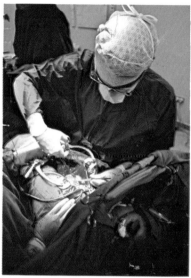

Left : Special heat-scan equipment produced this picture of a man's head and shoulders. The coolest areas such as the skin and hair, show up as blue and the hottest areas, such as the brain and glands in the neck, show up as white.

Below : Open-heart surgery uses the most advanced techniques and skills, and saves hundreds of lives every year.

the person who is to receive it. Blood has to be matched before any transfusion is given by making certain it is of the right 'group', and in the same way tissue typing will tell the surgeon whether the rejection process is likely to be strong, or weak enough to control with the help of special drugs.

The most successful organ transplants have been with kidneys, and there have been many cases where the donor has been a close relative of the recipient, making the chances of a good tissue match more likely. An international system called 'Eurotransplant' is in operation to record the tissue types of patients in Europe awaiting transplants. When a kidney becomes available, and sometimes they are from people who have died as the result of an accident, a computer identifies the person needing a transplant who is the nearest to a perfect match, and the kidney is then rushed to the hospital where the patient is waiting. Kidneys can be stored in ice for up to 12 hours.

In 1967, a South African surgeon, Christian Barnard, startled the medical world by carrying out the first ever heart transplant operation on a man who would have died soon unless something was done for him. Although the operation itself was a success, the patient later died from pneumonia which he may have caught as a result of the immunizing drugs he had to be given to prevent his body rejecting the new heart. Unfortunately, these drugs reduce the body's ability to resist disease, and so any transplant of vital organs is only attempted when the alternative is early death for the patient. Until some way is found of overcoming the immunizing problem without these side-effects, it seems that transplant surgery will always carry an element of risk.

Heart transplants must not, of course, be confused with 'open heart' surgery, when surgeons repair damaged valves in the heart, often isolating the heart during the operation by the use of a heart/lung machine. These wonderful machines take over the work of the heart and lungs by cleansing and pumping the blood round the body until the surgical team have finished their work.

The World Health Organization

The great improvement in health care is no longer confined only to the more advanced western nations of the world, thanks to the World Health Organization (WHO), one of the specialist agencies of the United Nations. WHO was established in 1948 to bring 'the highest possible level of health' to all peoples.

The headquarters of the organization is in Geneva, Switzerland, and it has six regional offices; in Egypt, the Republic of Congo, Denmark, India, the Philippines, and in Washington D.C. in the United States of America.

WHO has a number of main objectives. It provides a central clearing house for research services in medicine, and it has established a set of agreed rules for dealing with epidemics, and the quarantine regulations that are needed to limit outbreaks of infectious diseases throughout the world.

The headquarters staff send information to member countries about the latest developments, in vaccines, the control of dangerous drugs used by addicts, and keeps them up to date on recent advances in cancer research and other diseases.

Specialist medical teams working on behalf of WHO have visited many countries of the world, particularly the under-developed ones in Asia and the Far East, giving instruction to the local medical services on the use of antibiotics and insecticides, teaching them how to improve their water supplies and sanitation, and providing instruction on health education to people living in remote areas.

It helps to spread medical knowledge by setting up health centres in the poorer countries, and by giving financial aid to medical schools and nursing establishments.

Above: A WHO team arrives by helicopter to vaccinate people in the highlands of Ethiopia.

Below: The World Health Organization headquarters in Geneva.

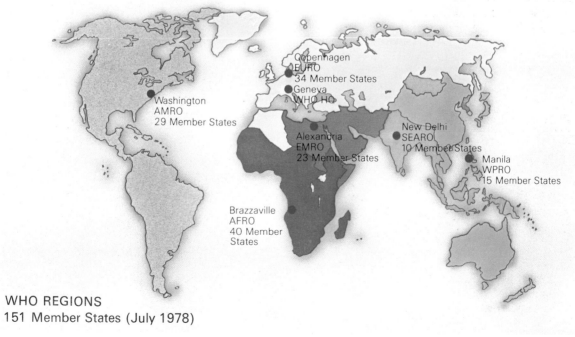

WHO REGIONS
151 Member States (July 1978)

Washington
AMRO
29 Member States

Copenhagen
EURO
34 Member States

Geneva
WHO HQ

Alexandria
EMRO
23 Member States

New Delhi
SEARO
10 Member States

Manila
WPRO
15 Member States

Brazzaville
AFRO
40 Member
States

Weapon technology

Missiles

One day in September, 1944, during the latter stages of World War II, a shattering explosion destroyed a number of buildings in a suburb on the west side of London. There had been no air raid warning, and there were no enemy aircraft in the sky. The explosion was caused by the world's first intercontinental ballistic missile – a German V-2 rocket.

The V-2 rockets were 13.8 metres (46 feet) long and 1.5 metres (5 feet) in diameter and had a total weight of 12 tonnes. The rocket motor worked from a mixture of alcohol and liquid oxygen, pumped under pressure into the combustion chamber. An automatic gyro-controlled device kept the rocket on course as it rose to a maximum height of 97 kilometres (60 miles), and then began its long, curved fall through the atmosphere to its target.

The rocket rapidly reached a *terminal velocity* of 3218 kph (2000 mph) about three times the speed of sound, which accounted for it giving no warning of its approach. In fact, the roar caused by its passage through the air arrived seconds after the sound of the explosion from its warhead.

The V-2's range of around 322 kilometres (200 miles) was a mere stone's throw compared with the distances that

Left : A German V-2 rocket of World War II being launched.

can be traversed by the Inter-continental Ballistic Missiles (ICBMs) of today. These sophisticated weapons with their nuclear warheads have ranges of around 8047 kilo-metres (5000 miles) and can truly be fired from one conti-nent to another. Their com-plex guidance systems ensure that they arrive within a few metres of their selected target despite their long journey, much of which takes place above the Earth's atmosphere.

The word *ballistic* comes from the Latin *ballista*, a large military engine used by the Romans for hurling missiles at the enemy, and the term is now used to define the science of what happens to shots fired from a gun, or the trajectories of rockets.

Some missiles are aimed at their targets by remote con-trol, while others are pro-grammed to guide themselves. Missiles that remain within the Earth's atmosphere on their way to a target often have a pair of wings similar to those on an aircraft, and the tail surfaces may also be pivoted so that they can be used to change the direction.

Other missiles make use of a method called 'vectored thrust' which means that the nozzles of their rocket engines can be moved to alter the direction of thrust. The massive ICBMs use this type of 'steering', which is effective both in outer space or within the atmosphere. ICBMs may rise to a height of 1600 kilometres (1000 miles) in their trajectory to reach a distant target.

Right : An American 'Minuteman' ICBM rocket takes off from its launch silo.

Some short-range weapons have a 'wire' guidance system in which the soldier has direct control over the missile by sending signals along one or two fine wires which are wound round bobbins at the firing point. These unwind rapidly as the missile heads for the target. Such anti-tank missiles are limited to a range of not more than 3 kilometres (2 miles) because of the added weight of the wire, and the fact

that the operator must be in visual contact with the target.

Certain types of anti-air-craft missiles are 'radar' guided to their target. This is an automatic system with two radar beams, one beam to track the target and the other to track the missile. Information from the reflected beams is fed into a computer. The resulting calculation sets the missile on a deliberate collision course with the target.

A system known as 'radio command guidance' can be used to fire a missile beyond visual range. The missiles have miniature TV cameras in their nose cones, and as they approach the target the operator actually sees the target on his cathode ray tube and can guide the missile with a high degree of accuracy.

Missiles are not, of course, always fired from positions on the ground. Some are fired from surface ships, either as a defence against aircraft, or as a weapon against other surface ships or submarines. Nuclear powered submarines carry missiles that can be fired from beneath the surface of the sea, already aimed at targets more than 2000 miles away.

Aircraft, too, are armed with missiles which may be used either against enemy aircraft, or against ground targets.

Perhaps the most formidable of all war weapons are the 'space bombs' and Multiple Re-entry Vehicles (MRVs). These missiles can be put into orbit round the Earth and then guided down on to a target at

Above: A helicopter gunship fires one of its anti-tank missiles.

Inset: A Polaris ICBM emerges from the water after being fired from a submarine.

will. The MRVs have a number of small nuclear warheads which can be released at intervals as the missile passes over a particular target area. It is rather a disturbing thought that there may be a number of these destructive weapons circling several hundred miles above our heads day and night.

MAIN BATTLE TANKS

Of all the weapons used by ground forces in modern war, armoured fighting vehicles (AFVs) are probably the most formidable. There are many different types of these metal monsters, from light, speedy Scout Cars, to mighty battle tanks like the 'Chieftain', one of the hardest-hitting tanks in the world.

The tank was a British invention, and first appeared on the battlefields of France during the First World War of 1914–18. It was intended to clear enemy trenches and help to protect advancing infantry. These early tanks were slow, cumbersome, and armed only with light machine-guns, although their sudden appearance demoralized the Germans.

Since the Second World War, many countries have developed larger and more heavily armed Main Battle Tanks (MBTs). In theory, there is no upper-limit to the size and weight of a tank, but in practice there would be little point in building one weighing more than 70 tonnes as it would be liable to sink into soft ground, or break up roads as it turned on

A Chieftain Tank

its caterpillar tracks and would need specially reinforced bridges to cross deep rivers.

In the early 1960s several major European powers began to develop new MBTs which were to be the tanks of the 1970s and 1980s, including the 'Leopard', the AMX 30, and the 'Chieftain'.

The 51-tonne Chieftain is armed with a high velocity 120mm gun which fires a variety of shells that can penetrate any known armour. The main gun is particularly accurate because it is linked to a range-finding machine-gun. The gunner fires a short burst from the lighter weapon and when he has found the target, the deadly 120mm gun is automatically ranged and ready to fire.

A powered mounting and stabilizer enables the Chieftain's gun to be fired accurately on the move during cross country running. The tank is manned by a four-man crew – commander, gunner, loader-operator and driver, who can shut themselves inside their protective shell of thick armour-plating and continue to operate the tank for 48 to 72 hours. They have electric cooking vessels and thermos containers, and there is sufficient room for two crewmen to lie down to rest at the same time.

The Chieftain also has an armoured infra-red searchlight for night fighting, and infra-red head-lamps to help the driver see in the dark. Like the German Leopard tank, the Chieftain can be adapted to travel on the bed of a river in water 4.56 metres (15 feet) deep. On land, its 750bhp engine can power it along at 40kph (25mph).

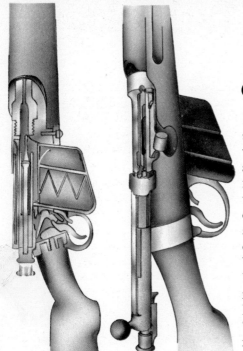

Above: Detailed drawings of a rifle with a breech-bolt loading mechanism. This type of rifle was introduced to the British Army in 1889 and was used for many years.

Below: A British soldier using an SLR rifle with an Image Intensification Sight.

Guns

In spite of all the highly sophisticated missile weapons which enable wars to be fought at long range, the role of the foot soldier is still an important one, and the infantryman of today is better armed than any of his predecessors. The old breech-loading rifles of World War II have long since been discarded in favour of the modern SLR or Self-Loading Rifle. The British SLR is of 7.62mm calibre, and has a magazine holding 25 rounds of ammunition. Larger magazines can be fitted when needed, and once the gun has been cocked shots can be fired simply by pulling the trigger until the magazine is exhausted. The normal SLR has an open sight, but certain special infantry forces have rifles with sights that enable targets to be seen at night and in poor light conditions. These sights incorporate a device known as an 'image intensifier', which has to be powered by a tiny battery, and as the name implies they improve, or intensify, an optical image when there is poor illumination.

Some rifles have also been fitted with infra red sights which operate on the same principle as that used in the gun on a Chieftain tank. This device is sensitive to the infra red light which is emitted from any warm object such as the human body. Some of these infra red sights depend upon a small searchlight which itself emits an infra red beam, and the equipment then detects the reflected heat rays.

High-explosive bombs

Although the best part of 2000 years separates us from the armies of ancient Rome, the word 'bomb' comes from *bombarda*, a huge catapult which Roman soldiers used for throwing boulders against the walls of cities they were attacking. Following the invention of gunpowder, which is attributed to the Chinese, the word bomb was applied to any hollow iron ball which was filled with explosives.

Bombs were first dropped from aircraft during a war in the Balkans in 1912. They were little more than small hand-grenades, and it was not until 1916 that Britain's Royal Flying Corps began developing bombs that were specially designed for aerial attacks.

Conventional high-explosive bombs probably reached their peak during the 1939–45 war. At the outbreak the heaviest was a 227 kg (500 lb) high-explosive bomb almost 1.8 metres (6 feet) long and 33 centimetres (13 inches) in diameter, but towards the end of the conflict the Royal Air Force was dropping bombs weighing 10 000 kg (22 000 lb). These enormous bombs, nicknamed Grand Slam by the RAF, were 7.6 metres (25 feet 5 inches) long and had a diameter of 1.1 metres (3 feet 10 inches). Most of these bombs were filled with an explosive called tri-nitro-toluene (TNT) although during the course of the war a more powerful form was used.

Despite the widespread damage they caused, the bombs used during the major part of World War II were relatively insignificant compared to the devastation caused by the first atomic bomb which was dropped on the Japanese city of Hiroshima in August, 1945. The uranium 235 fission bomb was devised to explode 610 metres (2000 feet) above the crowded Japanese city. Aerial photographs showed that 109 square kilometres (42 square miles) of the city were completely flattened. It was learned later that 80 000 people were killed outright, 10 000 people were listed as missing and never found, 37 000 were seriously injured. Many more were made ill by radiation sickness, and died later. Some people survived but the effects of the radiation are still shown in the deformed children who have been, and continue to be born.

The fundamental difference between ordinary high-explosive bombs and nuclear bombs is in the way energy is released. Atoms are made up of particles known as protons, neutrons, and electrons. Atoms also have a nucleus made up of protons and neutrons – except for hydrogen whose nucleus

Below: An area of Dresden in Germany which was badly damaged by bombing in the Second World War.

Centre: An early atomic bomb of the type dropped on Hiroshima in Japan.

Bottom: The devastation caused in Japan by a single atomic bomb. Only a few larger buildings remain standing.

consists of only one proton.

An Italian physicist named Enrico Fermi found that when a stream of neutrons is used to bombard the nuclei of a radio-active isotope called uranium 235, the nuclei of the metal split into two parts, forming two lighter elements. In 1938, two other physicists, one German and one Austrian, found that when the nucleus of the uranium atom splits into two parts, there is a great release of energy, and it is this sudden release of energy which is the basis of nuclear bombs.

Conventional explosive substances like simple gunpowder, for example, consist of a number of different chemicals which when mixed together are quite harmless. They only become dangerous when heat is applied to them in the form of a spark or flame and then they begin to burn – but they burn very rapidly indeed. It is when gunpowder is heated increasing the energy of the mixture, and the gases which result are confined inside a metal case like a bomb, that a violent explosion occurs.

The amount of energy released by the atoms in the gunpowder mixture trying to get away from each other as fast as possible is, however, infinitesimal compared to the amount of energy released when the parts of an atom of uranium are split into two, producing two or sometimes three new neutrons. These new neutrons can split more of the uranium nuclei resulting in what physicists call a 'chain reaction'. The whole process is called 'fission' and when it is controlled, as in a nuclear reactor, it is a useful source of power. Uncontrolled it can cause death and destruction, not only from the sheer force of the explosion, but also from the dangerous radiation which goes with it.

Hydrogen bombs are the result of the fusion – joining together – of two light nuclei to form one heavier nucleus with a resulting release of energy – causing an even greater explosion than that produced by 'fission' bombs.

Below: The Hiroshima A-Bomb was just 3.14 metres (10 feet) long. A small wedge of uranium-235 was driven down the barrel and exploded with a force of 20 000 tonnes of TNT
A Uranium target
B Radar antenna
C High explosive
D Uranium edge
E Gun barrel

Bottom: How a chain reaction builds up when a nuclear bomb is exploded.

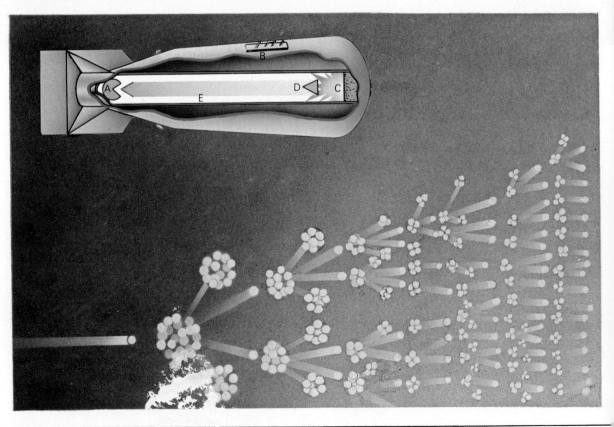

VTOL aircraft

The initials VTOL stand for Vertical Take-Off and Landing, and such planes do not need a runway as they can take off like helicopters. VTOL aircraft have conventional wings and control surfaces, i.e. ailerons, rudders and elevators, but can use their engines to lift them vertically off the ground before moving forward into normal flight.

Without doubt, the most spectacular success with this type of aircraft was achieved with the Hawker Siddeley Harrier, a military aircraft currently in service with the British Royal Air Force and the United States Marine Corps.

The Harrier was another 'first' for Britain in the world of aviation. It was the world's first fixed winged V/STOL (Vertical *Short* Take-Off and Landing) fighter to become fully operational, and the story of its development began in 1954 with an extraordinary looking contraption called the 'Flying Bedstead' which was built by Rolls-Royce.

Rolls-Royce were looking into the possibilities of using jet engines to achieve vertical take-off, and to this end had built a research vehicle called a Thrust Measuring Rig (TMR). One glance at the illustration overleaf will show you how it got its nickname!

The pilot had a somewhat

Above: A Royal Air Force 'Harrier' VSTOL aircraft fires an air-to-air missile during exercises.

Inset: A Rolls-Royce Pegasus 6 vectored thrust turbofan engine showing the jets that can deflect the thrust downwards when required.

precarious seat on the top of an open framework inside which were two Rolls-Royce Nene jet engines with a total thrust of 44.5 kn (10 000 lb). Forward and lateral control was achieved by the pilot using compressed air from four downward pointing nozzles.

The Flying Bedstead never really *flew* in the strictest sense of the word, but it did rise off the ground, and by adjusting the airflow from the small nozzles the pilot could manage

Above : The original Rolls-Royce Thrust Measuring Rig, which was used in vertical take-off experiments.

Below : A 'Harrier' can be easily camouflaged in wooded areas to hide it from enemy eyes.

limited movement in various directions. These tests led eventually to the development of an aircraft called the Short SC.1, a delta-winged research aircraft powered by no less than five Rolls-Royce RB.108 turbojets. Four of the jets lifted the aircraft off the ground while the fifth was used to thrust it forward.

Only a single engine – a Rolls-Royce Pegasus 6 vectored thrust turbofan is used to power the Harrier, and give it both lift and forward movement. The engine develops 84.6 kn (19 000 lb) of thrust – almost double that of the Nene engines of the 'Bedstead' – and there are four rotating nozzles which the pilot can adjust from inside the cockpit. In addition there are jets at the tip of each wing which enable the pilot to control lateral movement when the Harrier is slowly hovering.

The ability to take off vertically in a military aircraft is a tremendous advantage, because it means that there is no need to have large airfields with concrete runways. A small field is all that is required, and when the planes are not actually in use they can be camouflaged, or even hidden in clearings in a wooded area.

In spite of the success of the Harrier, it is doubtful whether the same principle will ever be successfully applied to large long-distance airliners. Experiments are continuing, however, and it is possible that one day passengers may be able to land on a small concrete 'apron' right in the centre of the city they wish to visit, instead of having to make a long journey by road or rail from an airport on the outskirts.

Transport and Travel

Contents

Flight

The one form of transport which eluded man, and which filled his dreams for centuries, was one that would enable him to rise off the ground and fly through the air as free as the birds.

It was only natural that man should try to copy the birds he envied so much, by designing wings similar in shape to those they used with such ease. This usually had disastrous results, for the human body is too heavy and the chest muscles are too weak for this kind of individual flight.

Strangely, man's first true flight was not achieved in a winged vehicle, but in a hot-air balloon. The balloon was built in 1783 by two Frenchmen, the Montgolfier brothers, and flown in by F. de Rozier and the Marquis d'Arlandes.

The first successful engine-powered, heavier-than-air machine was the result of many people's efforts, but history generally accords the success to two American brothers, Wilbur and Orville Wright. Their first true powered flight took place on a freezing cold morning on 17th December, 1903, and their machine, called *Flyer*, was a simple, but well-constructed biplane 6.3 metres (21 feet) long, with fabric-covered wings 12.2 metres (40 feet 4 inches) wide. With the help of a mechanic called Charlie Taylor, they had built and fitted their own four-cylinder petrol engine which supplied power to two 'pusher' propellers.

Above : An early artist's impression of the Montgolfier brothers' hot air balloon.

Below : The historic moment when the Wright brothers made their first flight.

Modern Aircraft

Today's aircraft are a far cry from the Wright brothers' flimsy, under-powered machine, for progress in aviation has been extremely rapid. Seventy-five years may seem a long time, but it is really only equivalent to one man's lifetime, and if it were possible to place a Wright *Flyer* alongside a Boeing 747 'Jumbo' jet-liner, and compare their size and performance, you would realise what has been achieved.

The Wright brothers' machine carried one person, and its 12 hp engine gave it a top speed of 48 kph (30 mph). A Boeing 747-200B can carry up to 516 passengers, plus a flight crew of three and cabin staff. Its four huge turbofan engines, each with a 222 kn (50 000 lb) thrust can take it more than 11 000 km at a speed of 965 kph (7000 miles at a speed of 600 mph). Passengers can watch films on two or three different screens, listen to a selection of music on earphones, be served three meals,

and even take a 'walk' to the upper deck where first-class passengers have their own bar.

Fifty years ago very few people had flown in an aeroplane, and many had probably not even seen one. Today flying is commonplace, and thousands of people travel by air every day. The Boeing 727, the BAC-111, the McDonnell Douglas DC-10, the Lockheed TriStar and the A-300 Airbus, are but a few of the familiar sights, all flying millions of passenger miles a year. Added to them now is the slim fuselage and delta wing of the Anglo-French Concorde, flying faster and higher than any commercial aeroplane has ever done before.

There are now about 650 airlines operating passenger scheduled and charter flights over air routes that stretch out to almost every corner of the world. Many of these are only small companies with perhaps two or three aircraft, but there are about 200 major airlines whose planes between them fly routes which encircle the globe.

Of course, modern aircraft do not only carry passengers. A great deal of cargo is also carried by air, and although much of it is flown in passenger planes that have been adapted for the purpose, there are some giant machines specially built for carrying cargo. One of these has the nickname 'Super Guppy' because of its shape which is rather like the guppy fish found in some parts of the world.

The Super Guppy is a specially adapted version of a four-engined Boeing Stratocruiser, a development from a military aircraft. An enormous extra section was added to the upper part of the fuselage which gave it headroom of almost 6 metres (20 feet). Like many cargo aircraft, the Guppy's nose can be swung open like a garage door to make loading into its 1400 cubic metres (50 000 cubic feet) of storage space easier.

The Guppies were first used to ferry sections of the huge booster rockets used in the American space programme. They have since been used

Bleriot's flimsy monoplane is dwarfed by a Boeing 747 'Jumbo' jet.

Comparative dimensions:
Bleriot XI
  Wing span : 7.8 metres (25 feet 7 inches)
  Length 8.00 metres (26 feet 3 inches).
  Gross weight : 300 kg (661 lb).
  Speed : Approx. 75 km/h (47 mph).

Boeing 747–200B
  Wing span : 59.64 metres (195 feet 8 inches).
  Length : 70.50 metres (231 feet 4 inches).
  Weight (empty) : 163 855 kg (361 216 lb).
  Speed : Max 978 km/h (608 mph).

to move fuselage sections of the McDonnell Douglas DC-10, and wings of the Lockheed TriStar, from the production plants to the final assembly shops.

One of the really great giants of the sky is the Lockheed C-5 Galaxy, a United States Air Force military transport aircraft designed to carry both men and weapons over long distances. The measurements and carrying capacity of the Galaxy are mind-boggling. The top of its tail is 19.5 metres (65 feet) above the ground – equal to the height of a six-storey block of flats! It has a wing span of about 67 metres (220 feet). The floor is specially strengthened so that battle tanks weighing 50 tonnes can be driven straight inside it, and it has a 28-wheel undercarriage to spread the weight of the aircraft, plus its load of cargo and fuel, when it lands on rough ground. Fully laden it can weigh as much as 340 tonnes! The Galaxy's fuel tanks hold 186 000 litres (41 000 gallons), and you could run a small family saloon car on that for 100 years!

Top : Super Guppy in flight.

Centre : Multiple wheels of the Lockheed Galaxy undercarriage.

Right : Tanks being loaded into the nose of a US Air Force Galaxy.

Pan Am Boeing 747-SP

TWA Lockheed TriStar

Laker McDonnell Douglas DC-10

TEA A300 Airbus

Bulgarian Airlines Tupolev 154B

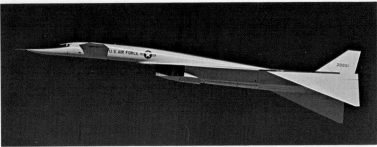

Top: The Concorde in flight.

Above: North American Rockwell Valkyrie bomber.

Right: The Russian Tupolev TU-144 supersonic airliner.

Below: The Lockheed SR 71A supersonic strike aircraft.

Opposite: The Bell X-15 experimental rocket plane

Supersonic aircraft

Concorde is the world's first supersonic passenger-carrying aircraft to go into commercial service, and was designed and built by French and British aviation experts working together. Although military aircraft had already broken through what had become known as the 'sound barrier' and a great deal was known about the problems associated with flying at speeds faster than sound, no one had tackled the greater problems involved with building a much larger supersonic aircraft – particularly one which had to carry ordinary fare-paying members of the public.

To give some idea of the immense difficulties that the designers had to overcome let us look at what happens when Concorde flies at Mach 2.02 – more than twice the speed of sound. The heat caused by the friction of air passing over the external surfaces of the aircraft raises the temperature of the skin to about 117°C at a point half way along the fuselage. The temperature reached at points such as the nose and the leading edges of the wings is even higher.

The heat problem was solved in a unique way. Fuel in the wing tanks was used to absorb the heat in the passenger compartment. The fuel tanks themselves had to be slightly pressurised because of the operational height – 18 300 metres (60 000 feet) – at which Concorde flies. The atmospheric pressure at that altitude is much lower, thus reducing the boiling point of liquids, and it would be disastrous if the aviation kerosene used in the powerful Rolls-Royce Olympus engines were allowed to boil!

A certain amount of fuel is also pumped from tanks at the front of the aircraft's wing to a tank in the tail, in order to alter the aircraft's 'trim' or attitude, which changes as the sound barrier is passed, and also when the plane is throttled back to subsonic speeds.

One feature of the unusual shape of Concorde, apart from its beautifully shaped 'delta' wing is its droop nose. A section of the sharply pointed cone in front of the pilot's cockpit has to be lowered for landing because of the unusually steep angle the aircraft adopts during this phase of flight. Without this hinged section, the pilot would not have a good forward view through the cockpit windows.

The first prototype Concorde rose gracefully into the air from the runway at Toulouse in France on 2nd March, 1969. It was here that the French company *Aerospatiale* were building the airframes. It was piloted by André Turcat, the French test pilot. The second Concorde, which had been assembled at Filton in England, took off on 9th April, some five weeks later, flown by the British test pilot Brian Trubshaw.

The lessons learned from the test flights were incorporated into two pre-production Concordes designated 01 and 02, which first flew in December, 1971, and January, 1973, respectively. Further changes were made to the design before the actual production models made their appearance. Altogether the first six Concordes had flown almost 4000 hours by the middle of 1975, including over 1200 at supersonic speed. It speaks volumes for the skill of the designers and builders of Concorde that that there were so few problems during the flight tests.

What is it like to fly in Concorde? Those who have been lucky enough to make a flight in this sleek, streamlined airliner say that it is the most stable plane they have ever flown in. It is impossible to tell at what moment the plane actually passes through the sound barrier, and the only indication the passengers have is when an airspeed indicator inside the passenger compartment registers a speed above Mach 1.

Concorde takes off at around 325 kph (202 mph) and climbs very fast at about 725 kph (450 mph), and more steeply than other airliners. When it reaches about 9150 metres (30 000 feet) it is high enough to begin supersonic acceleration. Reheat is turned on in the engines to boost the thrust, by injecting fuel into the exhaust gases, and as the plane continues to climb to its operational altitude, a speed of around Mach 2 is reached within a matter of minutes.

At that altitude the plane is well above any weather disturbance, and the passengers have a smooth flight in a sky that looks a deep violet colour. Concorde has shrunk the world for the air traveller by about half, crossing the Atlantic in a little over three hours, compared with about six hours for a subsonic jet.

Concorde is not the only supersonic aircraft, of course, although it is the only commercial aircraft in service capable of exceeding Mach 1 in level flight. Many military aircraft fly at speeds in excess of Mach 2, including the Tornado, a multi-role combat aircraft developed by Britain, Italy and Germany; and the incredible Lockheed SR 71A Blackbird, a high-altitude reconnaissance plane which can cruise at Mach 3.

The first aircraft to break the sound barrier was the American Bell X-1, a rocket-propelled experimental plane which reached Mach 1.015 in October 1947. The American X-15 rocket-powered research aircraft has reached a speed of 7297 kph (4534 mph), the fastest anyone has yet travelled in any vehicle other than a spacecraft.

Airports

Airports are fascinating places, and most airports provide facilities for spectators who like to see the aircraft taking off and landing.

Large airports, like London's Heathrow, New York's Kennedy Airport or the new Charles de Gaulle Airport outside Paris, all allow spectators, and if you have ever spent time looking around you will soon realise that they can be compared with a small city. A small army of highly trained and skilled personnel watch over a large and constantly changing population.

London's Heathrow Airport is one of the busiest international airports in the world. Because of its geographical location, Heathrow is a stopping-off place for passengers flying between the North American continent and Europe and countries to the east. More than 24 million people use it every year – and that is almost double the population of Australia! Seventeen million of the passengers are travelling to or from countries outside Britain.

The airport is divided into three separate terminals, plus a cargo handling complex. Terminal One is used by British Airways European flights, and one or two smaller airlines such as British Midland Airways, Aer Lingus, and Cyprus Airways. Terminal Two is used by foreign airlines operating to and from Europe, such as Air France, Lufthansa, Alitalia and KLM Royal Dutch Airlines. Terminal Three deals with the arrivals and departures of long distance

Above : The runway complex of Dallas Fort Worth airport U.S.A.

Below : A modern air terminal with loading bays.

Flood lights

Satellite lounge

Satellite lounge

'Airbridge' boarding ramp

Mobile steps

Catering vehicle

flights from such places as the United States of America, and those in the Near and Far East such as India, Malaysia, Australia and Japan.

Heathrow Airport is linked with the centre of the capital by a specially built underground station which has moving staircases and 'walkways' to help passengers move quickly and easily to and from the trains.

One of the largest airports in the world is the Dallas-Fort Worth complex in the state of Texas, USA. It has runways totalling nearly 10 kilometres (six miles) in length and the whole complex is 14.5 kilometres long and 13 kilometres wide (9 miles by 8). Because of the long distances that have to be covered inside the airport, the Americans have constructed a specially designed transport system called 'Airtrans' which links the terminals with the various car parking areas.

The Airtrans vehicles have rubber-tyred wheels which run along concrete guideways, and the coaches are all computer controlled. The system can transport up to 9000 people an hour together with their baggage, and is also used by people who work at the airport.

Building a large airport, and trying to keep it up-to-date can be almost a non-stop undertaking. Heathrow, for instance, began its active life as an airport shortly after World War II, although work on a new control tower did not begin until 1950. The adding of extra terminals, cargo handling areas, lengthened runways, fuel storage facilities, car parks, the underground railway, etc. has taken 28 years, and today changes are still being made to try to meet the ever-increasing demand on facilities at this busy airport.

The problem of handling passengers quickly and smoothly has been made more difficult by the size and speed of modern aircraft. Just two Boeing 747 Jumbo jets arriving within five minutes of each other can flood the reception area with almost 1000 people and their luggage. The problem will continue into the 1980s and beyond, when it is anticipated that super-jumbos carrying up to 700 passengers each will be landing and taking off from airports.

Flood lights

Domestic pier

Security check

Main check-in lounge

Customs immigration

Satellite lounge

AIR CANADA

Baggage trolleys

Cargo container

747 FLIGHT DECK

1 Director Horizon: displays the pitch and bank attitude of the aircraft, and flight director information to keep the aircraft on a selected flightpath.

2 Flight Compass: gyro-compass which shows aircraft heading, and also displays navigational information.

3 Airspeed Indicator: shows aircraft's speed in knots. In the centre is a Mach readout showing the speed as a fraction of the speed of sound.

4 Altimeter: displays aircraft height.

5 Vertical Speed Indicator: shows the rate of climb or descent.

6 Magnetic Compass: very basic standby compass.

7 Standby Horizon.

8 Standby Altimeter.

9 Radio Altimeters: very accurate altimeters which use radio waves.

10 Radio Magnetic Indicator: uses pointers to show the bearing of a radio beacon.

11 Distance Measuring Equipment: shows distance in nautical miles from some radio beacons.

12 Marker Lights: illuminate when the aircraft passes over the beacon.

13 VHF Navigation Frequency Selector: selects the frequency of the radio aid to be used.

14 VHF Communications Frequency Selector: selects the voice frequency to talk to the ground controllers.

15 Radio Selector Box: controls the input of radio signals to the pilots' headsets.

16 Inertial Navigation System: uses known aircraft position at the start of the flight and 'memorises' all heading and speed changes to give a continuous presentation of aircraft position.

17 Autopilot (A/P): can be used to select a course and height or speed to be flown and also to guide the aircraft when landing.

18 A/P and Flight Director Mode Indicators: show which facilities the pilot has selected.

19 A/P Trim Indicators: monitor the autopilot.

20 Undercarriage Selector: either up or down selected, and this also opens and closes all the doors around the undercarriage.

21 Undercarriage Lights: indicate whether the undercarriage is locked down (green) or not (red).

22 Flap Selector: selects both leading edge and trailing edge flaps to the correct position.

23 Flap Position Indicator:

shows the position of the various sections of flap.

24 Airbrake Selector: moves a slab-like wing section when a rapid speed reduction is required.

25 Stabilator Trim: reduces the load on the controls.

26 and **27** Flying Controls: pulling back on the control column moves the elevator, raising the nose. Pushing forward lowers the nose. Turning the handwheel deflects the ailerons and banks the aircraft.

28 Throttles: control the power generated by the engines, and also select reverse thrust.

29–32 Engine Instruments Number One Engine: show revolutions at two positions in the engine (N^1 and N^2 R.P.M.), temperature and pressure ratio which is a method of measuring the power produced.

33–35 Engine Instruments Numbers Two to Four Engines.

36 Outside Air Temperature: shows temperature of air around the aircraft.

37 Central Warning System: red light flashes warning of any system malfunction.

38 Smoke and Oxygen Masks: if the aircraft loses pressure oxygen masks drop out automatically in front of the crew.

Travelling by air

Preparing for take off

When you board an aircraft most of the people concerned with your flight have finished their tasks. But an hour before an aircraft takes off you will see it surrounded by vehicles and people – all with vitally important jobs to do.

The largest vehicle is usually the fuel tanker – the *bowser*. The flight crew use the information provided by a meteorologist to work out how much fuel they will require for the journey. A 'Jumbo' jet can carry about 180 000 litres (39 595 gallons) of fuel so some bigger airports have a pipeline system which takes fuel directly to the aircraft from the storage tanks.

Because of the high cost of fuel, aircraft are designed to be as economical as possible. The Boeing 747 uses 11 700 kg (25 800 lbs) per hour, and although this is twice the consumption of the older jets, the 'Jumbo' carries more than twice as many passengers as, for example, the Boeing 707. It is therefore more economical per passenger carried. Although Concorde burns almost 19 000 kg (40 000 lbs) per hour the supersonic jet travels over twice the distance of its subsonic competitor during that hour.

Supervising the fuel loading is an engineer who also checks the aeroplane for any faults before it leaves. Large aircraft have as many as 18 wheels, so just checking the tyre pressure can take some time, and adding air can also be a time-consuming task as the tyre pressures, even on the smaller airliners, are five times those on a car.

The flight crew, usually two pilots and a flight engineer, arrive about 40 minutes before departure. They have already studied the weather reports and navigation charts for their route, and they now work through the pre-flight checklist to prepare the aircraft. One crew member examines the outside of the aircraft, looking especially for hydraulic leaks, faults in the tyres or lights, and damage caused by ground vehicles. In winter he will look especially for any snow or ice which must be removed from the wings before take-off. The others will ensure that the aircraft systems are in working order including the hydraulics, air-conditioning and electrics. They will also check the radio receivers, transmitters and navigation units – the avionics.

In the passenger cabin the catering for the flight arrives by lorry from the kitchens near the airport. For a long flight the galleys heat up 400 meals. On some aircraft these galleys are below the passenger cabin and are reached by lifts. Sometimes the meals for the return journey will be loaded into the cargo holds and transferred to the galleys at the destination. This, combined with the aircraft bars and duty-free drinks for passengers to purchase, means that there is considerable weight of food and drink on board.

The cabin crew check that all is ready before the passengers are shown on board. Below the cabin the baggage is loaded into the holds, along with any freight being carried. It is very important that the weight of passengers, baggage and freight is properly distributed throughout the aircraft. It is the job of the aircraft despatcher to check the weight limits and direct the loading of the aircraft. He is also responsible for avoiding any delays to the departure of the aircraft.

Shortly before departure the captain checks the weight distribution worked out by the despatcher, then the doors are

Above : A Boeing Jumbo jet being re-victualled at London Airport.

Above left : A Lockheed TriStar being refuelled.

Above: Aircraft being plotted in an air-traffic control centre.

closed and he asks Air Traffic Control (ATC) for permission to start engines. For regular flights which may take place several times in a day ATC has the details, including the route to be flown, stored in a computer and this information is now made available to the controller. The controller gives permission to start engines,

and gives the captain a clearance with the height to be flown to avoid all other aircraft. He also gives a route along the complex system of taxiways to the runway in use. As aircraft have become larger, so the length of runway they require has increased. Most large airports have runways in excess of 3500 metres (11 480 feet).

Finally the controller gives the captain clearance to take off. On the aircraft all the crew's checks are completed, and the cabin staff have checked that all the passengers' seat belts are fastened – then they also take their seats. The co-pilot applies full power, and he and the flight engineer check all the indications on the instruments. The crew have calculated a speed called V_1 which alters with the weight of the aircraft. If any fault

develops before this speed the co-pilot will close the throttles and abandon the take-off. If all is well the aircraft accelerates along the runway to another pre-set speed at which the co-pilot calls, 'Rotate', and as the captain eases back on the control column the aircraft takes to the air.

As the aircraft climbs, the crew retract the undercarriage and reduce power to avoid making more noise than is necessary. Soon the aircraft breaks through the clouds into the bright sunshine above. When the 'fasten seat belts' signs are put out the cabin crew come round with refreshments and meals. On longer flights there may even be an in-flight cinema.

When they reach the cruising level, which for most jets is a maximum of about 13 000 metres (40 000 feet), although

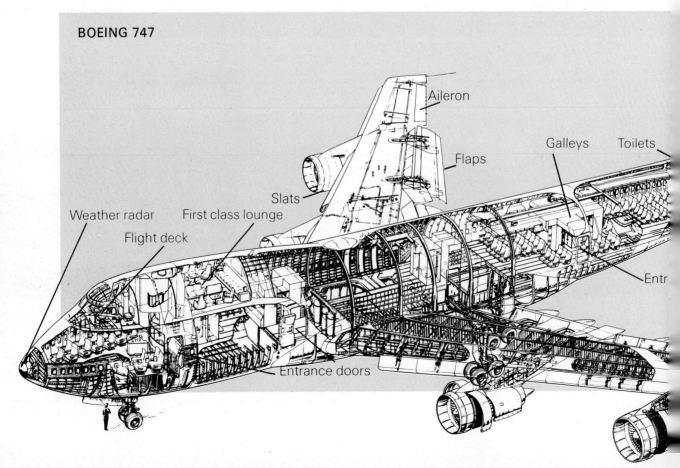

BOEING 747

Aileron

Galleys   Toilets

Flaps

Slats

Weather radar   First class lounge

Flight deck

Entr

Entrance doors

Concorde can reach 18000 metres (60000 feet), the flight crew check the weather reports and the en-route navigation of the flight. In busy areas like Western Europe 'airways' are well marked with radio beacons, but in more remote parts, like Africa, and on long over-water flights such as the north Atlantic, there are few aids to navigation so most aircraft flying these routes are fitted with *inertial navigation systems*. These work by knowing the exact position from which the flight started and 'remembering' every turn and acceleration of the aircraft so that they can give a continuous presentation of the aircraft's position.

Normally this cruising phase of the flight is quite relaxed for the flight crew, though they must always remain alert to deal with any sudden emer-

AIRWAYS

Airways are bands of airspace 16 kilometres (10 miles) wide, along which commercial aircraft are separated from each other by Air Traffic Controllers on the ground. On busy airways such as those in western Europe this separation is achieved using radar, which gives the controller a picture of all the aircraft in his area. With newer systems, the flight number and the altitude of the aircraft are also displayed. The controller will be in communication with his military counterpart to arrange clearance for military aircraft to cross the civilian airways clear of other aircraft.

The turning points of the airways, where a change of course is required by the aircraft, are marked by radio beacons. The pilot selects the frequency of the beacon and may select the course he wishes to fly to the beacon. His flight deck instruments then tell him whether he is right or left of the required course. There is another type of beacon where the pilot simply has a needle on his instrument panel which points to the beacon. This type is called a Non-Directional Beacon or NDB.

Height limits of the airways vary depending on their use. Those closest to the airports may start at about 610 metres (2000 feet). But the airways across the Atlantic may start as high as 7600 metres (25000 feet).

gency – for instance a rapid decompression if a window should blow out, or an emergency landing at the nearest airport due to a technical fault, or perhaps a passenger becoming critically ill on the journey.

Landing

As the flight approaches its destination the crew receive details of the runway for landing and are given a height to descend to in order to start an approach. In bad weather this stage of the flight will be done using the autopilot, although the human pilot is still kept very busy monitoring what is happening.

Modern autopilots are very complex, having two or three different 'channels', each of which is almost a separate autopilot, which cross-check each other, and will detect a fault and inform the pilot. The autopilot can maintain a height, speed and rate of descent fed into it by the pilot. It can also navigate, using radio beacons or inertial navigation units.

Bad weather often causes delays and the flight might have to 'hold' by flying a circular pattern over a radio beacon some distance from the airport. The crew know to the minute how long they can wait for permission to land before they must give up and divert to another airfield to avoid running short of fuel.

When the flight is finally given clearance to start on an approach to the airfield the aircraft descends to about 600–900 metres (2000–3000 feet) and the pilot uses the Instru-

Below: The slots and flaps on the trailing edge of a Boeing 747 wing.

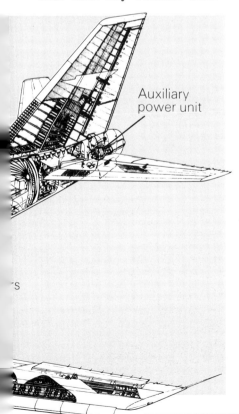

Auxiliary power unit

ment Landing System or ILS to guide him the rest of the way down. The ILS is another radio device which gives the pilot indications on his instrument panel of whether he is left or right of the runway approach and above or below the *glidepath* – the ideal descent to the runway.

As the aircraft slows the wing flaps are extended, changing the shape of the wing to make it more suitable for slow speeds. The undercarriage is lowered as the aircraft lines up with the runway and the aeroplane continues down until it reaches its decision height – the height at which a decision whether to land or overshoot and fly off again is made. This height is determined by the quality of the ILS equipment at the airfield and the standard of the aircraft's own equipment. Each runway has its own decision height for each aircraft. In aircraft fitted with complex automatic landing equipment, decision height can be as low as 4 metres (12 feet). If at decision height the crew still cannot see the runway they overshoot by applying full power, raising the undercarriage and flaps and climbing away, either to go round and try again if the weather improves, or to divert to another airfield with better conditions.

Normally the aircraft lands safely, but when it touches down its speed is more than 241 kph (150 mph) so it is fitted

Above: A Lockheed TriStar under construction in the United States of America.

with reverse thrust, which enables the pilot to use his engines to slow the aircraft down. There are also at least two wheel-brake systems fitted with sophisticated devices to prevent skids developing on wet runways. Some aircraft are fitted with airbrakes in addition, usually slab-like sections which extend from the wing to create as much drag as possible to slow the aircraft until it turns off the runway. It then taxis in to the terminal where a whole reception committee of engineers, baggage handlers and cleaners waits to prepare the plane for its next departure.

THE JET ENGINE

Jet engines are really heat engines in which a fuel, such as aviation kerosene, is sucked in through the front of the engine, mixed with compressed air, and burned in a combustion chamber where the hot expanding gases provide a thrusting force. A popular misconception is that it is gases streaming out from the tail pipe of a jet which move the plane along, but in fact, the atmosphere only supplies the oxygen needed to make the fuel burn. The actual thrust occurs *inside* the combustion chamber, pushing the engine forward, while the tailpipe serves only to allow the exhaust gases to escape.

The simplest jet is the ramjet, which must be first set in rapid motion through the air by another force. Once travelling through the air, the motion rams air into the front of the engine. Fuel is then added and ignited, and the burning gases leave at the rear.

The intake end of a modern jet engine consists of a huge air compressor, which is operated by the burning gases turning the blades of a turbine which is on the same drive shaft as the compressor. Some engines have two or more compressors driven by two or more turbines to give increased power.

The power of jet engines can be further increased when they are fitted with an 'afterburner', or re-heat system. When the pilot requires extra power, to accelerate the aircraft through the sound barrier, as in Concorde, he opens the throttles so that extra fuel is injected into a chamber beyond the main combustion area in the engines. Here, the fuel is ignited in the already intensely hot gases from the main combustion chamber, producing considerable, extra thrust.

Below left: An engineer is dwarfed by the enormous jet engine.

Below: A South African Airways 747 taking off.

Bottom: The 'Inside story' of a Rolls-Royce RB-211 turbofan engine.

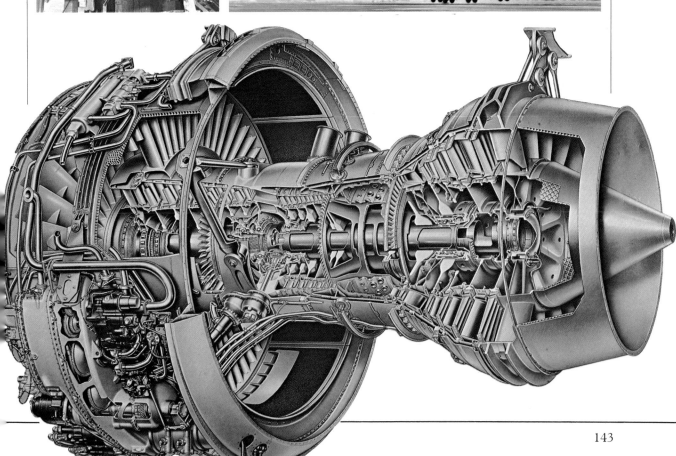

HOVERCRAFT

Amphibious vehicles, those that can move on both land and water, have been in use for a number of years, but while most of them were fairly fast on land, they moved quite slowly when they were functioning as boats. The only truly amphibious vehicle that can move with equal ease on both land and water is the hovercraft.

The hovercraft is the invention of an electronics engineer named Christopher Cockerell. Cockerell's hobby was sailing and he was interested in the problem of reducing the 'drag' or friction of water on the hull of a boat, and hit on the idea of designing a boat which would travel on a cushion of air.

The air cushion under a hovercraft is produced by a large fan which blows air downwards between the hull and the water or ground, and so lifts up the craft. The air is maintained at higher than atmospheric pressure by a flexible rubber 'skirt' around the bottom edge of the hovercraft, preventing leakage of air from the cushion. Because the hovercraft floats on the air cushion with no contact between the craft and the surface below, it can travel over flat, rough ground or water with ease.

Hovercraft are usually driven by airscrews like aircraft propellers,

which face backwards and 'push' the craft forwards, and can be turned to steer the hovercraft. Since there is no propeller dipping below the hull, hovercraft can travel up ramps out of the water, or land on beaches, and even move easily over swamps and marshes.

Cockerell's Air Cushion Vehicles, or ACVs, are now familiar to everyone and like all inventions, they have been improved upon. British Seaspeed hovercraft have been ferrying passengers and cars across the English Channel since 1968. They now have a 'stretched' version of their Mountbatten Class hovercraft which can carry up to 60 cars and 416 passengers between Britain and France in a little over half and hour.

A new, jumbo-sized hovercraft, designed and built in France, called the Sedam N500 or Naviplane, has now joined the Seaspeed fleet. The 155 tonne N500 is 50 metres long (162 feet) and 23 metres wide (76 feet) and can carry 65 cars, plus five coaches, together with 400 foot-passengers. When the sea conditions are ideal the N500 can reach 112 kph (70 mph).

A variation of the hovercraft principle is the sidewall ACV, which is more economical than the flexible skirt models, and easier to control, but it cannot be used on land. The United States Navy have been experimenting with warships based on the sidewall principle, and some of these may well reach a speed of 160 kph (100 mph).

Right: Hoverlloyd plying the English Channel.

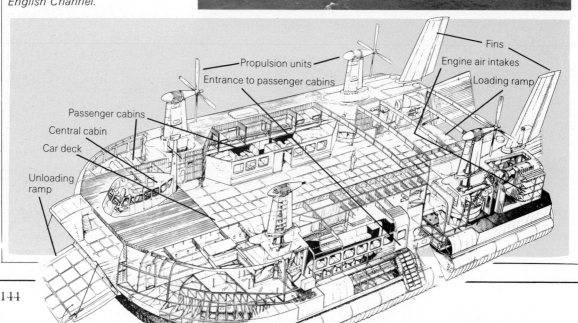

Ships

Ships are the largest man-made structures that move, and they still maintain their supremacy as a form of transport for carrying goods between countries which are separated by vast stretches of ocean. Where very long distances are involved, such as between Europe and Australia, or across the North Atlantic, ships remain the most efficient method of transporting large quantities of merchandise.

Container ships

In recent years, a whole new generation of cargo vessels have begun sailing the oceans of the world at speeds that in the past have been confined to fast passenger liners. They are known as container ships, 30-knot (one knot is equal to a speed of one nautical mile per hour) monsters with powerful engines developing up to 90 000 hp. The 'container' method of transporting goods has revolutionized maritime cargo carrying because of the speed at which the ships can be loaded and unloaded when they arrive at a port specially equipped to handle the containers. These containers look like giant-sized building bricks, and are made to a standard size.

Huge gantries on rails alongside the docks move to where the container ships are moored, and their massive 'arms' reach out to lift the containers off the decks and out of the holds, on to lorries or trains. This rapid mechanical handling is much quicker than the old

Above : A conventional cargo ship about to drop anchor. Note the derricks for loading cargo.

Below : The Mairangi Bay, *a modern container ship passing through the Panama Canal.*

SUBMARINE TANKERS

The use of submarines for other than military purposes has been considered for some time. Recently, an idea for underwater supertankers was put forward by General Dynamics (Electric Boat Division) of America for submarine oil tankers to operate in a part of the world which is normally closed to surface ships for most of the year – the Arctic.

Large, nuclear powered submarines up to 350 metres (1000 feet) in length could navigate under the ice to take on board the enormous quantities of much-needed crude oil which geologists believe lie beneath the sea bed in the north Polar regions.

This bold, imaginative plan would necessitate the construction of concrete oil terminals on the ocean bed off the coast of Alaska. The designers envisage tankers large enough to take on up to 170000 tonnes of crude oil which would be discharged at North Atlantic ports not enclosed by ice.

The super-subs would be 26.5 metres (88 feet) from keel to deck-top, and up to 45 metres (150 feet) wide. Oil could be stored in almost the entire hull except for a comparatively small 'pressure cylinder' in the centre containing the engines and nuclear reactor, and crew's living quarters.

The men manning the sub- marines would not have to face the hazards of surface vessels that are forced to crunch and bulldoze their way through ice-bound seas, not to mention the danger of colliding with drifting icebergs. The submarines would have advanced navigation and sonar systems with long distance detection ability which would enable their crews to avoid the deep underwater sections of icebergs.

Navigation under the ice has already been achieved by both British and American nuclear powered submarines. The Americans were the first to demonstrate that it could be done safely when the USS *Nautilus* journeyed from the Pacific Ocean to the Atlantic in 1958, passing under the ice at the North Pole on the way.

Left: HMS Sovereign, *a Royal Navy nuclear powered submarine breaks through the Polar ice. She is equipped with navigational instruments enabling her to travel under the ice.*

Below: Artist's impression of a super sub.

method of using dockside cranes which lifted comparatively small amounts of cargo out of the holds at a time and then left the cargo to be man-handled into warehouses.

The use of containers can cut a vessel's stay in port from weeks to hours and this means that a ship can make many more voyages in a year, and with larger ships which run faster, one ship will be capable of doing the work of up to eight ordinary cargo carriers.

One route which has proved the effectiveness of container ships is that between Northern Europe and Japan, where just 17 large vessels have replaced 100 conventional cargo ships. All these mighty ships can each carry more than 2000 containers – an enormous quantity of merchandise.

It is natural to think of ships as slow-moving, and therefore safe and easy to manoeuvre, but let's take a look at one of the fastest container ships in the world – the Japanese *Elbe Maru*. This vessel has three propellers driven by three huge diesel engines. The engines are under the control of one officer on the bridge of the ship. Each engine has 10 cylinders and is 15 metres (50 feet) long. When they are running at full speed they gulp 300 tonnes of fuel per day, thrusting the *Elbe Maru* through the sea at a speed of nearly 55 kph (35 mph), so that when she meets a sister ship travelling in the opposite direction in a sea lane their passing speed is 110 kph (70 mph). This does not give much time for either ship to take avoiding action if they find themselves on a collision course!

These modern container vessels are fitted with all the latest navigational aids and anti-collision radar equipment. In foggy weather the radar automatically plots the position and course of all ships in the vicinity. The information is fed into a computer which then calculates the course which must be steered to avoid a collision.

The captain of one of these super-ships has a great responsibility, and he must be particularly mindful of his cargo, much of which is carried on deck in the containers, which are sometimes stacked four-deep. Bad weather could seriously damage deck cargo so that the captain must adjust his speed, and perhaps even his course, to avoid damage. To help him steer clear of foul weather the captain will almost certainly have what is called 'facsimile weather equipment' which can print a weather map of the surrounding area in a matter of minutes.

Below : The bridge of the Liverpool Bay, *and (bottom) the control console of its spacious engine room.*

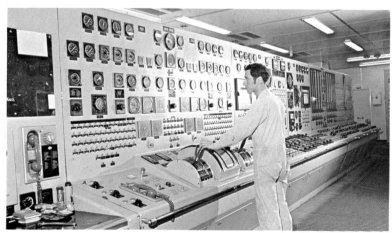

Oil tankers and passenger ships

Remarkable as the new container ships are, the real giants of the ocean are oil tankers. The first giant oil tankers were built in Japan in the early 1960s, and the first such vessel was launched in March 1968. Since then, the size of tankers being built has steadily increased. These enormous ships are known as Very Large Crude Carriers, or VLCCs, because of the crude oil they carry from countries surrounding the Arabian Gulf and elsewhere.

It is hard to imagine just how big these vessels are, but if you think of three football pitches placed end to end and then add a bit more, you have some idea of their length. With a deadweight tonnage of 250 000 tonnes, and sometimes more, they make a large passenger liner of 65 000 tonnes like Britain's QE2, seem a mere lightweight. (The deadweight tonnage indicates the weight of the load a ship can safely carry.)

Although the VLCCs may seem huge, there are a few tankers which are even larger! They are called ULCCs, or Ultra Large Crude Carriers, and some, like the *Globtik Tokyo* of almost 500 000 deadweight tonnes, are only a few metres shorter than the Empire State Building in New York, USA. In fact, the distance from the crew's quarters at the stern to the bow is so great (379 metres) that seamen have been known to use a bicycle to get to work!

Of course, comparing a beautiful passenger liner like the QE2 with a supertanker can be confusing, because each is designed to perform very different tasks. The tankers carry about 35 men in comfortable crew's quarters, where most of them have individual cabins, and where there is often the added luxury of a swimming pool. Apart from the engine room, the rest of the vast hull is simply a series of tanks for carrying the oil – in the case of supertankers as much as 580 million litres.

The hull of a super liner

Below : The Globtik Tokyo, *a London registered supertanker of almost half a million deadweight tonnes.*

like the QE2 contains all the elements of a floating town with a population of around 3000 people. The QE2 can accommodate 2025 passengers, and has a crew of 906, who maintain the ship and look after the passengers' needs. Apart from restaurants and cafeterias, there are: a theatre and cinema; four swimming pools; 5000 square metres (6000 square yards) of deck space; a hospital; a printing plant for the ship's daily newspaper; a dentist's surgery; a laundry; a variety of shops, including hairdressers; and even kennels for passenger's pets, with a special exercise area.

The QE2's 110000 hp engines make her the most powerful twin-screw merchant ship afloat, and give her a top speed of approximately 30 knots, while the big tankers with their single screws heave their way through the water at the much slower cruising speed of 16 knots. Nevertheless, because of their immense weight, tankers have to be handled carefully, particularly in congested waters like the English Channel. Ships have no brakes, and a supertanker continues to travel ahead for almost three miles before she can stop, even when her engines are in full reverse. Despite her single propeller she has a turning circle of less than three times her length.

Below : The British Petroleum tanker British Patience *of 250 000 tonnes.*

Bottom : The graceful and elegant lines of Cunard's QE 2.

OPENING OF THE FIRST ENGLISH RAILWAY BETWEEN STOCKTON AND DARLINGTON, SEPT. 27TH 1825.

TREVITHICKS,
PORTABLE STEAM ENGINE.

Catch me who can.

Mechanical Power Subduing
Animal Speed.

Top: A contemporary artist's impression of the opening day of the Stockton & Darlington Railway, and the famous Rainhill trials which were won by George Stephenson's 'Rocket'.

Above: Richard Trevithick's locomotive.

Below: A Beyer Garrett steam locomotive at work on South African railways.

Railways

Each form of transport in its turn seems to have drastically changed the lives of people all over the world, and railways are no exception. The first man to make a steam-driven engine which ran on rails was Richard Trevithick. His 'locomotive' was used at an iron works near Merthyr Tydfil in Wales, in 1804, where it hauled a 20-tonne load at 8 kph (5 mph). The adaptation of steam-power to railway engines did not really come into its own until the British engineer George Stephenson built the historically famous 'Rocket' locomotive.

Britain's first railway line was built between Stockton and Darlington in north-east England. It ran a distance of 60 kilometres (37 miles) and was opened in 1825 when a Stephenson's engine weighing 8 tonnes hauled a train at a speed of 26 kph (16 mph). A later model of a 'Rocket' in 1829 reached a speed of 46.6 kph (29 mph).

Railways expanded rapidly in Europe in the 19th century, and the country with most railways per square kilometre was at one time Belgium, although the network has now been considerably reduced for economic reasons. British Rail still operate over 17 700 route kilometres (11 000 route miles), and in recent years large amounts of money have been spent in modernising both rolling stock and track.

The exciting and romantic steam locomotives belching smoke and sparks as they thundered about their business, remained the kings of speed on the railways for well over 100 years, but since the 1950s steam traction has been replaced by diesel-powered locomotives. Electric locomotives have also been introduced, and have proved to be some of the fastest trains.

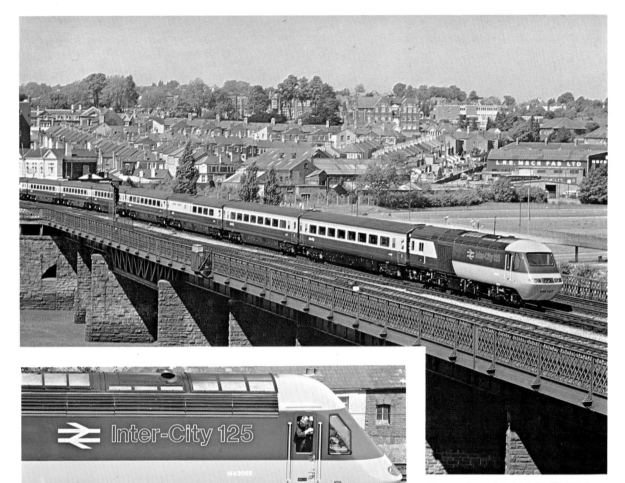

Above : One of British Rail's High Speed Trains leaving Newport, Gwent, Wales.

Left : Close-up of HST engine.

High speed trains

High Speed Trains (HST) are a major advance in diesel/electric traction. A prototype in Britain began its early trials in 1976, running between London and Bristol. The HST covered the distance of 190 kilometres (118 miles) between the two cities in only 82 minutes, cutting 25 minutes off the previously scheduled time, and giving an average speed of 140 kph (87 mph) for the journey, at times reaching 200 kph (125 mph).

Motive power is supplied by two light engines, one at each end of the train. This spreads the weight and provides plenty of power. The overall weight has been reduced by the use of light materials such as aluminium for the fuel tanks, and glass fibre panels for the train ends. Each driving coach has a powerful 12-cylinder pressure-charged and air-cooled diesel engine which generates electricity through dynamos to power the traction motors. High Speed Trains have to

be brought to a halt safely and smoothly, and the HST not only has air brakes fitted throughout, but they are applied automatically unless the driver depresses a lever in the cab every 60 seconds. A buzzer sounds to warn him to do this, and it is a safety device in case the driver collapses at the controls.

Unlike some modern train projects, the HST can run on existing lines without any major alterations to the rails themselves, although some improvements have been made

on the high speed inter-city routes to allow the trains to maintain their top speed most of the way.

Several countries have built a number of high speed trains although none of them incorporates the unique suspension system of the British advanced passenger train the APT.

High speed passenger services have been given great attention in both Germany and Japan. In West Germany the Class 103 electric locomotive is capable of reaching speeds of around 200 kph (125 mph) and has been in service for a number of years, and new high-speed railways with better quality track are planned for the future. Passenger trains on these new inter-city routes should achieve impressive speeds of 300 kph (190 mph).

Japan has a famous high speed train service known as the New Tokaido Line. *Hikari*, or lightning trains, run between Tokyo and Osaka, a distance of 515 kilometres (320 miles).

As a result of the carefully laid track and gentle curves the trains can keep up a speed of 210 kph (130 mph) for practically the whole journey.

Top: An elevated electric commuter railway in Chicago, USA.

Above: The German Intercity-Zug Hermes, High Speed Train.

Above right: A Japanese Tokaido express at speed.

Right: An American 'Amtrak' locomotive at Union Station, Los Angeles.

ADVANCED PASSENGER TRAIN

When you travel by train you may have noticed that the rails on which the locomotive and coaches run are tilted or 'banked' on curves. This is done to counteract the centrifugal forces which act upon the train when it has to go round a corner. Railway engineers avoid sharp corners when laying track, and gentle curves are always used, particularly on high speed sections.

When trains travel at speeds approaching 160 kph (100 mph) and beyond, it is essential that the track is carefully maintained, and when a driver approaches a steep curve he will normally have to reduce the speed of the train otherwise it would leave the track, with disastrous consequences.

British Rail's Advanced Passenger Train (APT) is capable of travelling at 240 kph (150 mph) on ordinary lines, although its eight powerful British Leyland gas turbine engines, each generating 300 hp, could whisk it along at 320 kph (200 mph) on specially built high-speed track.

These tremendous speeds are only possible because of the new technology used in the APT. If ordinary diesel or electric loco-motives attempted to reach these very high speeds, their tremendous weight would make their wheels act like grindstones against the metal rails. This would not only damage the wheels, but eventually the track itself would need replacing.

The APT solves these problems in two ways. Its light construction, using aluminium in both the coaches and locomotive, reduces the total weight by half. This decreases the strain on the rails, but in addition to this, the APT has a clever computer-controlled system which has the effect of guiding the flanges on the wheels away from the rail edges.

The APT also has a unique body-tilting mechanism. As the train rounds a corner hydraulic 'jacks' tilt it into the curve. This does not affect the train speed or safety, but prevents passengers being thrown sideways.

In 1979, APTs were temporarily introduced on to the passenger service run between London and Glasgow and were electric with overhead power lines, unlike the original experimental model with its gas turbine engines. Although the APTs are not in service at present, they are still providing useful information on the effects of high speed rail travel.

Below: British Rail's APT-E on trials on Western Region track.

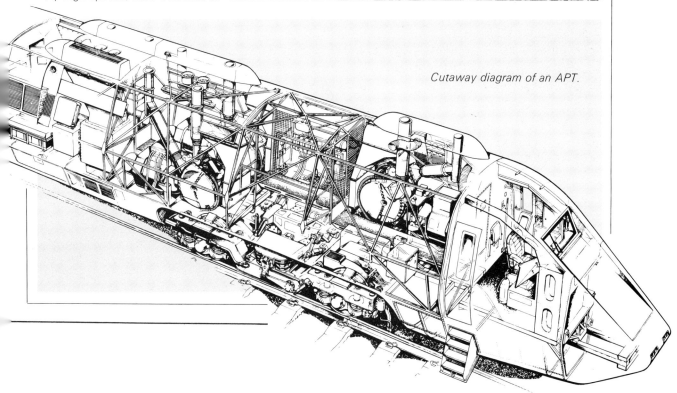

Cutaway diagram of an APT.

Hovertrains

At the beginning of the 1960s development engineers in Britain began planning an entirely new type of transport system called hovertrains. A hovertrain is a combination of a hovercraft and a train. Instead of running along a conventional railway track on the ground, the hovertrain travels along a 'T' or 'U' shaped concrete beam. Fans inside the train suck in air and direct it downwards onto the beam 'track' so that the coaches float on a cushion of air. Two more air cushions exert pressure against the low sides of the beam to guide the train along.

In 1973, in a demonstration test run along a specially built 6½ kilometre (4 mile) length of track, a full scale hovertrain reached a speed of 170 kph (107 mph). It was called the RTV 31, and was a remotely controlled test vehicle which had no driver. The train was 22 metres (73 feet) long, 3.6 metres (12 feet) wide, and weighed 21 tonnes. The motive power was supplied by a linear induction motor, which pushes the train magnetically along the track. Plans were in hand to extend the track to a distance of 19 kilometres (12 miles), and it was anticipated that the hovertrain would be able to achieve its top speed of 480 kph (300 mph), but unfortunately the project was cancelled, and what might have been the beginning of an entirely new era of high-speed travel came to an abrupt end.

France also experimented with the hovertrain idea, called the Aerotrain. An 18 kilometre (11 mile) length of test track was built north of Orleans, and several prototypes were built and tested successfully between 1965 and 1971. Speeds of more than 420 kph (260 mph) were reached, and over 10000 passengers were carried. In 1973, an Aerotrain was fitted with a turbo engine, and a year later it established a new world record for air-cushion rail vehicles when it reached an amazing 426 kph (265 mph).

Although there were plans for a commercially operated Aerotrain to run on a 24 kilometre (15 mile) route between Paris and the new town of Cergy-Pointoise, the French Government, like the British, changed their minds and the project was abandoned. Tests are still going on in France, and in the United States of America, but the world has yet to see its first fully operational hovertrain.

Hovertrains can be built on concrete 'stilts' so that the track is above the ground, an advantage when the line has to run into congested city centres. Overhead monorail systems have the same advantage, and there are a number of these in use in different parts of the world, particularly in Germany. Monorail trains were also considered to be the answer to travel in congested city areas, but because of the high cost of building overhead track, and the existing ground rail (and underground) systems already well established, it seems unlikely that they will be extended in the near future.

Right : The French prototype Aerotrain.

Below : A cutaway diagram of a typical air-cushion train.

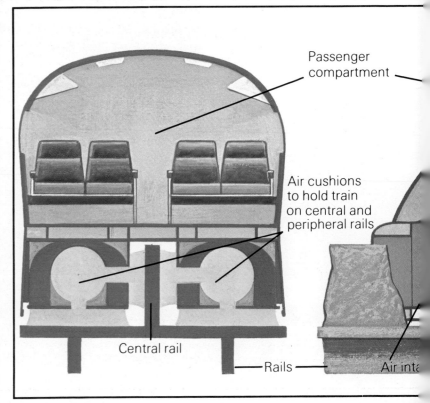

Passenger compartment

Air cushions to hold train on central and peripheral rails

Central rail

Rails

Air inta[ke]

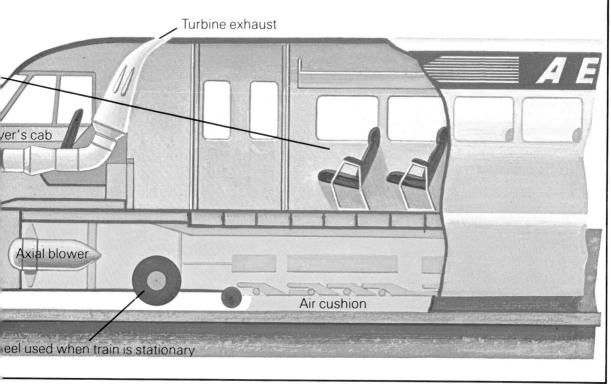

Turbine exhaust

A E

Driver's cab

Axial blower

Air cushion

Wheel used when train is stationary

Motor Cars

In the early 1900s, an American engineer named Henry Ford founded a motor manufacturing company at Detroit in the United States of America. His aim was to produce a light, fast car at the lowest possible price, and Ford realized that to achieve this his vehicle would have to be produced quickly and in large numbers – and so the idea of mass production was born.

Assembly line production

Ford's genius lay in the fact that he realized cars could not be built on a 'one-off' basis if the price was to be brought down within the reach of the average man, and he knew that there were a limited number of people with sufficient money to buy expensive models. The only way of building cars that would be cheap enough to enable the millions of ordinary wage earners to buy them was to standardize them. In this way the engines and component parts could be made in large quantities, and then brought together in one vast factory where trained workers could assemble them.

The cars were put together in sequence – one worker, one part – with the cars passing from worker to worker along a moving conveyor.

Top: One of Henry Ford's first Model 'T' cars.

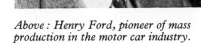

Above: Henry Ford, pioneer of mass production in the motor car industry.

Below: An early production line in the Morris factory in Britain where the famous 'bull-nose' models were made.

So that Henry Ford could make everything needed for his cars, he bought mines, mills and factories for the supply of steel, wood, glass and leather. He also acquired interests in railway, steamship and aircraft lines so that his finished products could be transported. His methods proved so successful that between 1908 and 1925 some 15 000 000 of his Model 'T', or 'tin Lizzie', were sold to an eagerly awaiting public.

The famous Model 'T' was not particularly comfortable or elegant by today's standards, but Ford had brought motoring to the masses, and the basic principle of his production methods has not changed in more than 50 years. Motor manufacturing plants of today, of course, are much larger than even the forward-looking Henry Ford could have dreamed, and world production is in the millions.

Cars which would have been considered expensive luxury models 50 years ago, are now built on the assembly line principle, and often most of the component parts are made in one vast factory complex. There is a foundry where engine blocks are cast, and where moving parts such as

Below and right : Various stages in the production of cars.

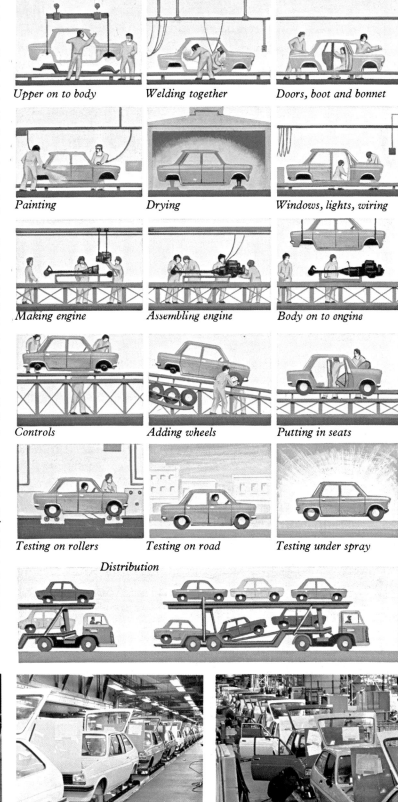

Upper on to body

Welding together

Doors, boot and bonnet

Painting

Drying

Windows, lights, wiring

Making engine

Assembling engine

Body on to engine

Controls

Adding wheels

Putting in seats

Testing on rollers

Testing on road

Testing under spray

Distribution

gear wheels have to be hardened. The hardened parts are ground and polished to fit exactly into the engines. The engines themselves have to be put together and then fed into the main assembly line system.

Meanwhile, in the body shop, enormous 'presses' stamp out the different metal parts of the car bodies such as doors and wing panels. These are then welded together until the complete shell is ready.

As the main assembly line moves along, every single item of the car is methodically fixed in position; the engine is lowered from a moving line overhead, all the electrical wiring is installed, axles, wheels, transmission, instrument panels, upholstery, carpets, windscreens, windows, lights, and bumpers are all added until the completed car is ready to be rolled off the line.

Roads

As the motor car began coming on to our roads in ever increasing numbers during the first half of the 20th century, it soon became evident that the roads themselves would not only have to be increased in number, but improvements made in the technique of building them.

When the need for faster transport came with the Industrial Revolution, heavier steam-driven road vehicles began to appear, and many roads were not good enough to stand up to the pounding they were getting. A hundred years ago most roads in towns and cities were made by laying down small, square stone blocks, and in some instances even wooden blocks. In wet or icy conditions these were dangerous for horses, and

when cars and bicycles started to use them, skids were frequent. Such roads soon crumbled under the speed and weight of cars and lorries, and a new method of construction had to be found.

A widely used method today is first to bulldoze away the topsoil and then lay a thick foundation of stone mixed with ash, up to 1 metre (3 feet) deep. When this is rolled hard and compacted, a surface of small stones coated with a natural tar, or a similar substance called bitumen, is added. This type of road can be easily resurfaced and will last many years.

A far better method is needed, however, for motorways, which have to take a pounding from high-speed cars and huge, heavily loaded trucks. The foundation for this type of road is again

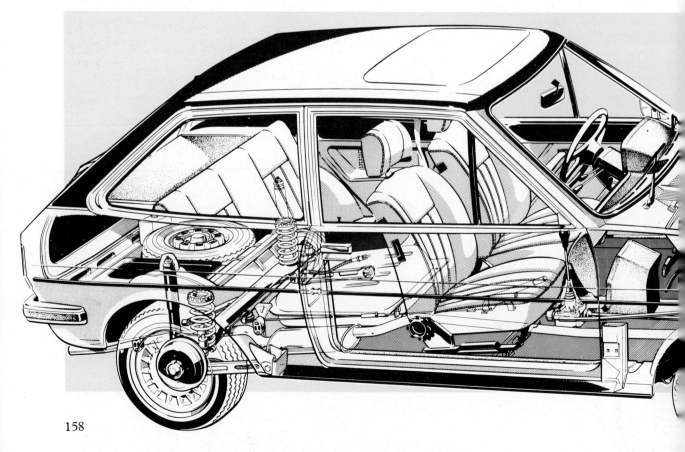

stone mixed with ash, frequently with a weak cement mixture added to hold it together. A special road-making machine then lays concrete slabs, beneath which is a network of steel mesh to give added strength. The concrete slabs are at least 15 centimetres (6 inches) thick, and each one may be up to 30 metres (100

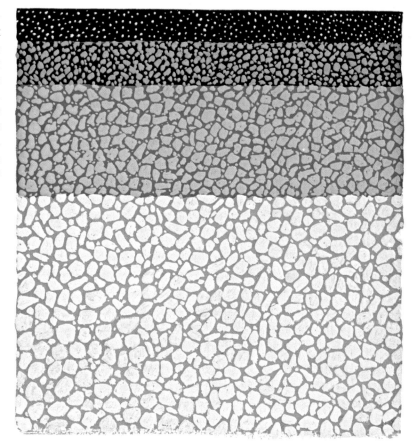

1.
2.
3.
4.

Right : The construction of a modern road.
1. Wearing course (20–40 mm coated macadam)
2. Basecourse (50 mm dense bitmac)
3. Road base (250 mm thick macadam)
4. Sub base (crushed stone gravel up to 600 mm thick)

Below right : Modern roads take a pounding from international juggernauts.

Below : Cutaway diagram of a left-hand drive Ford Fiesta.

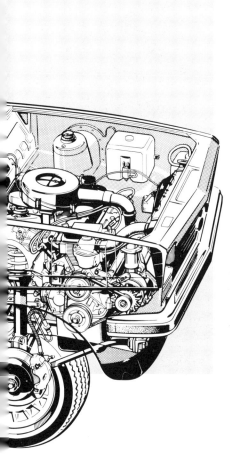

feet) long. A layer of asphalt 5 or 6 centimetres thick is added, and a final 4 or 5 centimetres of hot-rolled asphalt forms the actual driving surface.

Above : A giant road-scraper used for the first stage of levelling in the process of modern road building.

Below : Britain's famous 'spaghetti junction' near Birmingham where two motorways intersect.

The motorways of Britain, the autoroutes of European countries, and the mighty six-lane highways of the United States of America form a communication network that would have astounded people of 100 years ago. They would have been even more astonished by the complicated junctions, underpasses and fly-overs which have been built to link one road system with another, so that vehicles can change over safely without having to reduce speed. A fine example of one of these complex junctions is in Birmingham, Britain, where a system of overhead roads joins the M6 and the A38(M) and has the nickname 'Spaghetti Junction'.

The Natural World

Contents

Millions of years ago, there was no life on this planet. In fact, there was no planet as we would recognise it today – it was just a ball of flaming gases. These gases were in a state of considerable chemical turmoil, reacting together to form and reform chemicals. As time passed, the gases cooled, became liquid and eventually a thin crust was formed over the surface. Beneath this crust, the centre of the earth was still, and remains today, a molten mass of rocks and metals with a solid core. The planet was still an inhospitable place, with frequent storms and volcanic eruptions, and at first there was no life on it.

First signs of life

In the unsettled conditions and electrical storms, the chemical disturbance continued. Minute particles called atoms combined to form molecules, split apart and joined again in new combinations of atoms.

At some time in this 'natural laboratory' carbon, hydrogen, oxygen and nitrogen combined to produce a stable protein molecule which had an amazing new property. It could reproduce itself. It was the first sign of life. In time, more complex molecules formed which were able to eat, move, feel, excrete and breathe as well as reproduce. It is these six functions that separate the non-living from the living.

As the environment changed, some of these first protein molecules adapted themselves and changed with it. They became more complicated and were slowly organized into cells, with each cell having a nucleus to control its activities. Two important chemicals emerged; these were the nucleic acids, deoxyribonucleic acid (DNA) and ribonucleic acid (RNA), which carry the blueprint of the living cell to the next genera-tion and ensure that the new cells grow and behave in the same way as the parent cells.

With the living proteins or cells adapting to the changing environment and the DNA carrying the information to the next generation, life became

Below left : Molecules had to evolve, just as plants and animals evolved. The water molecule is quite simple. Glucose has more atoms in it. DNA is very complex.

Below : Mendel was the first person to understand the Laws of Inheritance. The red flower has genes for red colouring. The white flower has genes for white. Their offspring have both genes and all the flowers are pink. Their offspring may be pink, white or red, half the new flowers being pink, a quarter red and a quarter white.

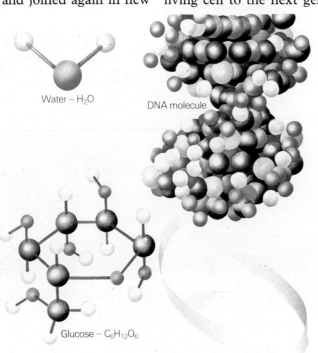

Water – H_2O

DNA molecule

Glucose – $C_6H_{12}O_6$

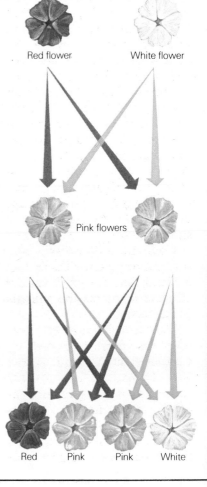

Red flower   White flower

Pink flowers

Red   Pink   Pink   White

THE MAN WHO NAMED THE LIVING WORLD

Before 1753 it was difficult for scientists to talk to each other about plants and animals because, even if they spoke the same language, every plant or animal had more than one name. A bat was called a flittermouse in one country, and something completely different in another. There was a great deal of confusion about exactly which plant or animal was being described. Then a Swedish scientist called Carl von Linné clarified the situation. He was born in 1707 and lived until 1778. He was a botanist and he invented the method of naming plants and animals that is still in use today.

In 1735 von Linné, or Linnaeus, as he is usually known, wrote a book called the *Systema Naturae*. It was written in Latin, because Latin was the international language of the day, and that is why his name changed from Carl von Linné to Carolus Linnaeus. The names were all in Latin too, and that tradition has remained. Linnaeus gave each plant and animal two names. First came the surname, or generic name, followed by the specific, or species, name. This method of naming plants was called the binomial system (bi = 2, nomial = name). Plants and animals which are closely related have the same surname, or generic name. They are grouped together in a *genus*. Each kind of plant is given a specific name, and is called a *species*.

For example, the generic name of the woodpeckers is *Dendrocopus*. The Great Spotted Woodpecker has a scientific name of *Dendrocopus major*. The Middle Spotted Woodpecker is *Dendrocopus medius* and the Lesser Spotted Woodpecker is *Dendrocopus minor*. If a scientist publishes a paper about the Greater Spotted Woodpecker, he will write about *Dendrocopus major*, and German scientists, who call the bird a 'Buntspecht', French scientists, who call it a 'Pic épeiche' and Swedish scientists, who call it a 'Större hackspett', will all know exactly which woodpecker the scientist is writing about. By his invention of the binomial system, Linnaeus began modern scientific investigation.

still more complex. Some cells evolved a green pigment called *chlorophyll* with which they trapped the sun's energy, to make their food, and became plants. Others broke down the chemicals from their surroundings to obtain their energy, and became bacteria. Still others fed on their fellow creatures, and became animals. Each group included many different types; some of them were not successful, and became extinct, but left traces in the rocks, called fossils, to show that they once existed.

Over the millions of years, the first protein molecules had evolved into the great variety of bacteria, plants and animals living today.

The theory of how life evolved was first suggested by Charles Darwin and Alfred Russel Wallace in 1858. It caused a great argument, because the religious leaders believed that God had created the world in seven days and that it had not changed since the Creation. Darwin collected a great deal of evidence to show that plants and animals adapted to their surroundings, that only the fittest survived and that characteristics were handed on to their offspring. This he published in 1859 in his famous book *On the Origin of Species by Natural Selection*.

Gregor Mendel lived at the same time as Darwin, but it is unlikely that they knew each other. Mendel was a monk, who studied the plants growing in the monastery garden and from them, worked out the Laws of Inheritance. Mendel founded the study of genetics, showing how living things handed on their characteristics to their offspring.

Below : The fossil of an ammonite, Asteroceras obtusum lias. *This fossil, which is between 135 and 180 million years old, was found at Lyme Regis, England.*

Bacteria

Bacteria are tiny, one-celled creatures, without a definite nucleus. They are so small that they cannot be seen with the naked eye and can only be studied properly with an electron microscope. Although they crowd about us in the air, the soil, the water, in our food and even inside our bodies, people did not know they existed until the last century.

Microscopic creatures were first investigated by a Dutch merchant named Antony van Leeuwenhoek. He made the first microscope in 1675. Through this he saw and described bacteria, fungi, protozoans and other tiny creatures. Despite this early discovery the great importance of bacteria was not then fully realized.

The harmful bacteria were the first to be investigated. Two doctors, Pasteur and Lister, emphasised that diseases could be caused by bacteria, and that it was necessary to sterilize everything that came into contact with disease, to prevent the disease from spreading. Each disease-causing bacterium had to be killed. In order to do this the habits of that bacterium had to be investigated, and so the study of bacteriology came into existence.

The work carried out on harmful bacteria often makes us forget that there are as many useful bacteria as there are harmful ones. They play an important part in making our planet work. Without them the processes of decomposition and the recycling of elements could not take place. The bacteria in the soil help to trap nitrogen from the air and turn it into nitrates, so that it can be used by plants. They help to decompose dead plants and animals, and by living off the debris in rivers they help to clean polluted water, making the planet habitable. All animals have some bacteria living inside them. Without them cattle could not digest the grasses on which they feed. We use bacteria to make yoghourt and cheese, two commer-

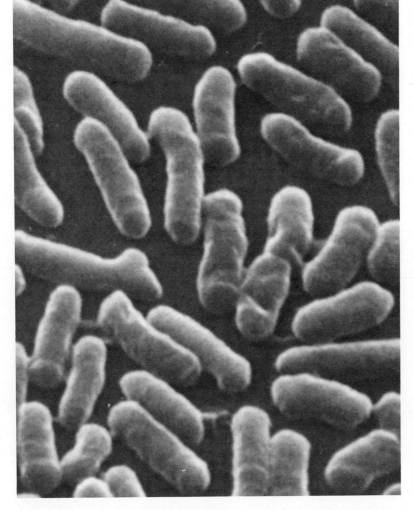

Left : A picture of bacterial cells (the bacillus Escherichia coli) *magnified 32 000 times.*

Below : These bacteria, which cause the disease of scarlet fever, are the rounded coccus type. Here they have formed chains.

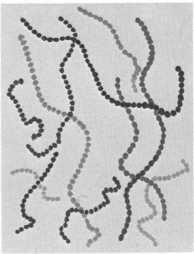

cial ways of preserving milk.

Under a microscope, a bacterium can have one of three shapes. It may be straight (a *bacillus*), rounded (a *coccus*), or twisted (a *spirillus*). All these shapes may be found in one group or family of bacteria. There are about 50 families, divided into 10 orders. They live in different ways. Some get their energy from the chemicals in the mud in stagnant water, releasing a smell similar to rotting cabbages in the process; some are found in milk and help in the making of cheese, while others cause diseases such as the Black Death, diphtheria and pneumonia, or can cause food poisoning.

Bacteria feed in different ways. Some can manufacture their own food, as plants can, others use chemicals around them for food. Some need oxygen, while others can live without it. They reproduce by dividing in half, and can reproduce very quickly. A bacterium can divide every 20 minutes! That means that one bacterium will become eight at the end of an hour, and as each of those also divides there would be millions by the end of the day.

Viruses

Viruses are even smaller than bacteria, and are the simplest known forms of life. They are not able to live by themselves. They live as parasites in bacteria, animals and some plants. So far, no viruses have been found in fungi, mosses, liverworts, or ferns. Viruses invade the cells of their hosts and simply take them over. The DNA in the virus takes over the DNA in the host cell and

Above : The patterns of colour in these tulips are due to a viral infection.

Right : Although a virus is a living thing, it can have a non-active form which is like a crystal. The tail on this virus acts as a syringe, injecting chemicals into host cells to infect them.

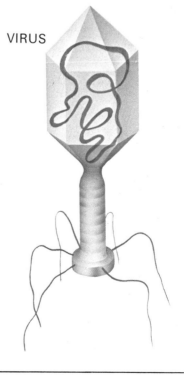

VIRUS

changes the instructions, so that the host produces more viruses.

There are a large number of diseases caused by viruses, such as influenza, measles and smallpox in men, rabies and foot and mouth disease in animals and tobacco mosaic disease in plants. Some tulips have a viral infection in their petals which gives an attractive colour, and this infection is bred into the tulips to improve their appearance.

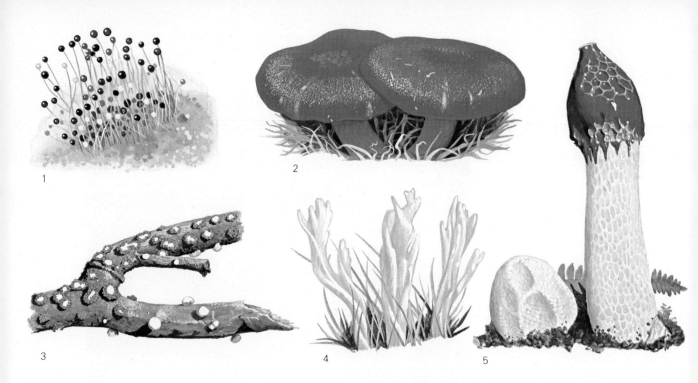

1

2

3

4

5

The fungi

Fungi look like plants, but many people classify them separately because fungi are unable to make their own food. They feed by dissolving and digesting plant and animal materials outside their bodies and absorbing the food matter through their *hyphae*. Hyphae are the main 'building blocks' of a fungus and appear as long, thin, thread-like branches which grow through the food material on which they feed. Hyphae appear as fine white hairs when viewed through a magnifying glass. The mass of hyphae together are called a mycelium. The familiar mushrooms and toadstools are produced by the hyphae to carry the 'seeds' – which are really spores – above the ground, so that they can blow away to grow into new fungi. These structures are called *fruiting bodies*. There are four large groups of fungi.

The Phycomycetes

This group contains the Potato Blight Fungus, which in 1846 rotted potatoes and caused famine in Ireland, and the Black Bread Mould, which can grow even in a refrigerator, spoiling food that is kept there. The Pin Mould is also a phycomycete. Many fungi in this group play an important part in decomposing organic matter, particularly in breaking down animal dung.

The Ascomycetes

This group includes attractively coloured fungi like the Orange Peel Fungus, the Scarlet Elf Cup, the edible morels, and the most useful fungi to man – the yeasts. Brewers' yeast has been helping men to produce beer for hundreds of years, and bakers' yeast has been used as far back as history records. In the past, when fresh food was difficult to obtain in the winter months, the vitamins in bread and beer were an important part of the diet, and it was yeast that supplied them. Some scientists believe that yeasts will play an important part in feeding the world of the future. If the population continues to increase at its present rate, it will not be possible to grow enough plants or animals conventionally to feed so many mouths, and yeasts and soya beans will be used as staple foods.

The Basidiomycetes

The familiar field mushroom and the cep, are included in this group. It also contains the pretty, but poisonous Fly Agaric, bracket fungi, such as the Beefsteak Fungus, which is tough and nothing like beefsteak to eat, and the dainty umbrellas of the fungus *Psathyrella gracilis*. Rusts and smuts, which are plant parasites that can destroy crops, are also in this group.

The Fungi Imperfecta

A collection of widely differing fungi; they include *Penicillium*, which provides man with the useful drug penicillin, but also with *Macrosporum*, which is an unpleasant parasite causing ringworm on human skin.

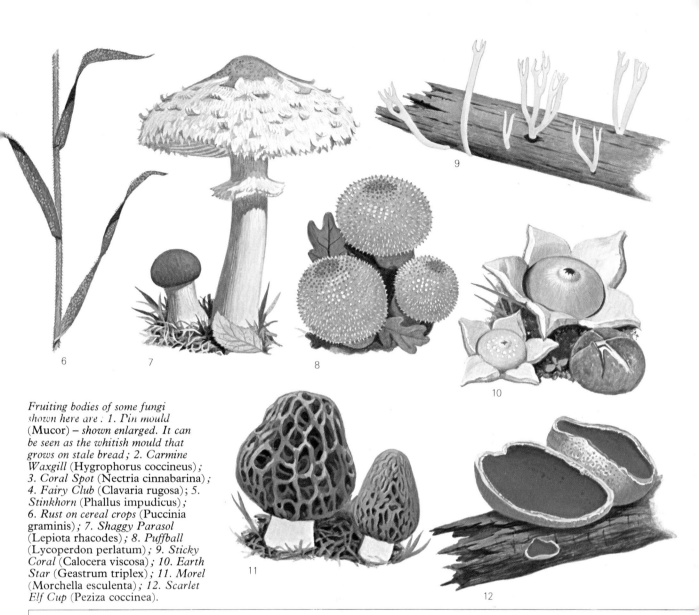

Fruiting bodies of some fungi shown here are: 1. Pin mould (Mucor) – *shown enlarged. It can be seen as the whitish mould that grows on stale bread; 2. Carmine Waxgill* (Hygrophorus coccineus); *3. Coral Spot* (Nectria cinnabarina); *4. Fairy Club* (Clavaria rugosa); *5. Stinkhorn* (Phallus impudicus); *6. Rust on cereal crops* (Puccinia graminis); *7. Shaggy Parasol* (Lepiota rhacodes); *8. Puffball* (Lycoperdon perlatum); *9. Sticky Coral* (Calocera viscosa); *10. Earth Star* (Geastrum triplex); *11. Morel* (Morchella esculenta); *12. Scarlet Elf Cup* (Peziza coccinea).

PLANTS THAT HEAL

Many of the plants that are poisonous in large quantities are useful medicinally if taken in very small quantities. Foxgloves are poisonous if eaten, but the drug *digitalis* is extracted from the plants, and this is used to treat people with heart diseases. The Deadly Nightshade gives belladonna which is used as a sedative and the Nux vomica tree supplies strychnine, which can increase appetite. However, both of these medicines must be taken in small doses; they are poisonous if that dose is exceeded. Before men could manufacture drugs, plants were their only source. The Chinese were using opium, from poppies, and the South American Indians chewing coca leaves as pain-killers long before the appearance of drugs called heroin and cocaine. Now that these drugs are distilled from the plants and used at greater strengths, they have become addictive drugs, causing as much distress as relief from pain. Other drugs are not as dangerous. Quinine, which helps to bring down fever, is extracted from the bark of the cinchona tree, which grows in South America. Camphor, castor beans and cloves all give oils with medicinal uses, and these are only a few of the many plants used to ease illness. Another fungus must be included here, the *Penicillium* fungus, which gives penicillin, an invaluable antibiotic.

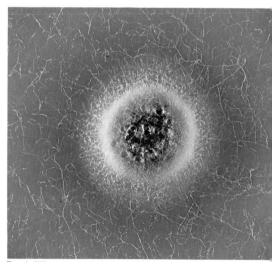

Penicillium notatum *mould growing on agar, a jelly-like substance.*

The Plant Kingdom

Plants play a vital part in the ecology of our planet, for they provide food and shelter for an enormous variety of animals. Most plants are green in colour, and this green colour comes from one of the most important chemicals in the world, *chlorophyll*. A few bacteria have chlorophyll, but no animal has it. With chlorophyll, it is possible to convert carbon dioxide and water into sugar, which forms food for the plant. Chlorophyll traps the energy from the sun's rays to provide energy for the sugar-making process. Animals have to rely on plants to supply the food, and hence energy that makes living possible.

This major difference in feeding explains the difference between plants and animals. Plants need air, water, sunlight and trace elements from the soil to supply their nutrition. All these requirements surround them. Plants do not hunt for food, so they do not have to move from place to place. Providing a plant has good soil, shelter and a suitable climate, its main problems are the fertilisation of its eggs and the spreading or *distribution* of its seeds. If all the seeds simply fell to the ground close to the parent plant, there would not be space for many to grow. The seeds must land at a distance from the parent, so they must be mobile, even if the plant is not.

Plants do make movements, however. They turn their leaves to the sun, open and shut their flowers and wind tendrils round supports. Plants that have no flowers produce little sex cells, called *gametes*,

TYPICAL FLOWERING PLANT

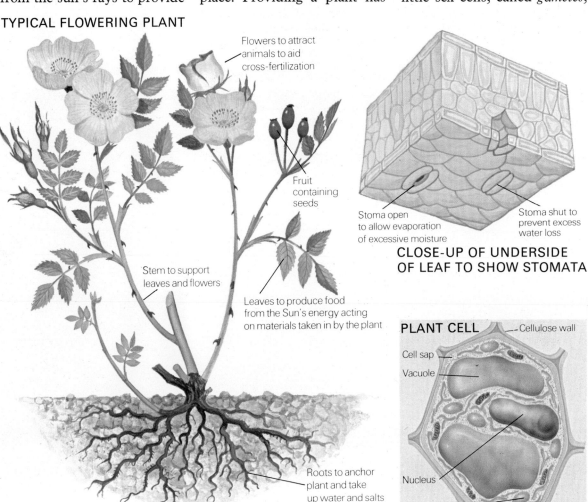

Flowers to attract animals to aid cross-fertilization

Fruit containing seeds

Stem to support leaves and flowers

Leaves to produce food from the Sun's energy acting on materials taken in by the plant

Roots to anchor plant and take up water and salts

Stoma open to allow evaporation of excessive moisture

Stoma shut to prevent excess water loss

CLOSE-UP OF UNDERSIDE OF LEAF TO SHOW STOMATA

PLANT CELL
Cellulose wall
Cell sap
Vacuole
Nucleus
Chloroplast

which swim about. These small movements do not, however, use up the large amounts of energy required by animals whose lives are much more active.

Photosynthesis

The food that plants need is made by a process called *photosynthesis*. This is an extremely complicated chemical process, which can be shown by a simple formula.

The formula (shown above) does not show the many energy changes or the stages of photosynthesis, however. Simply, the plants combine carbon dioxide from the air with water to make sugar. This sugar is stored as carbohydrate, and is used later by the plant to provide energy for growth and flower production. From the formula, you can see that oxygen is a waste product from photosynthesis. When the plant needs energy the carbohydrate is combined with

$$6CO_2 + 6H_2O \xrightarrow[\text{chlorophyll}]{\text{sunlight}} C_6H_{12}O_6 + 6O_2$$

carbon dioxide   water   sugar   oxygen

oxygen, releasing energy and forming water and carbon dioxide again. This last process is called *respiration*, and it also takes place in animals to provide the energy they require in order to live.

Plant cells

There are two main differences between plant and animal cells. Plant cells contain green chlorophyll and they have thick, rigid cell walls, made of a substance called *cellulose*. Plants do not need the thinner, flexible walls found in animal cells because they do not move in the same way. Inside the walls, a plant cell has protoplasm with a nucleus embedded in it, and there are often large spaces called *vacuoles*, filled with a liquid called *cell sap*. The plant is

kept in shape by the pressure of the sap on the cell walls rather like the shape of a balloon is maintained by the air inside.

These cells build up into tissues which have different

Below : Bubbles of oxygen being released from the leaves of a water plant, starwort, during photosynthesis.

Below left : The leaves of trees in a European forest. Without sunlight photosynthesis would be impossible.

tasks in the plant. The supporting tissue is called *xylem*. It is xylem that makes up most of the trunk of trees. The xylem is the transport system that carries the water and dissolved salts from the roots to the leaves, where the food is made. This food is then transported to other parts of the plant in another system of tubes, the *phloem*. Between these two layers is the *cambium*, whose cells divide to form either new xylem or phloem.

These tissues, together with the outer layer of the plant, the *epidermis*, and some strengthening and packing cells, build up into the whole plant. A typical flowering plant has roots, a stem, leaves and flowers. The roots hold the plant in the soil and take up water and salts. The stem supports the leaves, so that they get enough sunlight to produce food. The flowers attract animals so that the egg cells and pollen will cross-fertilize to produce fruit and seeds. The fruits surround the seeds and help to disperse them, so that they land in a new place, germinate and grow into new plants.

Plants do not have nerves, to carry messages through their bodies. They send signals in the form of chemicals called *auxins*. These auxins move through the plant cells by a process called *diffusion*. Diffusion is a slow process, and plants cannot react quickly, as animals can. The auxins control the speed with which cells divide, which affects the growth of a particular part of the plant and causes it to bend and grow in another direction.

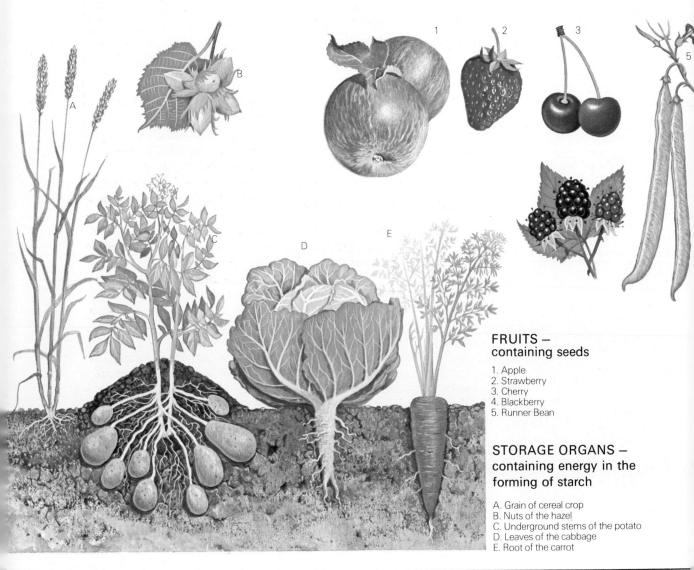

FRUITS —
containing seeds

1. Apple
2. Strawberry
3. Cherry
4. Blackberry
5. Runner Bean

STORAGE ORGANS —
containing energy in the forming of starch

A. Grain of cereal crop
B. Nuts of the hazel
C. Underground stems of the potato
D. Leaves of the cabbage
E. Root of the carrot

DIAGRAM OF PLANT STEM

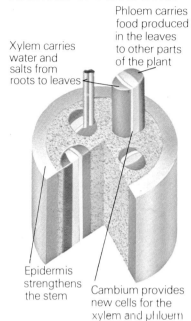

Xylem carries water and salts from roots to leaves

Phloem carries food produced in the leaves to other parts of the plant

Epidermis strengthens the stem

Cambium provides new cells for the xylem and phloem

Above : Cross-section of a plant stem showing the waterproof outer covering (epidermis) and the phloem and xylem cells which carry food and water.

Below : When a seed first germinates it sends out a shoot called a 'coleoptile' and a root called a 'radicle'

SEED GROWTH

Cotyledons (seed leaves) providing young plant with food

Leaves

Coleoptile

Tough outer coat

Radicle

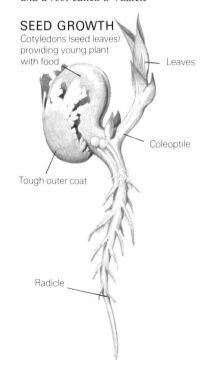

MEAT-EATING PLANTS

Some plants live in conditions that do not supply them with all the salts needed to make their own food and to grow. These plants have turned the tables on animals —they have become insectivores. The plants cannot stalk and pounce on their prey, so they set traps for them.

The sundew is a small plant found growing on heaths, in damp situations. Its leaves have hairs round the edges with droplets of liquid on them. This liquid attracts flies, which land on the leaf. The damp, slightly sticky hairs then close over the insect, trapping it. The plant then oozes digestive juices on to the fly and absorbs its body proteins. Other plants trap insects in various ways. The pitcher plant has leaves which form containers like pot-bellied vases. These leaves are partly filled with a liquid that attracts insects, which fall in and are digested. Bladderwort traps underwater insects in a similar way while the Venus Fly Trap has spiked leaves which close over

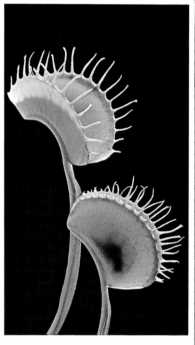

The spiked leaves of the insect-eating Venus Fly Trap.

insects which land on them. All these plants absorb the nitrates from the animals' bodies.

How a seed grows

When a seed falls on a suitable piece of ground, it does nothing until there is moisture and a favourable temperature. The tough coat keeps out the cold and protects the seed until the conditions are right, when the seed begins to germinate. The warmth and the moisture start the auxins working, and the cells inside the seed begin to divide. The first outward sign of germination is the appearance of the root-like *radicle* which grows downwards. The next part to appear is the *coleoptile*, which grows up and, in time, the first leaves unfold. The radicle anchors the seedling in the soil and the coleoptile carries the leaves up into the light, where the chlorophyll turns green and the little plant begins to make its own food. Until then it has been living on the food stored in the seed by the parent plant. The tip of the stem continues to grow and more leaves are produced. Roots grow from the radicle, and a complete plant is formed, which makes enough food to produce flowers and eventually fruits. The fruits, containing seeds, are distributed to begin the cycle again.

Most flowering plants follow this pattern, but not all plants have the same life cycles. The plant kingdom, like the animal kingdom, has evolved, and some of the plants are the last remaining members of much larger groups.

Plant groups

Although the flowering plants have a greater variety of species than the other plant groups, they do not necessarily have greater numbers. In fact, the most primitive plant group, the Algae, make up a large proportion of the plants on the planet. Most algae float in the seas. Many millions of tiny, one-celled algae float on the surface, and make up an important part of the minute animal and plant life called *plankton*. As the seas cover 7/10ths of the surface of the planet, the algae have plenty of room in which to live. Algae are the only plants to reign in the salt waters. On land there are the modern representatives of groups that were more numerous in the past, adding their variety to that of the flowering plants.

There are four major groups of plants, containing seven main families. These are: the Algae; the Bryophytes containing the liverworts, or Hepaticae, and mosses, or Musci; the Pteridophytes including the club-mosses, or Lycopodinae, the horse-tails, or Psilotinae, and the ferns, or Filicinae; Spermaphytes including the cycads and conifers, or Gymnosperms, and the flowering plants, or Angiosperms.

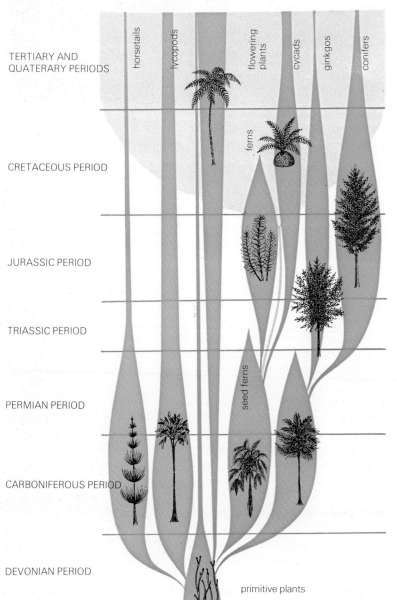

Above : Algal bloom on the surface of a pond.

Left : Diagram to show the evolution of land plants.

Algae

The algae are the oldest of the plant groups. They are divided into the blue-green algae, the yellow-brown algae, the green algae, the brown algae and the red algae.

The blue-green algae, or Cyanophytes, are very much like bacteria, but are true plants, with chlorophyll, able to make their own food. The group lives in damp soil, and fresh and salt waters. Apart from these fairly conventional habitats, blue-green algae are found in hot springs, cold cave waters and on rocks in fast flowing waterfalls. Some of the species are one-celled, others

live in colonies of balls or chains.

The remaining algae are not as difficult to classify as the blue-green algae. Some are very small, one-celled plants. The yellow-brown algae, or dinoflagellates, are unusual because they swim about by means of little whips, or *flagellae*. The yellow algae, the *euglenids*, and some of the green algae are also mobile. They live in the soil and in water.

Not all algae are small. The seaweeds are algae, and the kelp seaweed forms great underwater forests along the shore lines of the Atlantic and Pacific Oceans. The seaweeds consist of green, red and brown algae. These large algae do not have the same structure as the flowering plants. They have *holdfasts*, which anchor them to rocks, a long *stipe* instead of a stem and a *thallus* instead of leaves. The thallus forms the broad part of the seaweed.

Algae can reproduce *vegetatively*, which means that a piece of the plant can break off and grow into a new plant. They can reproduce *asexually*, by cells simply dividing in half to give two new cells, or they can produce *sexually*, with cells dividing and halving their chromosomes to produce male and female sex cells called gametes, which combine with the gametes of other, similar plants to grow into a new plant.

Lichens

Lichens are an unusual plant group, because they are a combination of fungi and algae. Lichens are made up of a network of fungal hyphae, protected by a layer of fungi cells, with algae cells bound up in the threads of fungi. The algae contain chlorophyll, and make food for both themselves and the fungi. The fungi provide shelter for the algae. Together, they make an extremely hardy plant, able to survive in the most exposed conditions. Lichens are often the only plants found on mountain tops or on rocks in the polar regions.

Above : Red, green and brown seaweeds growing on a rocky shore.

Below : Lichens are often found growing on old stone walls or, as shown here, on gravestones.

173

Bryophytes

The liverworts and mosses are grouped together because they have similar life cycles. They are an interesting group because they are at one end of an evolutionary trail that leads to the flowering plants. They have a double life-cycle. The tiny green plants of mosses and liverworts found in damp habitats are called the *gametophyte* generation, because they produce gametes. The male gametes swim to the female gametes through the thin film of water on the plants and their surroundings. A male gamete fertilizes a female gamete to form the beginning of a new plant. This plant is called the *sporophyte generation*, because it produces spores. The sporophyte plant grows on the gametophyte plant and takes its food from it. The spores are thrown out of the capsule on the sporophyte plant and fall to the ground. There they begin to grow into new gametophyte plants. This pattern of life cycles is called *alternation of generations*, and although it is not always so readily seen, it occurs in all kinds of plants.

In the bryophytes the gametophyte generation is the most prominent one. As we go through plant evolution, we see that the sporophyte generation becomes more and more important, until it takes over from the gametophyte generation as the prominent stage in the life cycle.

The Hepaticae or liverworts, are a very small group of plants. They live in damp woodlands, on the banks of streams or actually in the water. There are two kinds of liverwort. One group, the *thalloid liverworts*, still look rather like seaweeds. They have flat, lobed bodies branching over the ground, anchored by rhizoids. The leafy liverworts look more like land plants, having a stem and leaves. They are also anchored by rhizoids.

The Musci or mosses, are the more familiar bryophytes. They can be seen on stones and trees in damp places, and on mountains and moorlands. They have alternation of generations with the sporophyte generation appearing as a long stalk with a capsule on it supported by the green gametophyte generation which has a stem and leaves, but, like the leafy liverworts, it has rhizoids instead of roots.

The bryophytes are an ancient group, but there is not much fossil evidence to prove this. The plant tissues are so soft that they do not make good fossils. Scientists believe that there were bryophytes on the planet 300 million years ago, in the middle of the Carboniferous Period. Pieces of leaves which resemble the *Sphagnum* moss leaves of today are found in Cretaceous rocks, 120 million years old.

Opposite top: A Pinga treefern growing in New Zealand. One of the few remaining large ferns. Modern pteridophytes are much smaller.

Below: Liverworts, such as Lunularia curciata, live by damp river banks.

Below left: Sphagnum moss, a member of the Bryophytes.

LIFE CYCLE OF A FERN

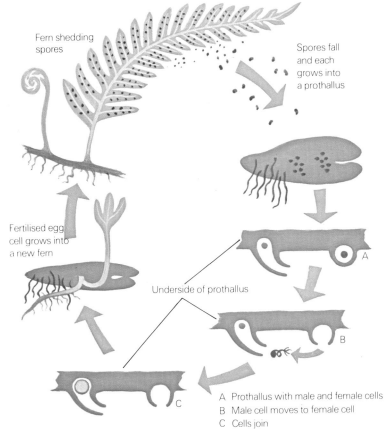

Fern shedding spores

Spores fall and each grows into a prothallus

Fertilised egg cell grows into a new fern

Underside of prothallus

A

B

C

A Prothallus with male and female cells
B Male cell moves to female cell
C Cells join

Pteridophytes

The next three groups, the Lycopodinae or club-mosses, the Psilotinae or horse-tails, and the Filicinae or ferns, have evolved further than the bryophytes. Their gametophyte and sporophyte generations are quite separate. Each generation produces its own food. The sporophyte generation is larger than the gametophyte.

In the pteridophytes, the woody tissues make better fossils than the soft tissues of the algae and bryophytes, and fossil pteridophytes have been found. There were pteridophytes in the Silurian Period, 350 million years ago. Ferns first appeared in the Carboniferous Period, 280 million years ago. The club-mosses and the horse-tails are even older than that. Fossils show that the plants were much larger than they are now. There were great forests of giant club-mosses and horse-tails at the beginning of the Carboniferous Period, 310 million years ago.

The modern pteridophytes are much smaller plants. They are the familiar ferns, and the less familiar club-mosses, horse-tails and quillworts. These plants are the sporophyte generation, and carry the spores on special leaves in *sporangia*. The spores are dispersed and fall to the ground, where they grow into a small separate plant, called a *prothallus*. In a similar way to the bryophytes, the male gamete swims through the film of moisture to reach the egg cell, and fertilize it. The resulting plant grows into the sporophyte generation.

All the pteridophytes have to live in damp surroundings, so that the male gamete can swim to the egg to fertilize it. The male gametes cannot swim very long distances, so the plants' distribution is not increased much by the gametophyte generation. It is the spores that have to colonize new ground for the plants, so that each new plant has room to grow. Some of the sporangia can throw out the spores to quite a distance, but the pteridophytes cannot spread quickly over large areas.

The modern Lycopodinae or club-mosses are small creeping plants found on mountains and moorlands, or sometimes in woods. They are very easy to overlook, when compared to the giants of the past.

The Psilotinae or horse-tails are easily recognised, because their leaves grow in whorls

Right : Equisetum palustre *(horse-tails) in leaf.*

round the stem. The skin, or *epidermis*, has glassy crystals in it, so that the plants feel rough to the touch. They were once used to scour dishes, and are often called scouring rushes. They are fairly quick to colonize new ground, and are found on wasteland and in road or rail cuttings. Some are water plants.

The Filicinae or ferns are a group of beautiful plants, which today grow much larger than the other pteridophytes. They grow in damp cracks in rocks and walls. Like horsetails, they grow readily on waste ground. Ferns such as *Pteridium* (bracken) appear quickly on burnt ground. This is because they have underground stems, called rhizomes, which are not easily damaged by fire.

Coal formation

The Carboniferous forests have played an important part in the economy of the modern world. The green plants made their food and stored it, just as plants do today. The climate was very damp and the plants grew in swamps. When they died, the plants fell into these swamps, which were not suitable for the fungi and decomposing bacteria to work in, and the giant club-mosses did not

Left : Artist's impression of a forest in the Carboniferous Period.

rot away. They turned to peat. As time passed the peat built up into thick layers. Other rocks formed over the peat, and the pressure converted it into coal. There is a limited amount, however. Only the remains of the great, prehistoric forests supply coal and once they have been used up, there is no more. Even if the conditions that produced the first forests could be repeated, men could not wait the millions of years needed to convert plant remains to energy-rich black rock.

Spermaphytes

The spermaphytes include the greater part of modern land plants. The group is divided again into the gymnosperms (the cycads, conifers and gingkos) and the angiosperms (flowering plants). All the spermaphytes have the sporophyte generation as the largest and most noticeable generation. The gametophyte generation is reduced to a tiny plant always enclosed in the cones of the conifers or the flowers of the angiosperms. Also all the spermaphytes have seeds, which are a more efficient way of distributing new plants.

Gymnosperms

The gymnosperms' seeds are not produced in fruits but are carried in cones. The cones are grown on the sporophyte generation. The female spores are fertilized by the wind-blown pollen, and the seed which results grows into a new sporophyte plant. The gymnosperms can therefore grow in much drier places than can bryophytes or pteridophytes. The first fossils appear in the Triassic Period rocks, 200 million years old.

The Cycadaceae or cycads, were the most important group in the Jurassic Period, which is often called the 'Age of Dinosaurs', 175 million years ago. There are very few left today. They grow in tropical areas, where some are believed to live for 1000 years. The cycad stems are covered by old leaf scars, with a crown of leaves on top – they look rather like pineapples.

Above : Cycads can still be found growing in tropical regions. This one is in South Africa.

Below : Pine trees (conifers) retain their waxy leaves even in the harsh winters of southern Lapland.

The Coniferae or conifers, are a very successful group; they live in dry, cold conditions and are found at the tops of mountains and in the colder parts of the world. Their leaves have a waxy covering and are curled, to prevent water loss. This helps them to survive in conditions where water lost from the leaves could not easily be replaced by the root system. The conifers are known as evergreen trees, because most of them do not lose all their leaves in the autumn. The plants do drop leaves, but a few fall all the year round, not all of them at once. The leaves do not rot very quickly and the ground in a coniferous forest is usually covered by a carpet of pine needles. Very few smaller plants can grow under coniferous trees.

PINE CONES AND NEEDLES

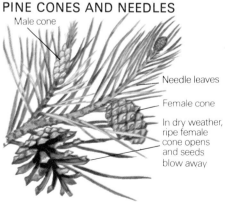

Male cone

Needle leaves

Female cone

In dry weather, ripe female cone opens and seeds blow away

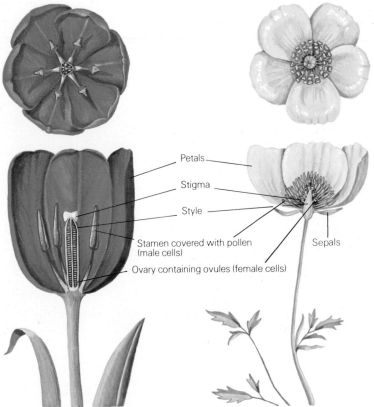

Petals

Stigma

Style

Stamen covered with pollen
(male cells)

Sepals

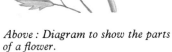

Ovary containing ovules (female cells)

*Below : Bluebells growing in
deciduous woodland in England.*

*Above : Diagram to show the parts
of a flower.*

*Flowering plants have adapted to
widely differing habits.*

*Top : Edelweiss, a flowering plant
found in the European Alps.*

*Centre : A garden pool surrounded by
water-loving plants*

*Above : Desert plants growing in
Death Valley, California, USA.*

Angiosperms

The angiosperms, or flowering plants, are by far the most successful group of plants. The first fossils appear in the Cretaceous rocks, 120 million years old. Fossil trees very like modern figs, magnolias, poplars and planes have been found.

The purpose of the flowers is to ensure that the egg cell contained within it is fertilized. Flowering plants sometimes rely on wind or water to get the male cell to the female cell, but usually they use animals as 'porters'. The large, brightly coloured flowers contain nectar or other substances attractive to small animals, and when bees and other animals collect this substance, pollen is brushed off on to their bodies. When an animal then visits another flower, some of the pollen brushes off. In this way the female cell of one plant is fertilized by the male cell of another plant. Bees and butterflies play an important part in the lives of many flowers, but larger animals, such as humming-birds, pollinate some flowers. This method, called *cross-pollination*, gives us a great variety of flowering plants.

Flowering plants come in many shapes, sizes and colours; they grow in a variety of different habitats, from the

Right : As the planet has changed, so the life on the planet has changed too. The living things adapted to changes and to different ways of living, producing the great variety of shapes, sizes and life styles found today.

DEVELOPMENT
OF LIFE ON EARTH

PRECAMBRIAN PERIOD

CAMBRIAN PERIOD

ORDOVICIAN PERIOD

SILURIAN PERIOD

DEVONIAN PERIOD

CARBONIFEROUS PERIOD

PERMIAN PERIOD

TRIASSIC PERIOD

JURASSIC PERIOD

CRETACEOUS PERIOD

TERTIARY PERIOD

QUATERNARY PERIOD

Above left: This colourful orchid is an epiphyte, that is, it always grows on another plant. Orchids belong to the monocotyledon group of plants.

Above: Gorse is a dicotyledon. It has prickles to protect it from being eaten by animals.

Left: Many wild flowers such as Ragwort and Willow Herb are dicotyledons.

DAFFODIL LEAVES
Monocotyledon

ROSE LEAVES
Dicotyledon

Above: It is easy to identify the two different kinds of flowering plants. Monocotyledons have narrow leaves and parallel veins. Dicotyledons have broad leaves and branching veins.

hot deserts to the mountains and the cold arctic tundra.

Flowering plants make up the bulk of the tropical rain forests and the deciduous woodlands. There are many freshwater angiosperms. The only unconquered region is the sea. There is really only one truly marine flowering plant, the Eel Grass, *Zostera*.

The angiosperms are divided into two main groups. The plants that have a single leaf in the seed are called *monocotyledons* and those that have two seed leaves in the seed are called *dicotyledons*. It is easy to tell which is which by looking at the true leaves. The monocotyledons have strap-like leaves with parallel veins running down them, and flower parts, such as petals, in threes or multiples of three. The dicotyledons have broader leaves with the veins branching all over them from the stalk, and flower parts in groups of fours or fives, or multiples of those numbers (e.g. 20 and 25).

The monocotyledon group includes the grasses, lilies, rushes, orchids, daffodils and tulips.

The dicotyledons include all the larger plants, the trees and most shrubs, as well as many wild and garden flowers. Buttercups, daisies, primroses, gorse, violets and roses are a few of the many beautiful plants in this group.

Flowering plants are very successful, mainly because of their methods of pollination and the way they scatter the seeds. Some plants have fruits which again use animals as carriers and ensure that the seeds travel long distances from the parent plant. The fruits, which have seeds inside them, may be attractive to animals as food, or catch on their coats. Other fruits are explosive or winged, scattering seeds or carrying them well away from their parent.

Right : A field of wild grasses. Grasses are monocotyledons.

PLANTS THAT FIGHT BACK

Being unable to move, plants are easy prey for animals. Some plants have evolved means of defending themselves in order to survive.

In some cases the means are mechanical. The plants have leaves or twigs adapted to form spines or thorns. In Africa the acacia trees are covered by sharp thorns which keep away most herbivores. In deserts, cacti, such as the Prickly Pear, have juicy stems with long spines for leaves. Many members of the rose family, which includes the blackberries, defend themselves and their fruits with thorns.

Other plants use chemicals to defend themselves. Some have spines which inject acids into would-be diners. Stinging nettles are a good example. When touched the leaves inject formic acid causing a sharp pain. Some plants have fruits that are poisonous if they are eaten. The nourishing potato produces poisonous berries on its stems if left long enough. The attractive berries of the Deadly Nightshade are extremely poisonous. Although the fungi are not true plants, the famous poisonous toadstools must be mentioned here. The Death

The poisonous Spotted Fly Agaric.

Cap, *Amanita phalloides*, is probably the most poisonous fungus in the world, and many of its relatives in the *Amanita* family are dangerous to eat, including the very pretty Spotted Fly Agaric.

Seed dispersal

The word fruit conjures up a picture of oranges, strawberries, plums and bananas. These are all fruits, but they are not the only kind. Nuts, pea-pods and sycamore keys are also fruits, and so are tomatoes and cucumbers. A fruit describes anything that is formed from a flower and helps to protect and distribute the seeds.

Seeds are scattered by a variety of different methods. The delicious apples, raspberries and blackberries are eaten by birds and mammals. The seeds in the fruit are either dropped before eating, or pass through the animal's digestive system unharmed, to be passed out of the body a long way from the plant. Other fruits use animals in different ways. Some fruits are sticky when they are wet, or have tiny hooks on them like goosegrass, so that they catch on animals' fur or birds' feet and are carried away. They then drop off when they become dry or when the animal cleans its coat.

The wind plays an important part in the dispersal of some fruits. These have wings or parachutes to carry them off on the air currents. Sycamore, thistle, dandelion and cotton are all wind distributed. The wind plays a different part for other fruits. It shakes them, like a rattle, and shakes the tiny, dry seeds out of the fruits, scattering them about. Poppies use the wind in this way.

Some fruits, like gorse and broom, actually explode, shooting their seeds away from them. Water plants may float their seeds away, or their seeds may stick to the feet of ducks or similar birds.

Adaptation to life on land

Another reason for the success of the angiosperms is that they have evolved ways of saving their water. They have a waterproof 'skin' covering them and a waxy layer on their leaves which keeps moisture inside their bodies so that they do not dry up in dry conditions. In winter the deciduous trees would lose a large amount of water through their broad leaves, so to prevent this, they lose their leaves in the autumn, when the winds increase and

Above : The splitting seed capsule of Rosebay Willow Herb. These seeds are dispersed by the wind.

Left : Hazel nuts have a hard outer shell to protect the seed.

Below : Burdock fruits have hooks which catch in animals' fur, in this way they are carried away from the parent plant.

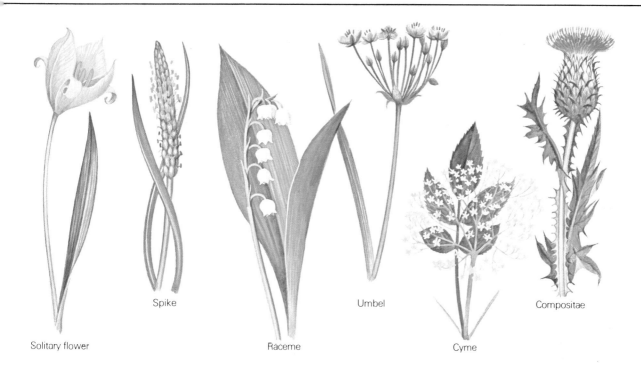

Spike

Umbel

Compositae

Solitary flower

Raceme

Cyme

the temperatures drop, and spend the winter leafless. In the spring, when conditions improve, new leaves start to grow.

Plants and man

The angiosperms, many with edible fruits and seeds, and the food stored in roots or stems to last through a long winter, supply animals and man with a great deal of food. Men have taken the wild plants and bred and cross-bred them to give bigger seeds, or roots or leaves. The once wild wheats now grow large ears of grain to give us flour.

Root crops such as carrots and turnips, underground stems such as potatoes and the leaves of the cabbage family are larger than their wild ancestors. The rose family has provided an enormous variety of fruits; apples, plums and cherries to name but a few.

Above : The word 'flower' describes a single bloom. Some flowers grow in groups which are called inflorescences.

Below : Improved varieties of wheat and barley (see inset) feed millions of people throughout the world.

Peanuts drying in India. These nuts have a very high protein content and so can be used as a substitute for meat in the diet.

Plants are used in other ways as well. Trees are used for timber and paper, and logs are burnt as fuel. Most of the spices and many of our drugs come from flowering plants. Quinine is distilled from oak bark and cocaine first came from the leaves of a South American shrub. Opium, of course, comes from poppies. Nutmeg, pepper, cinnamon and ginger are all flowering plants.

Man has changed the distribution of the plants that are useful to him. When discoverers adventured across the seas to different continents, they took familiar food plants with them and brought back exotic foods. Potatoes and tomatoes, along with maize, came to Europe from America, in the 16th century. Rubber, coffee and bananas were carried round the world by traders. Sometimes when new plants were introduced to a country, the balance of nature was upset. This happened when the prickly pear was taken from America to Australia, where it almost took over the agricultural land. Eventually scientists introduced a caterpillar which ate the prickly pear and checked its headlong advance. With man taking a hand, the distribution and the appearance of many plants have been changed completely. The essential part that plants play in the world is unchanged, however. They still provide the fuel that maintains the life of the planet.

GIANTS OF THE PLANT KINGDOM

The largest flower in the world is found on the *Rafflesia* plant, a parasite which lives in South-east Asia. The plant grows in the tropical rain forests, where the brownish petals reach a diameter of 91 centimetres (3 feet) and weigh 7 kg (15 lb).

The largest tree in the world is the Californian *Sequoiadendron giganteum*, named 'General Sherman'. It is 83 metres (275 feet) tall, and measures 24 metres 11 centimetres (79 feet) round. The tallest tree in the world is found in California too. It is a *Sequoia sempervirens*, which is 111 metres 60 centimetres (366 feet) tall.

The longest seaweed is the Pacific Giant Kelp, *Macrocystis pyrifera*, which has fronds 60 metres (196 feet) long.

A giant Rafflesia *plant from Sumatra.*

The Animal Kingdom

Animals evolved after plants and bacteria. As they cannot make their own food, they could not exist until there were plants for the first plant-eating animals to feed on. In their quest for food, animals have evolved into a great variety of different shapes, sizes and colours. They can be as small as the one-celled protozoans or as large as the elephant, *Elephas*, on the land, or the Blue Whale, *Balaenoptera musculus*, on the seas. The colours range from the sober grey of the hippopotamuses (Hippopotamidae) to the brilliantly coloured humming-birds (Trochilidae). The shapes to be found in the animal kingdom are just as varied – think of the differences between worms, crabs, insects, jellyfishes, fishes, birds and mammals, for instance.

Most animals have to actively search for their food, and those that are mobile need keen senses. Animals such as sponges (porifera) and sea squirts (ciona), which are filter feeders, have lost the ability to move, and draw food particles into their bodies by producing water currents.

Plant-eaters have to be able to search for suitable plants, hunters to find and kill suitable animals. These activities have led to the great variety in animals.

Above and Below : The big cats are hunters ; they actively search and kill for food.

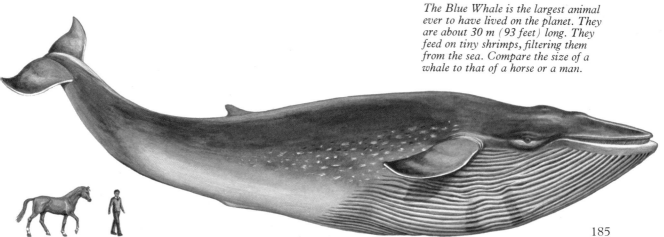

The Blue Whale is the largest animal ever to have lived on the planet. They are about 30 m (93 feet) long. They feed on tiny shrimps, filtering them from the sea. Compare the size of a whale to that of a horse or a man.

ANIMAL CELL

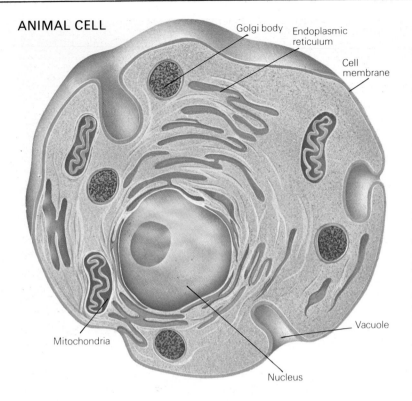

Golgi body
Endoplasmic reticulum
Cell membrane
Mitochondria
Vacuole
Nucleus

Zebras are herbivores. This herd is in Tsavo Park, Kenya.

Animal cells

The most noticeable difference between plant and animal cells is in the cell wall; in animals it is thin and flexible, and in plants it is more rigid. In the *cytoplasm*, the cell fluid, there are several structures: the nucleus containing a nucleolus, the Golgi body, the endoplasmic reticulum and mitochondria. The basic cell is adapted to form several different tissues.

These tissues build up into organs and systems in the animal's body. The bones form a skeleton to support the rest of the body in the animals with backbones. Those without backbones have shells outside their bodies to protect and support them, or they rely on water pressure inside their bodies, as do plants. The muscles contract, enabling the animal to move. The nervous system carries the information which tells the muscles to contract.

In the most highly evolved animals, the body is controlled by the brain, which is a highly developed part of the nervous system. The blood system carries food and oxygen around the body, and collects the poisons which are produced by the body when it is respiring and moving. The blood is pumped round the body in the circulatory system by the heart. The heart is not always a single structure (some animals have a line of hearts) but the heart is always a pump. The poisons are cleaned from the blood through a filter, the kidneys, and passed out of the body through the excretory system. Oxygen is taken into the body through the lungs, which work in air, or gills, which work in water; these are part of the respiratory system. The digestive system converts the food eaten by the animals into chemicals which can be used by the body. The reproductive system produces the female egg cells and male sperm cells, which combine to produce a new animal.

In most animals there are two sexes, the male cells are produced by the individuals of one sex, the female cells by the other. In a few animals, however, both eggs and sperm are produced in one animal, called a *hermaphrodite*. One such animal is the tapeworm. In even fewer animals, asexual reproduction takes place. The greenfly, or aphid, often gives birth to a daughter who is already pregnant.

Carnivores and herbivores

One of the most important activities of animals is feeding. There are two major divisions in the animal world: the plant-eaters, or *herbivores*, and the meat-eaters, or *carnivores*.

Within the herbivores, there are animals which live mainly on fruit, and others which live mainly on grass. There are animals which will eat one particular plant, for example Koala Bears (*Phascolarctus cinereus*), eat mainly eucalyptus leaves, and Giant Pandas (*Ailuropoda melanoleuca*) eat mainly bamboo.

Among the carnivores, there are insect eaters and fish-eaters. Some animals, man included, can eat both plants and animals. They are called omnivores.

The herbivores have a completely different way of life from carnivores. Their food does not run away from them and so food capture is not a problem. The problem is digestion. Plants are very difficult to digest and herbivores usually have much longer intestines than carnivores. The cell walls of plants are made from cellulose, and no animals have the chemicals needed to digest the substance – only bacteria can do that.

Grazing animals have bacteria living in their intestines to digest the cellulose for them. Cattle have three extra chambers, apart from their stomachs; they chew the cud, a process which involves food being chewed and stored in a chamber, then brought back to the mouth for further chewing. This method ensures that the grass is digested. Rabbits

Top : Barren Ground Caribou live on the sparse vegetation in the tundra of Alaska, USA.

Above : Koala feeding in a eucalyptus forest in Eastern Australia.

Above: The Hobby, a member of the falcon group, has the typical hooked beak and sharp talons of a bird of prey.

Right and Below: Teeth are adapted for the work that they do. The cheetah's teeth bite and cut. The horse's bite and grind.

CHEETAH

HORSE

eat their food twice. The first time the grasses pass through the rabbits' digestive systems to emerge as soft green pellets. The rabbits eat these pellets again, and the digestive process is repeated. The final pellets of undigested food are hard and brown.

Herbivores need teeth that will grind the plants thoroughly, breaking the tough cell walls. It is possible to identify herbivores by looking at their teeth. The teeth have flattened tops, ideal for grinding the plants into a paste.

Carnivores, on the other hand, often use their teeth to kill their food. They have sharp, piercing teeth at the front and cutting teeth, like scissor blades, at the back, to cut up the meat. Fish-eating animals need sharp, needle-pointed teeth to grip their slippery prey. The beaks of birds also indicate the type of food they eat. Birds of prey have hooked beaks to tear their

food; seed eaters have powerful, 'nutcracker' beaks and insect-eating birds have small, fine pointed beaks.

As there is usually plenty of food available for herbivores they can live together in large groups, relying on numbers to protect them. Most carnivores, however, have to search for their food. They do not usually live in large groups, because

there are not usually enough food animals living together to feed a group of carnivores. There are exceptions, however. On the African plains, the enormous herds of antelopes and zebras allow lions to live in groups called prides. In most cases carnivores live alone, or in twos, the young leaving an area as soon as they can fend for themselves.

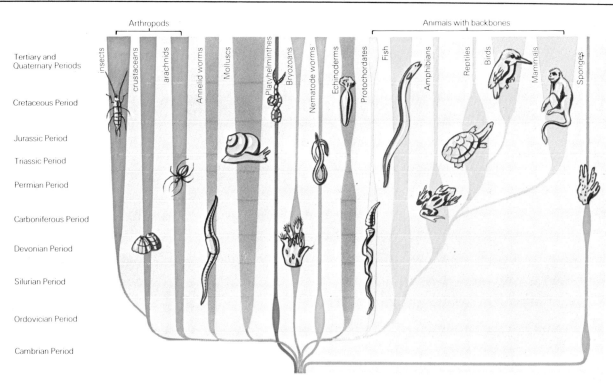

Tertiary and Quaternary Periods

Cretaceous Period

Jurassic Period

Triassic Period

Permian Period

Carboniferous Period

Devonian Period

Silurian Period

Ordovician Period

Cambrian Period

Arthropods — insects, crustaceans, arachnids

Annelid worms, Molluscs, Platyhelminthes, Bryozoans, Nematode worms, Echinoderms, Protochordates

Animals with backbones — Fish, Amphibians, Reptiles, Birds, Mammals

Sponges

Animals of the past

In the process of evolving from one-celled animals to the complex animals alive today, millions of animals have become extinct. Extinction is a natural process. As conditions and climate on the planet changed, so did the plants. Animals that could not adapt to the new conditions or to competition from new animals died out. Some of these animals left their fossil remains behind in the rocks, but many have left no trace of their existence.

The first traces of animal life are found in rocks of the Precambrian Period, 600 million years old. These are only traces, worm tracks and imprints of jellyfishes. The first definite fossils are found in Cambrian rocks. There, extinct animals called grapto-

lites and trilobites, both of which had hard skeletons, have left evidence. Both these groups of animals did not have backbones; they are called *invertebrates*. They lived in the seas on the planet for about 250 million years, before becoming extinct at the end of the Devonian Period. Most of the other groups living in Cambrian times still have representatives alive today. Brachiopods (lamp-shells) and molluscs (mussels, oysters, snails, squids, etc) left fossils behind them and worms and jellyfishes left signs of their presence. Corals, sponges, echinoderms (starfishes, sea-urchins and sea-cucumbers) and crustaceans (lobsters, crabs, etc) all lived in the seas with the rest of the Cambrian plants and animals.

These invertebrates were the only inhabitants of the seas for about 200 million years, until the end of the

Silurian Period. Then, 450 million years ago, the first animals with backbones, the *vertebrates*, appeared. They were fish-like animals. The period following, called the Devonian, is often called the

Above : The evolutionary tree to show the development of animals.

Below : This fossil trilobite from Australia dates from the Cambrian Period.

189

'Age of Fishes', because the numbers of fishes increased so rapidly. These fishes were covered by heavy, bony armour and made good fossils.

The next period, the Carboniferous Period, is also called the 'Age of Amphibians'. The seas were drawing back and swampy land appeared. The great forests of club-mosses and tree-ferns, which later turned into coal, were growing and the amphibians evolved and moved about these forests. They were not the small newts, frogs, toads and salamanders alive today. Like the early fishes, they were heavily armoured, and some, such as *Eogyrinus*, grew to $4\frac{1}{2}$ metres (15 feet) long. In the seas, the sharks flourished, and fossils of the first insects which were like cockroaches and dragonflies, are found in Carboniferous rocks. At the end of the Period, the first reptiles appeared.

In the Permian Period, which lasted from 270 to 225 million years ago, the amphibians lived side by side with the first reptiles on the land and the forerunners of the mammals evolved. The insects were more numerous, and modern groups, such as beetles, bugs and cicadas, left fossils in the rocks. During the following Period, the Triassic, reptiles became more common, crocodiles and turtles being among them. The ancestors of the Australian monotremes (egg-laying mammals such as the platypus) lived at the same time. Insects, scorpions and crustaceans were alive and lung-fishes, very like those alive today, lived in the streams and lakes.

In the Jurassic Period, which began 180 million years ago and lasted for 45 million years, the reptiles became more important than the amphibians. The dinosaurs, or 'Terrible Lizards' appeared, along with the flying reptiles, the pterosaurs. Crocodiles and turtles still lived in the waters. The giant herbivores, *Brontosaurus* and *Diplodocus* were Jurassic reptiles. On land the conifers and cycads were growing. The first birds appeared, the fossil of *Archeopteryx* being found in Jurassic rocks. The first mammals, which were small, rat-like creatures, lived

In the Jurassic Period reptiles like the Allosaurus, Brontosaurus, Camptosaurus and Stegosaurus ruled the earth and the first birds appeared.

during the Jurassic Period.

The Cretaceous Period, which began 135 million years ago, is the 'Age of Reptiles'. The reptiles were the dominant land animals. The great carnivorous dinosaur *Tyrannosaurus rex*, probably the largest land hunter ever, lived in the Cretaceous Period. The strange *Triceratops* and *Iguanodon* were herbivores alive at this time, and *Pterodon*, the huge pterosaur, swooped about in the air. A fossil bird is preserved in Cretaceous rocks. It did not compete with the pterosaurs, because *Hesperornis* is a flightless bird, a swimmer which ate fishes. By the end of the Cretaceous Period, 70 million years ago, all the dinosaurs became extinct. Scientists do not really know exactly why this happened. It may have been that the climate changed and their food plants died out.

The crocodiles and turtles survived, however, and so did small lizard-like reptiles. Frogs and toads had evolved, but the glories of the reptiles and amphibians were over. It was now the turn of the mammals.

The next periods, the Paleocene, Eocene, Oligocene, Miocene and Pliocene make up the Tertiary Era, which is the 'Age of Mammals'. Recognisable rodents, whales, elephants, cattle and pigs appeared. The first tiny horse, *Eohippus*, which had four toes and browsed on leaves, gradually evolved into the fast, tall modern horse. Giant rhinoceroses, *Baluchitherium*, the elephant *Deinotherium* and the mastodon *Tetralophodon* were some herbivores of the time, which have since become extinct. Carnivores such as the bear-like *Arctocyon* and the earlier sabre-tooth, *Apatarlurus*, fed on the herbivores.

The first man-like mammals lived in the Pleistocene Period, which began 3 million years ago. *Homo Erectus* (see page 35), appeared about $1\frac{1}{2}$ million years ago and man as we know him today, *Homo sapiens*, probably evolved about 100 000 years ago.

Man has evolved very rapidly in the relatively short time that he has lived on the planet. Like mammals he has hair on his body and feeds his young with milk. Man's brain has evolved very quickly within a body that is easily able to adapt to a variety of different activities. Man may not be as strong as an elephant or as fast as a cheetah, but he has learnt to build machines which can compete with these mammals. He cannot compete with the insects in numbers, but if, in the distant future, some descendant describes the Period in which we are living now, it may well be called, the 'Age of Man'.

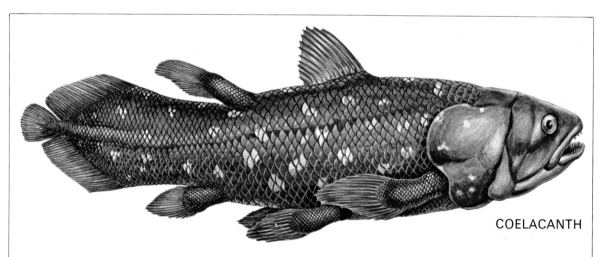

COELACANTH

LIVING FOSSILS

Some plants and animals are called living fossils because they have survived unchanged for millions of years. The deep sea mollusc *Neopilina galatheae* is one of these. There are fossils of this mollusc in rocks 500 million years old. It was thought to have become extinct 320 million years ago until a research vessel found a specimen in 1952. The lampshell *Lingula* is another living fossil because the group to which it belongs, the Brachiopods, first appeared 600 million years ago, in the Cambrian Period. Most of the animals in this group became extinct at the same time as the dinosaurs, 70 million years ago. The ginkgo tree, *Gingko.biloba*, is the only survivor of a group which flourished 160 million years ago, in the Jurassic Period. The coelacanth, *Latimeria*, was thought to be extinct until a scientist recognized one in a fisherman's boat off the coast of South Africa. Later investigations discovered many of the fishes living near coral reefs off the African coast. Specimens were caught in 1952. The coelacanth is interesting because it is related to the ancestors of the land vertebrates.

Animals of today

Of all the hundreds of groups of animals that have evolved during the millions of years of life on this planet, there are still a large proportion with representatives living today. These can be divided into two large groups, the animals without backbones, the *invertebrates*, and the animals with a backbone and a nerve cord inside it, the *vertebrates*. Although there are a great many small groups of animals here we will consider only the important larger groups.

The invertebrates – animals without backbones

The main groups of invertebrates include the Protozoa, or one-celled animals; the Porifera, or sponges; the Coelenterates, or jellyfishes and corals; the Platyhelminthes, or flat-worms and flukes; the Annelids, or true worms; the Arthropods, or insects, arachnids and crustaceans; the Molluscs, or cockles and snails; and the Echinoderms, or starfishes, sea-urchins and sea-cucumbers.

Protozoa

Some of the protozoans are very much like the one-celled algae, except that they cannot make their own food. The protozoans are very varied, despite their small size and single celled body. Some are covered by tiny hairs, which row them along. The slipper animalcule, *Paramecium*, is one of these. Some, like *Euglena*, are propelled along by two little whips, called *flagellae*, growing at one end of the cell. The amoebae simply flow along, and feed by flowing round their prey.

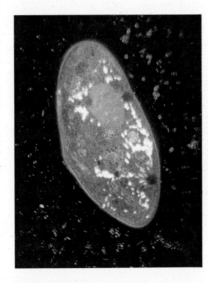

The one-celled protozoan Paramecium.

Some protozoans are enclosed in beautiful shells. The heliozoans have a spherical shell, with parts of their bodies forming spikes which look like the rays of the sun. Another group look like tiny snails, while still others look like bells on long stalks.

Some protozoans are parasites. A parasite is a plant or animal that lives in another plant or animal, taking all its food from its host and often damaging its host.

Some of the protozoans cause diseases in man. *Trypanosoma gambiense* and *T. rhodesiense* cause sleeping sickness. *Plasmodium vivax* causes malaria and there are many more diseases caused by protozoans.

The free-living protozoans live in damp places. Many are found in the plankton in fresh and salt waters. Some live in damp soil or on damp tree-trunks. Protozoans reproduce sexually, forming male and female gametes by meiosis, or simply divide in half by mitosis, thus reproducing asexually.

Porifera

The porifera, or sponges, are very strange animals. To begin with, they are *sessile*, which means that they live fastened to a rock, unable to move. Although there are several sessile animal groups throughout the kingdom, the sponges' lack of tissues is unique. Sponges are not organized in the same way as other many-celled animals. Their cells live together, but they are not closely connected. A sponge can be pushed through a sieve without killing it. The broken cells simply clump together again and form new sponges. The skeletons of sponges are made up of tiny clusters of spikes, called *spicules*. A sponge catches food by drawing water into its vase-shaped body through holes in its sides, and pushing it out through the hole at the top. Any one-celled plants or animals, or fragments of plants or animals, are trapped by cells inside the sponge. Sifting the water for food like this is called *filter feeding*, and it is quite a common method of food capture in the animal kingdom. Even the giant Blue Whale is a filter feeder. Sponges all live in water, a few in fresh water but most in the sea. There they are found along the shore, and down as far as the abyss, the deep, dark parts of the ocean.

*Above : The Lion's Mane Jellyfish
showing its stinging threads and
umbrella-shaped bell.*

*Below : A sponge covered with
brittlestars* (Echinoderms) *in the
waters of the Caribbean.*

Coelenterates

The coelenterates include the
jellyfishes, the corals, the sea
anemones and the hydroids.
They trap food for themselves
by using small cells which
shoot out a stinging thread or
dart, if they are touched. These
dart-firing cells then pump
poison into their victim to
paralyze it.

The coelenterates are more
advanced than the sponges,
having muscles in their bodies,
the cells being organized into
tissues. Like the sponges, the
corals, sea anemones and hydroids are sessile, but the
jellyfishes are mobile, drifting
and swimming through the
seas. The coelenterates show
an alternation of generations.
The sessile stage is called a
polyp. It feeds by means of the
ring of tentacles round the
mouth on the top of the body.
The tentacles are armed with

batteries of the stinging cells described above. *Hydra* is a typical polyp. On polyps such as those of *Bougainvillea*, buds appear on the body. Saucer-shaped discs called *medusae* are budded off. The medusae are free swimming. They produce male and female gametes, which combine and grow into a new polyp. Among the jellyfishes, the medusa has become the most important generation, the polyps often being lost completely.

The polyps are the most important generation in the corals and sea anemones. Corals are interesting because they build a strong skeleton from lime, which lasts long after the polyp has died. In warm seas they build up great reefs along coastlines. Jelly-fishes, on the other hand, have no skeleton at all. Some of them are both beautiful and dangerous. The Portuguese Man-o'-war, *Physalia*, and the Sailor-by-the-wind, *Vellela*, drift on the surface of the seas, moved by currents and wind. They can sting very painfully.

The sea anemones are common seashore animals, found in rock pools, looking like flowers. They have stings in their tentacles which stun their prey so that they can draw it into their mouths.

Below : Coral from the Red Sea.

Inset : A peacock worm, perhaps one of the most beautiful of the annelids.

The Natural World

Platyhelminthes

The platyhelminthes are worm-like animals that include some very unpleasant parasites, the flukes and tapeworms. The free-living platyhelminths are called *flatworms*. They are found in fresh and brackish waters, gliding over stones and plants.

The flukes have complicated life histories and have been parasites for millions of years. The Liver Fluke (*Fasciola*) which is a parasite in sheeps' livers, spends part of its life as a parasite in a freshwater snail. *Schistosoma*, a parasite in man, does the same. Tapeworms also have two hosts. The common tapeworm (*Taenia*) lives in the intestines of man, but passes through the pig in its life cycle, which is one of the reasons that pork should always be well cooked before eating. Since it is impossible for two adult tapeworms to meet (there is only one worm in a host animal), one animal produces both eggs and sperm, and sperm from one segment fertilize the eggs of another. Apart from the reproductive system, the tapeworm is very simple. With its hooked head buried in the wall of the host's intestine, surrounded by liquid food, the animal does not need senses or a digestive system. The worm consists of a long series of segments, which are budded off from the head, and fall off when they reach the end of the worm. By that time, they are nothing but a bag of fertilized eggs.

Right: Coral can grow to enormous size, as in this reef off Mauritius in the Indian Ocean.

Annelids

The annelids, or true worms, are quite highly evolved animals, with circulatory, digestive, nervous, excretory and reproductive systems. The annelids include the earthworms, the marine ragworms, the lugworms, leeches and the beautiful peacock-worms. The worms burrow in the soil or the bottom of the sea or lakes. Some of them are free swimming. Many of them produce both eggs and sperm, but they do not fertilize themselves. Cross-fertilization takes place, a pair of worms exchanging sperm. Some of the annelids are parasites, feeding on blood obtained from the outside of the host's body.

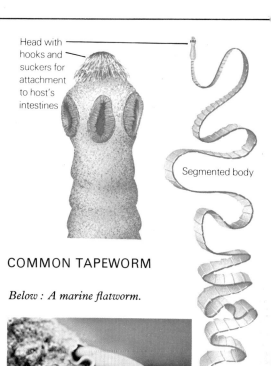

Head with hooks and suckers for attachment to host's intestines

Segmented body

COMMON TAPEWORM

Below: A marine flatworm.

195

Arthropods

The arthropods make up the largest group living today. Animals in this group have a jointed external skeleton, which covers their bodies like armour, moved by muscles attached to the inside. They include the classes Insecta (insects), Arachnida (scorpions, spiders and ticks, etc) and Crustacea (crabs, lobsters and prawns, etc).

The Insecta is the largest of all the animal classes, with nearly $\frac{3}{4}$ million species in it. Between them, the arthropods live in every available habitat on the planet. The insects are supreme on the land. There they are found burrowing in the ground, or in plants, feeding on carrion, swimming in streams and ponds, flying, living in caves, in old books and feeding on man's vital crops. The arachnids live in some of the harsher habitats, mites are found living in the snows of

All the animals pictured here are arthropods.
Above: The Wood Ants and the bee they are dragging are insects.

Inset: A Trapdoor Spider (arachnid) gripping the door of its hole.

Antarctica, while scorpions are desert animals. The crustaceans have the seas and fresh waters as their territory, although a few, such as the woodlice, live on land. On the shores, crabs are common, and prawns have been found even in the deep sea.

The insects are easily recognized; they have three-part bodies and three pairs of legs. They usually also have two pairs of wings. The arachnids have four pairs of legs and two part or one part bodies. The crustaceans have ten pairs of legs or more.

The insects include the familiar flies, butterflies, moths and beetles. These are all winged insects. Some insects, such as the little springtails, do not have wings. The insect's life cycle is either like that of the cockroach, in which the egg hatches into a larva called an *imago*, which moults (grows larger during several exoskeleton sheddings) to become an adult or, like that of the butterfly, in which the egg hatches into a caterpillar, or larva, which becomes a chrysalis, or pupa, from which the adult insect emerges.

The crustaceans include the crabs, lobsters, shrimps, prawns, barnacles, sandhoppers and woodlice. They also lay eggs which hatch into larvae. The life histories are complicated; the larva often going through several stages before becoming an adult.

The arachnids include the spiders, ticks, mites and scorpions. The group also contains a 'living fossil', the King Crab, *Limulus*, which has lived unchanged since the Triassic Period, 220 million years ago. Arachnids have life histories as complex as those of the crustaceans, particularly the parasitic ticks, but spiders and scorpions lay eggs which hatch into small adults, which they carry on their backs.

Above: Prawns are crustaceans – a group which includes mainly marine creatures.

Below: The carnivorous Praying Mantis (an insect) devouring a small day-flying moth.

Molluscs

Molluscs have soft bodies protected by external shells or, occasionally, they have an internal shell. There are three main groups: the one-shelled gastropods; the two-shelled lamellibranchs; and the cephalopods, which usually have internal shells. Molluscs lay eggs which have two larval stages before growing into adult molluscs.

The gastropods include the land-dwelling molluscs – the slugs and snails. These, as gardeners know, are herbivores, but there are carnivores among them, that feed on earthworms. The land snails breathe by means of a lung. The freshwater snails are mostly herbivores. They are an interesting group, because some of them have lungs, like the land snails, and some have gills, like the marine snails. These molluscs may be in the process of evolving into land animals. Most of the molluscs live in the sea. The winkles, topshells and limpets are a few of the more familiar seashore species. Some of the gastropods, such as the conches and turban shells, are very beautiful. They live in the warmer waters.

The lamellibranchs, or bivalves, have two shells. They are all aquatic, and most of them are marine. They are usually burrowing animals, although some, such as the scallop, can swim along the sea bed. Cockles, clams, carpet shells, razor shells and shipworms are marine bivalves. Oysters and mussels, which

are very good to eat, live in estuaries. There is also a freshwater mussel. Bivalves are filter feeders, sweeping the surface of the sand with tubes called siphons. They 'vacuum clean' the sand, taking water and food particles into one siphon and squirting it out of the second.

The cephalopods use their siphons to propel themselves at high speed through the water. When disturbed, they shoot out a cloud of ink and jet away while the attacker investigates it. The group includes the octopuses, the squids and the cuttlefishes. Squids are highly evolved

animals with eyes and nerves very similar to those of the vertebrate animals. They do not have external shells. The shells are small and are inside their bodies. Some cephalopods look after their eggs, cleaning and protecting them.

They live in the sea and are found at all levels, from the surface waters to the abyssal depths. Squids are an important source of food and are hunted by large numbers of animals, from penguins to whales.

Echinoderms

The echinoderms are believed by some scientists to be related to the ancestors of the first vertebrate animals. The adults do not show any similarities, but the larva of the sea-cucumber is very much like the larva of *Balanoglossus*, the acorn worm, which is a primitive chordate.

The echinoderms are all marine, and lay eggs which hatch into free swimming larvae. The adult echinoderms

Opposite above : The Garden Snail is a gastropod mollusc.

Opposite centre : This lamellibranch clam of a tropical reef has algae living in the folds of the mantle. The mantle produces the shell and can be seen around the edge of it.

Above : An octopus crawling over sand.

Right : A Common Starfish moving over Sea Lettuce.

include the starfishes, the sea-urchins, the sea-cucumbers and sea-lilies. Over 5000 species have been recorded. Echinoderms can be found on the sea bed, under rocks or crawling over coral reefs. They are sometimes difficult to see because their colouring and shape blend with the rocks.

They are all built on a pattern of a five-rayed star. They move and capture their prey by means of their *tube-feet*. The tube-feet are tiny, water-filled cylinders that are all linked together by canals inside the adult echinoderm. The canals are called the water vascular system. Some starfishes use these tube-feet to pull open the shells of the

bivalves on which they feed. They feed by turning their stomachs inside out and enclosing the food with the stomach.

These groups represent a few of the invertebrate animals, and they are arranged in the order in which scientists think that they evolved.

Towards the vertebrates

The groups called the Proto-chordates and the Hemichord-ates are halfway between the invertebrates and the verte-brates. The acorn worms which look like ordinary worms, live buried in the sand on sea shores. They show links with the primitive fishes. The sea-squirts are another sea-shore species. They look more like sponges than vertebrates as adults, being sessile filter-feeders, but their larvae have nerve cords along their backs, like the vertebrates.

The vertebrates – animals with backbones

The vertebrates are the fishes, amphibians, reptiles, birds and mammals. They are called vertebrates because they have a nerve cord running along their backs, enclosed by a column of bones called *verte-brae*. The first vertebrates were dependent on water, to lay their eggs in and to keep their skins moist and prevent them from drying up. As time passed they evolved waterproof eggs that could be laid on land then waterproof skins which pre-vented them from drying up. They also developed lungs to enable them to breathe air. Gradually they adapted to the changes in the climate of the planet, the mammals evolving fur, and the birds feathers to keep them warm when the planet grew colder. Most im-portant of all, their brains evolved, and the animals slowly became more intelli-gent, the peak of brain devel-opment being reached in the highest order – the mammals.

Sea-squirts take in water through the siphon at the top, filter out food particles and then squirt out the water through the siphon at the side.

POISONOUS ANIMALS

Several groups of animals have members who protect themselves by producing poison, or venom. Among the invertebrate animals jellyfishes all have some poison sacs in their tentacles. Many of them are too small to harm man, but some are dangerous. Two box jellyfishes, *Chiropsalmus* and *Chironex*, both of which live in the Indian and Pacific Oceans, round Australia, are extremely venomous. Anyone stung by either of these can die within three minutes.

Several arthropods are venomous, particularly the centipedes and spiders. The American Black Widow Spider, *Lactrodectus mactans*, is probably the most venomous, closely followed by the Australian Funnel-web Spider, *Atrax robustus*, but several other spiders found in hot regions have killed people.

The fishes are another group with venomous members, the stonefishes producing the most powerful venoms. They have poison sacs connected to the spines in the fins on their backs.

Many of the amphibians are poisonous, even the Natterjack Toad oozes venom from its skin. The arrow-poison frogs, *Phyllobates*, are the most venomous, producing the most deadly known poison, batrachotoxin, from their skins. They are so-called because the Indians of Central and South America smear this venom on their arrow tips, causing paralysis to the shot animal.

The snakes are perhaps the best known of the venomous animals. Poisonous snakes produce two types of venom. The vipers produce venoms that attack the blood system. The cobras and sea snakes produce venoms that attack the nervous system, so that the body stops working. The most venomous snake is probably the sea snake *Hydrophis belcheri*.

Poisons are unusual among birds and mammals, although the male platypus has a poison spur on his thigh.

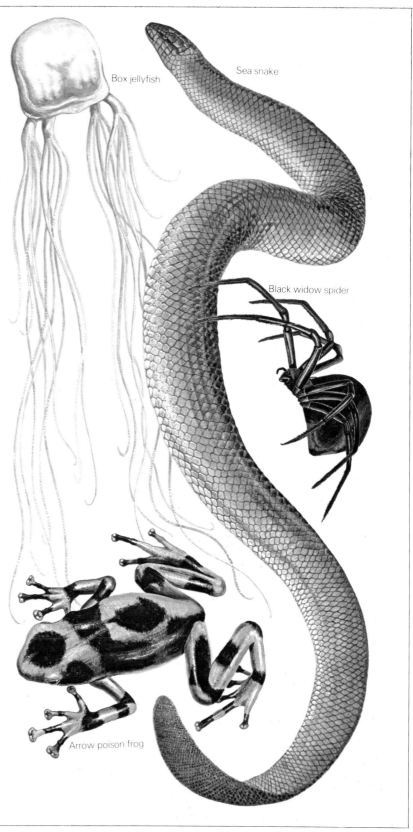

Box jellyfish

Sea snake

Black widow spider

Arrow-poison frog

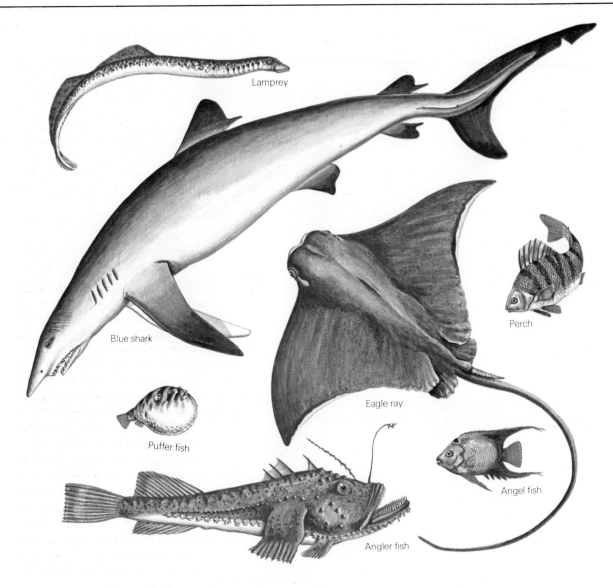

Lamprey

Blue shark

Puffer fish

Eagle ray

Perch

Angel fish

Angler fish

Fishes

The fishes were the first verte-brates to evolve. There are three groups of fishes living today. They are the jawless fishes comprising the lampreys and hagfishes; the cartilagin-ous fishes (sharks and rays); and the bony fishes (fishes with scales). Their skins are not waterproof. The jawless fishes have slimy skins, the cartilaginous fishes have tiny bony teeth embedded in their skins and the bony fishes are covered with overlapping scales.

The fishes cannot control their body temperature. They stay at the same temperature as the water around them. Most of them cannot control the water balance in their bodies. If a freshwater fish is put into the sea, it loses water to the sea from its body, 'dries up' and dies. If a marine fish is put into fresh water its body takes in too much water and it 'drowns'. Some fishes can control the water balance in their bodies. Eels, salmon and flounders are examples of fishes that can live both in the sea and in fresh water.

The fishes lay large numbers of eggs with very little food stored in them for the young fish to use. In most cases the eggs are just laid and then left by the female. Many of them are eaten by other animals and so are a large proportion of the larvae that hatch from the eggs. However, as fishes lay enor-mous numbers of eggs, some survive to grow into adults.

Opposite : The lamprey is one of the few remaining jawless fishes. The Blue Shark and Eagle Ray are cartilaginous fishes. The other fishes shown here indicate the enormous variety of bony fishes to be found.

Above : Common Frog.

Below : Toad croaking. The vocal sac is enlarged to produce a loud sound.

Amphibians

The amphibians that have survived until today fall into three groups: the Caudata – amphibians with tails, such as newts and salamanders; the Salientia – amphibians without tails, such as frogs and toads; and the Gymnophonia – strange blindworms that look like giant earthworms.

Most amphibians lay their eggs in fresh water, or in very moist surroundings. The eggs themselves are usually embedded in jelly. Some tree frogs lay their eggs in cocoons of spittle and some blindworms do not lay their eggs, but hatch them inside their bodies, to give birth to live tadpoles. If the eggs are exposed to dry air, they shrivel up quite quickly. A few amphibians, such as the midwife toad and some blindworms, look after their eggs, but most parents desert them, relying on the large numbers to ensure that some survive to the tadpole stage and that sufficient tadpoles survive to become adults and lay more eggs. Tadpoles are an important food item for several animals.

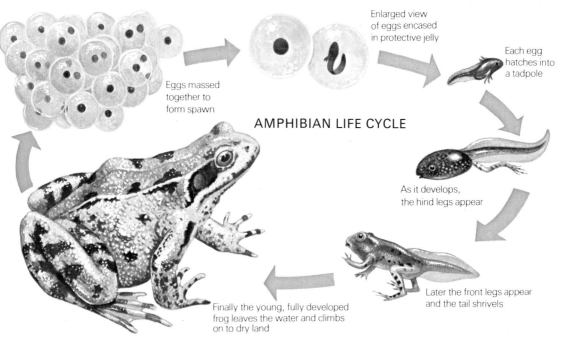

Enlarged view of eggs encased in protective jelly

Each egg hatches into a tadpole

Eggs massed together to form spawn

AMPHIBIAN LIFE CYCLE

As it develops, the hind legs appear

Later the front legs appear and the tail shrivels

Finally the young, fully developed frog leaves the water and climbs on to dry land

THE OLDEST LIVING THINGS

The oldest living thing on our planet is a tree. It is a Bristlecone Pine growing in California, USA, and its age is about 4900 years. It was nearly 3000 years old when Christ was born. It was already 350 years old when the first pyramid was built in Egypt.

The oldest animal ever to have lived cannot claim the same great antiquity. It was probably the giant tortoise that was kept as a mascot by soldiers stationed on the island of Mauritius. The tortoise arrived on the island in 1766, and it is recorded in the garrison records until it was accidentally killed by falling into a gun emplacement in 1918. It was then older than 152 years.

The Royal Tongan tortoise may have been older than the giant tortoise. It was said to have been presented to the King of Tonga by Captain James Cook in 1773, and to have lived until 1966, but the records may not be accurate.

Man is the only other really long-lived animal. The only authenticated record of longevity is that of a Canadian named Pierre Joubert, who was born in 1701 and died 113 years later.

A giant tortoise from the Galapagos Islands.

Reptiles

The reptiles are characterized by their scaly skins and their numerous, sharply pointed teeth. There are four main groups of reptiles alive today: the Crocodilia (the crocodiles, alligators, caimans and gavials); the Chelonia (the turtles); the Squamata (the snakes and lizards), and the Rhyncocephalia (the tuatara).

The tuatara is the only surviving species in the last group, a living fossil, found on islands off the coast of New Zealand. There it lives in old burrows, often sharing them with a sea-bird.

The tortoises, terrapins and turtles are heavily armoured reptiles, living inside a shell from which their legs and head protrude. The freshwater terrapins and the land tortoises are not in any danger of extinction, but the sea turtles are in danger of extinction because their nesting grounds are too disturbed by man.

The crocodiles have survived for 250 million years. Some of the species, such as the alligator, are in danger of extinc-

Left : Tuatara on Stephens Island, New Zealand.

tion because they are hunted for their skins.

The lizards and snakes are related to one another, but lizards have retained their legs and a tail, while the snakes have lost their legs. Snakes move along by means of their powerful body muscles, their ribs and their scales. Some snakes have overcome the difficulty of capturing and killing their food by developing a poison which they inject into their prey by means of their specialized teeth. Other snakes capture their food by dropping on it from above, and coiling round it. They slowly tighten the coils until the animal cannot breathe, and dies. Cobras and vipers belong to the first group, constrictors and pythons to the second.

The reptiles, like fishes and amphibians, cannot control their body temperatures, so they cannot live in extreme cold or heat. They do not have to live near water, however, because they lay eggs in leathery, waterproof shells. In fact, turtles and some sea snakes come ashore to lay their eggs, in warm sand. Some reptiles stay near their eggs to protect them, but many simply leave them. The eggs hatch into small adults, without a larval stage. Many of the little reptiles are eaten before they reach maturity.

Above right : A wild tortoise on the Greek Island of Corfu.

Right : The Copperhead Racer-Snake is found in Indonesia. Its raised head and inflated neck indicate an aggressive mood.

Below right : Pythons, like this Green Tree Python, are constrictors.

Below : The Salt Water Crocodile can be found in the Gulf of Carpentaria, Australia.

Birds

The last two vertebrate groups, the birds and the mammals, are much less dependent on their surroundings than the other vertebrates.

Birds and mammals can control the temperatures of their bodies, their fur and feathers keeping them warm in the cold, and sweating helping to cool them in the heat. They do not lay large numbers of eggs, or have many young, but they look after the few that they have, so that many more of them survive to become adults. This 'parental care' is a factor which has helped to make them successful groups.

The birds have evolved feathers to keep them warm, and their two forelegs are adapted to form wings. Like reptiles, birds lay eggs in rigid, waterproof shells. Most birds build a nest in which to lay their eggs, and one or both parents sit on the eggs to keep them warm. The eggs hatch into small birds which do not have feathers suitable for flight. One or both parents feed the chick until it has grown adult plumage. Many birds then teach their young to fly, before leaving them to look after themselves.

Birds are a successful group which makes use of most of the habitats available. They have even joined the herds of herbivores on the grasslands. In the African savannah lives the ostrich, *Struthio camelus*, a large bird that has lost the power of flight. It is the largest bird alive today. In the South American pampas, a very similar bird, the rhea, *Rhea americana*, occupies much the same niche. By contrast, the swift, *Apus apus*, spends most of its life airborne, feeding on the wing by capturing flying insects. The penguins are flightless birds, their wings being used under-

Above : Young birds, such as these Song Thrush nestlings are cared for by their parents until they are able to fly.

Left : A Royal Albatross. Despite its large wingspan, it is not an efficient flier.

water, as flippers. The albatross, *Diomedea*, spends most of its life at sea, circling the southern hemisphere, where it uses the wind to aid its flight. The Wandering Albatross, *D. exulans*, despite its enormous wingspan of $3\frac{1}{2}$ metres (12 feet) is not an efficient flier. The tiny hummingbird, *Trochilidae* is much better, actually able to hover in the air like an insect. The swifts and swallows are splendid aerobats.

The nests of birds show great variation, ranging from the guillemot, which lays its egg on a bare, rocky ledge, through the enormous platforms built by the storks and the neat mud constructions of the martins to the exquisitely made nests of the weaver birds and oven birds.

Birds have adapted to survive in every part of the world – The Magnificent Bird of Paradise comes from New Guinea (top), the flightless Ostrich lives on the hot plains of Africa (below) and the Adelie Penguins live in the cold, inhospitable regions of Antarctica (below right).

Mammals

The mammals are, together with the insects, the most successful group of animals on the planet at the moment. The group owes its success to its large brain and increased intelligence, its ability to control its temperature, and the care that it takes of its young. Female mammals produce milk in their bodies with which to feed their young.

Mammals have exploited all of the available niches. They are found in the cold polar regions, the tropics, the deserts, in woods and forests, in fresh waters and in the sea. The bats have taken to the air and many mammals, such as the moles, live underground. The mammals survive and breed in conditions that would kill fishes, amphibians and reptiles. Although they are air-breathers, the Sperm Whale, *Physeter catodon*, has been found 1134 metres (3720 feet) under the sea. The Yak,

Above: The Spider Monkey spends much of its time in the tree tops.

Left: The icy wastes of the Arctic are the home of the Polar Bear.

Below: The kangaroo-rat lives in desert regions, and can survive without ever drinking water.

Opposite bottom: Mammals even take to the air. These bats were pictured in flight in Trinidad, West Indies.

Bos grunnius, lives at 6100 metres (20 000 feet) in the Tibetan mountains. The Polar Bear, *Thalarctos maritimus*, swims in the icy Arctic seas and rests on ice floes.

Most mammals are four-legged and have tails, similar to the reptiles from which they evolved. There are still a few very primitive mammals living in Australia. The extraordinary Monotremata, the platypus and spiny ant-eaters, still lay eggs.

The Marsupialia, or pouched mammals, give birth to live young, but the young are tiny, embryo-like creatures, and crawl into pouches on their mothers, where they remain until they are fully formed marsupials. Kangaroos, *Macropus*, and Koala Bears, *Phascolarctos*, are among the best known marsupials.

The remaining groups of mammals give birth to live young which are fully formed, if helpless in some cases. They include the Insectivora (moles and hedgehogs); the Chiroptera (bats); the Edentata (armadilloes and sloths); the Primates (monkeys, apes and man); the Rodentia (rats and mice); the Lagomorpha (rabbits and hares); the Cetacea (whales); the Carnivora (the tigers, lions, cats, dogs, wolves, bears, otters and seals); the Perissodactyla (horses, tapir and rhinoceroses) and Artiodactyla (pigs, sheep, cattle, deer, antelopes, giraffes and camels). These animals all feed their young with milk and look after them until they can fend for themselves. For some mammals, such as the House Mouse, *Mus musculus*, this is only a few days, but in the case of man and elephants it can be for several years.

Top right : These Atlantic sea lions are at home on land and sea.

Right : This forbidding landscape does not deter the sure-footed Chamois.

Language

Animals communicate with one another by means of body language and by sounds. Body language can show that an animal is frightened, angry or friendly. The Primates have a series of expressions which inform their companions of their moods, such as the yawn from a baboon, which is a warning of anger, or the chest beating of a gorilla, which indicates a challenge.

Man has evolved the most effective communication system of all: words. In a relatively short time, man has learnt how to put his thoughts and feelings into words, and has developed languages. Man can communicate just for fun, he can sing, too, a sound which is purely for entertainment. In historical times, man has gone even further, and discovered how to communicate with people he will never see. You are using one of the oldest means of long distance communication now. I am very unlikely to meet many of the people reading this book, but I can communicate with you using the written and printed word.

More recently, man has invented radio, telephones and television. These inventions speed up the spread of information throughout the planet. Knowledge can be stored as books or films, so that it can be consulted when it is needed. It would be very time-consuming if everything had to be started from scratch, as it did in the past, before man learnt how to pass on his experience and knowledge.

It is difficult for us to imagine a world where news was spread by pedlars and carriers and a book was a rare and precious thing, but that was not so very long ago.

JEWELS FROM NATURE

Although the really precious stones, such as emeralds, diamonds and rubies, are minerals, a few jewels are made by plants or animals. The most precious of all the natural jewels is made by an animal. It is the pearl. Pearls usually come from pearl oysters found in warm sea waters. The largest pearl in existence came from a Giant Clam and was 24 centimetres (9½ inches) long and weighs 6.378 kg (14 lb 1 oz). Coral is becoming increasingly valuable as the animals that make it become more and more rare. The lovely red coral has been over-collected and its population is falling. The jewel is made by polishing the skeletons, or polyps, of tiny animals. Coral can also be pink or white. Cameos are jewels cut from sea shells. Like coral, the trade in cameos first came from the Mediterranean Sea. Ivory is made from the teeth of large mammals. Elephant ivory is the most usual kind, but Eskimos carve walrus and narwhal tusks to make statues and ornaments. Plants contribute amber to the jewellers' windows. The amber is fossilized pine resin and insects are often found trapped in the stones and so preserved — making a rather macabre ornament.

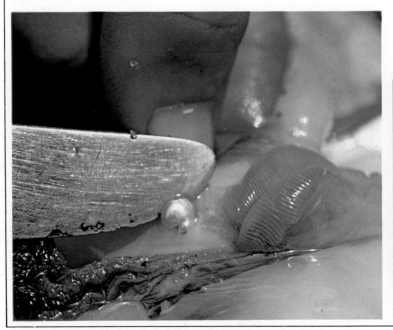

Pearls are formed in the flesh of oysters and clams, and are used in some of the world's most priceless jewellery: as seen in the Grand Imperial Crown of Russia.

Useful animals

Man can now change his surroundings to suit his needs. He builds houses in which to live and heats them or cools them as he wishes, so that the temperature of his environment is no longer so important. Man has discovered which plants and animals are useful to him and has cultivated them to make them even more useful. He discovered that dogs could help with his hunting about 10 000 years ago. As time passed, he found other uses for the dog, and they now work as sheep dogs, pull small carts, find lost travellers and guard properties. They comfort lonely people and even use their sight to help the blind, by acting as guide dogs. Man has bred the dog into a number of different shapes and sizes, very different from the wolf-like ancestor. Man has also domesticated cattle and sheep, breeding them to give more milk, meat and wool.

Some species have been exterminated by thoughtless killing. The dodo is a famous example of man's carelessness. It was killed to provide sailors with fresh meat. Today the whales are endangered by man's greed, and many of the beautiful spotted cats are in danger of extinction because they are killed for their fur, which is used to make coats.

Until recently, man has treated his fellow creatures rather badly. They are still often kept in poor conditions simply for man's amusement. Circuses, racing stables, aquaria and dolphinaria are usually commercial establishments, where making money comes before the welfare of the animals, and, to their shame, some zoos come into this category. Many zoos, however, are scientific establishments, dedicated to studying the lives of the animals in them and to saving endangered species from extinction by breeding them in the safety of the zoo, and so learning ways of protecting the species as a whole.

In the last half of this century, man has realized that the other plants and animals on the planet are part of a pattern, and all have an important part to play in the working of the planet. The pattern was established long before man appeared, and if he upsets the balance, then his own place on this planet is endangered. The study of the pattern of life on the planet is called ecology.

Animals are used by man for both entertainment (below) and for food (bottom picture).

MIGRATION

Throughout the animal world, and in a small part of the plant world, groups of individuals move off at regular intervals on long journeys called *migrations*. Millions of plants do migrate, but they are not often seen by men. The tiny plants in the marine plankton regularly migrate upwards during the hours of darkness, to the surface of the sea. When the sun comes up they move downwards again, being at their deepest at midday.

Some kind of migration is found in almost every animal group but it is most obvious among insects, fishes, birds and mammals. The fragile butterflies and moths undertake long migrations, the Monarch Butterfly, *Danaus plexippus*, travelling from North America down to Central and South America, crossing ranges of mountains in the process. Insects such as locusts do not migrate regularly, but every now and then great swarms of them take off to wreak havoc among the crops wherever they land. Fishes' migrations are carefully studied by fishermen, who follow their regular journeys from deep water feeding grounds to shallower breeding grounds. The most spectacular of the fish migrations is that of the American and European Eels. These eels breed in the Sargasso Sea, where the adults mate and presumably die. The fertilized eggs hatch into transparent larvae which begin an incredible journey back to their parents' home. These tiny creatures cross the Atlantic Ocean, the American eels returning to America and the European eels to Europe. When they reach land, they swim upriver, wriggling across wet fields to colonize ponds, lakes and even wells.

There, the fishes eat and grow until they are mature, when they travel to the nearest river and make their way back to the coast and the Sargasso Sea.

Birds make long migrations from one side of the world to another. Many birds fly from the temperate regions in which they breed to the tropics where they can find food in the winter, returning to the cooler parts in the spring. Swallows spend their summers in Europe and their winters in Africa, as do the storks. The American Golden Plover migrates from its breeding grounds in the Arctic Circle to South America, or even New Zealand, and so spends all its life in summer. Perhaps the most impressive migration is that of the Arctic Tern, which flies 19 300 kilometres (12 000 miles) from its breeding ground in the Arctic to the Antarctic and Australia.

MAP SHOWING MIGRATORY ROUTE OF THE ARCTIC TERN

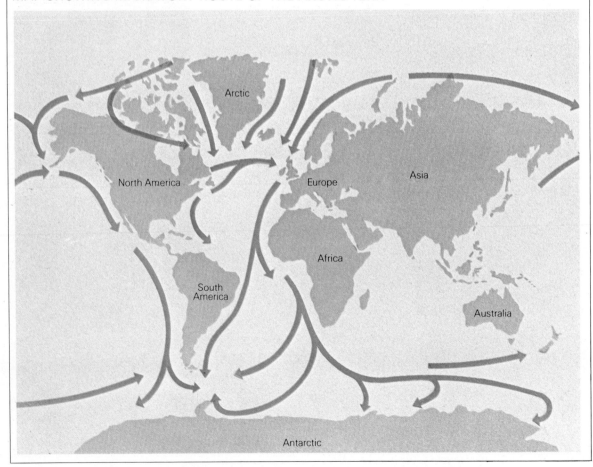

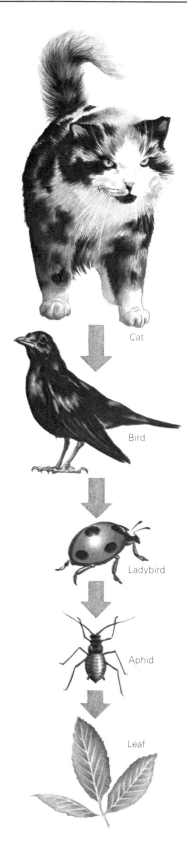

Cat

Bird

Ladybird

Aphid

Leaf

The balance of nature

The lives of animals and plants cannot really be studied separately. They have evolved side by side on the planet, and one cannot describe the life of an animal without including the influence of plants, and vice versa. The dependence of plants and animals on each other is only a part of the picture. Both plants and animals are affected by their surroundings. The amount of sunlight shining on a plant, the warmth of the climate and the water supply, together with many other considerations, make up the environment in which plants and animals live. The study of the environment is called *ecology*. Just as geology is the study of the structure and formation of the planet, zoology is the study of animals and botany is the study of plants, so ecology is the study of plants and animals and their relationships with their surroundings.

The study of the environment begins with an investigation of the soil. The rocks on the planet's surface play a vital part in the life above them. Some plants will grow on acid soils, such as those produced by granite. Other plants prefer alkaline soils, such as those formed by limestone. Each plant has evolved to suit a particular type of soil, so that the soil type dic-

Left: This is a long, simple food chain. The leaf is the producer. The aphid is the primary consumer. The ladybird is the secondary consumer. The bird is the tertiary consumer and the cat is the quaternary consumer.

Below: The presence of some animals indicates the underlying soil. This butterfly is only to be found on chalk hills, on which grow the plants it prefers.

tates the plants which grow there.

The type of animal present in a habitat depends on the type of plants. The structure of the rocks is important too. They can form ridges and caves which offer shelter and shade. The ridges can break the force of strong winds or keep off the direct rays of a hot sun. Mountains cause rain to fall, affecting the local climate and the water supply. Winds can dry an area or bring clouds. The climate, the rocks, the water supply and the winds all act together to shape the lives of the plants and animals.

An excellent example of the

Right : Flowering plants can be pollinated by birds as well as insects. This hummingbird is feeding from the nectar at the base of the petals.

way in which plants and animals have come to rely on one another is shown in the pollination of flowering plants. Plants such as grasses, and a few trees, are wind-pollinated. This is a wasteful method of pollination, because the plant has to produce a large amount of pollen to make sure that some reaches the stigmas of other flowers. Most of the pollen is simply blown away.

The most efficient method of pollination is insect pollina-

tion. In this method, insects looking for food carry the pollen from one flower to another. The insects are attracted to the flowers by the bright colours, which advertize the nectar. The nectar is usually

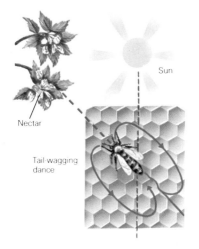

Nectar

Sun

Tail-wagging dance

Round dance

in nectaries at the base of the petals of the flower. The insects have to crawl right inside the flower to reach them. In doing this, the insect brushes against the stamens, which grow in a position that ensures that the insect must touch them. The pollen sticks to the insect, which then moves on to another flower. The stigma of the next flower is again in a position which makes sure that the pollen on the insect touches it. The pollen is transferred to the stigma and the plant has been pollinated. The position of the stigma, the stamens, the nectary, and the shape of the flower have adapted to the in-

Opposite : This is a deciduous woodland community. The animals would not usually be seen together. Some, the badger, fox and tawny owl, for example, feed at night. Each animal eats different food and occupies a niche in the woodland habitat.

sects as they, too, evolved, to ensure that pollen from one flower is carried to another. The insects benefit from the nectar and the plants benefit from the pollen transfer, and the plant and the insect now depend on each other.

This is only one example of the interdependence of plants and animals. There are innumerable other cases. Plants need animals to help with pollination and distribution and animals need plants for food, and often for shelter. Plants have come to depend on each other too. Trees shelter smaller plants from torrential rain or the heat of the sun, while the smaller plants bind the soil together and prevent all the water from evaporating too quickly, or draining away.

Once plants begin to grow in an area, they alter the air about them. In the process of

Above left : When a bee finds a new supply of nectar it returns to the hive and performs a tail-wagging or round 'bee dance' that tells the other bees the exact position of the nectar in relation to the sun.

Above : A honey bee feeding, and at the same time pollinating a flower.

respiration, carbon dioxide and water are released. The carbon dioxide is used again in photosynthesis, but the water vapour escapes and moistens the air. The moisture adds to the water in the clouds, and so affects the weather.

Plants can change the environment, and, as animals can change the plant population, they have an influence as well. The parts of the environment are balanced and if one part is changed, it can upset the balance and have widespread, and often unexpected results.

Ecological terms

Ecology is a science, and, like all sciences, it uses words which are strange to new-comers. Some of these words have already been used, and it would be sensible to explain them.

Habitat The word habitat describes the type of sur-roundings in which an animal or plant is usually found. For example, a rabbit's normal habitat is an open meadow with soil which allows for easy burrowing. A seaweed's habitat is a ' rocky shore. A Death Watch Beetle's habitat is dead wood. Dogwood grows on soil with lime in it and a trout lives in a fast flowing stream.

Niche This also describes a way of living. For example in a grassland community a small herbivore such as a vole, feeds on the grass stems, roots and seeds. There is only room for one species with these feeding habits. There may be other animals with slightly different eating habits living in the area, but they do not compete for food with the vole. If another species with identical eating habits appears in the habitat, the two species will compete for the *niche*. Normally there would not be enough food to

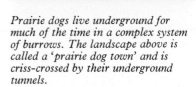

Prairie dogs live underground for much of the time in a complex system of burrows. The landscape above is called a 'prairie dog town' and is criss-crossed by their underground tunnels.

support two such species and one would either move away or die out. This is what is meant by *competition*. It is competition that has caused the extinction of so many species in the past. Plants compete as well as animals. They compete for space, water and the correct amount of sunlight and shade to enable them to grow properly.

A **community** consists of the plants and animals that live together in one place. If it is in a wood, then it is a woodland community. There are also desert communities, lake communities, seashore communities, river communities and grassland communities.

When an ecologist thinks of a grassland community, for instance, particular plants and animals spring to mind; grasses, of course, with a few trees. In North America, Bison and Pronghorn antelopes graze in the grasslands. In Africa, Wildebeest and Antelopes would be found; both are large herbivores, like their American counterparts. In North America, the Cougar would be the predator, while in Africa it would be the Lion. Although there is an ocean between the continents, the communities are similar. When a community has reached a stable condition, with a majority of its niches filled, it is called a *climax community*.

Grassland is grazed by different groups of large herbivores in different parts of the world: by buffalo in North America (below left); by gazelles in the plains of Africa, and by kangaroos in Australia (bottom).

Population describes the numbers of animals or plants of one species living in an area. A population does not always remain the same size. If the rainfall is very low one year, so that the plants do not grow, then there is a shortage of food for the herbivores. Some will die and not many offspring will be produced, and the population will be reduced. This, in turn, will mean that there is less food for the carnivores, and the carnivore population will also be reduced. If, on the other hand, there is a good growing year, plant food will be plentiful and first the herbivore population, then the carnivore population will increase.

If the growing conditions are exceptionally good, there may be a *population explosion* which means that there is a sudden, large increase in the numbers of animals. This large population eats all the food, and there is not enough shelter for them all, and some die. So the numbers fall again. Sometimes the population explosion causes the animals to migrate in search of food and shelter.

The Norwegian Lemming, *Lemmus lemmus*, is a famous example of this. When the lemming population increases to a certain level, some of the animals set out on a migration. Some of them find a suitable habitat and stay there. Others do not, and they continue to search. They ford streams and swim rivers and travel long distances. When they reach the sea, they do not realise that it is not another river and so they begin to swim it. They do not reach more land before they are exhausted, and so they drown. The rest of the lemming population has enough food and space, and it survives. These increases and decreases in a population are called *population cycles*, and are found in many animals.

Lemmings set out on migrations when the population becomes too great for the food supply.

THE WATER CYCLE

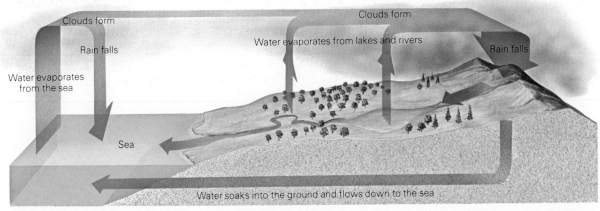

Clouds form

Clouds form

Rain falls

Water evaporates from lakes and rivers

Rain falls

Water evaporates from the sea

Sea

Water soaks into the ground and flows down to the sea

Cycle is also used to describe the re-use of the elements used in the living world. This planet is like a spaceship isolated in space; it cannot receive extra supplies, because there is nowhere for them to come from. The only supply that the planet receives from space is heat from the sun. Everything else that is needed by living things is here, but it is only available in limited amounts. Each element has to be re-used by the next generation, the carbon, nitrogen, oxygen, hydrogen, phosphorus and other atoms being used again and again. Each element has its own cycle. The carbon cycle is one of the most important.

THE CARBON CYCLE

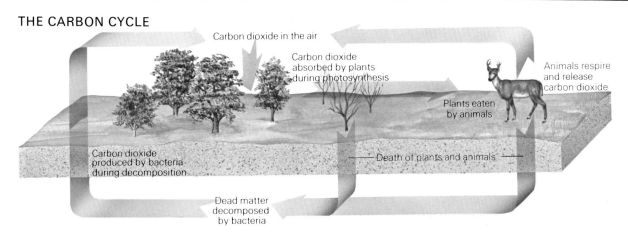

Carbon dioxide in the air

Carbon dioxide
absorbed by plants
during photosynthesis

Animals respire
and release
carbon dioxide

Plants eaten
by animals

Carbon dioxide
produced by bacteria
during decomposition

Death of plants and animals

Dead matter
decomposed
by bacteria

Carbon cycle

The atmosphere of gases which surrounds the planet is made up of nitrogen, carbon dioxide, oxygen, water vapour and a few other gases, including a precious layer of ozone, which protects life on the planet's surface from the dangerous ultra-violet rays from the sun. When plants photosynthesize, they take carbon dioxide from the air and combine it with water to make carbohydrates. The carbohydrates are built up into cells and tissues, and combined with nitrogen to make proteins. The plants are eaten by animals and the carbon enters the animal's body. There it is built into the cells, or stored as fat or used in respiration. During respiration, carbon dioxide is given off, and passes out of the animal's lungs into the air.

The carbon that is incorporated into the animal's body stays there until the animal dies. The body may be eaten by another animal or may decompose. Decomposition is very important, because it releases the elements for re-use. After the predators have eaten their fill, followed by the scavengers, the decomposers such as sexton beetles get to work, and break up the body. Then the fungi and bacteria take over, and feed on the remains. The carbon is either re-used or given off as carbon dioxide. It returns to the air where it can be taken in by plants again, and the cycle continued.

Nitrogen cycle

Nitrogen is an important element in protein, and it is also one of the most difficult elements for plants to obtain. There is more nitrogen in the atmosphere than any other gas, but plants cannot trap nitrogen when it is a gas. They can only use it when it is in the form of the compound, called a *nitrate*. Nitrates are found in the soil, and the plants take them in through their roots, with their water supply. There are a few, very important, bacteria, algae and fungi that can trap nitrogen. They are

THE NITROGEN CYCLE

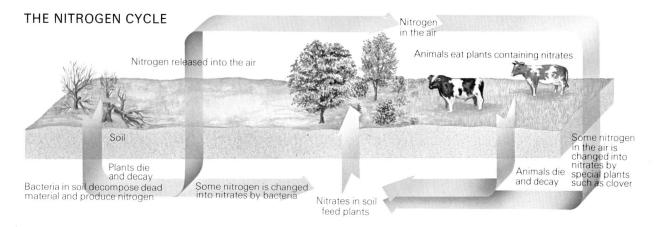

Nitrogen
in the air

Nitrogen released into the air

Animals eat plants containing nitrates

Soil

Plants die
and decay

Bacteria in soil decompose dead
material and produce nitrogen

Some nitrogen is changed
into nitrates by bacteria

Nitrates in soil
feed plants

Animals die
and decay

Some nitrogen
in the air is
changed into
nitrates by
special plants
such as clover

called nitrogen-fixing organisms, and the life on the planet would cease without them. They can change the nitrogen gas from the air into nitrates. Some of these nitrogen-fixing organisms live in the soil, while others live in the roots of plants such as clover. The plants build the nitrates into proteins which are, in turn, eaten by animals. When the plants or the animals die, the decomposers release most of the nitrates into the soil, where they can be used again. Some, however, are used by denitrifying bacteria, which break down the nitrates to release nitrogen, which escapes into the air, where plants cannot reach it.

Most fertilizers contain nitrates, to encourage plant growth. If too much fertilizer is used, then it will wash off the land into streams and rivers, and upset the balance there. The plants grow too quickly, use up all the oxygen in the water and the river becomes polluted. It is, therefore, very important to make sure

that the right amount of fertilizer is used on crops.

These are only two examples of the many cycles that exist in the natural world. Some take only a few months; others are very slow, taking millions of years. The carbon cycle can be slow, if the carbon is trapped in coal. It is only now, 300 million years later, that

Above : When oil leaks from tankers, many sea-birds, like this gannet, become oiled and die.

Left : Wheat crop being sprayed with insecticide by helicopter to kill aphids.

the carbon trapped by the Carboniferous club-mosses is being released into the air. Carbon dioxide is given off when coal burns.

Man has to be careful not to upset these cycles. It is easy to change something to suit himself, and discover later that there are dangerous side effects. Plastic is an example of this. Man invented plastic, and uses it a great deal. Unfortunately, when it was first developed, the types of plastic in use would not rot, because there are no decomposers to break it down. Scientists now spend a great deal of their energies in trying to produce substances that will decompose when discarded. Such materials are called *biodegradable*.

Another substance that man has introduced into the planet with unexpected consequences is DDT. DDT is an insecticide which man began to use on a wide scale in the 1950s. It was sprayed on crops to kill insect pests, and sprayed to kill mosquitoes which cause malaria. The results were excellent; the crops thrived and malaria was reduced. After some time, naturalists began to notice that some of the birds of prey were less common. The population was falling for no apparent reason. The naturalists investi-

THE DDT CYCLE

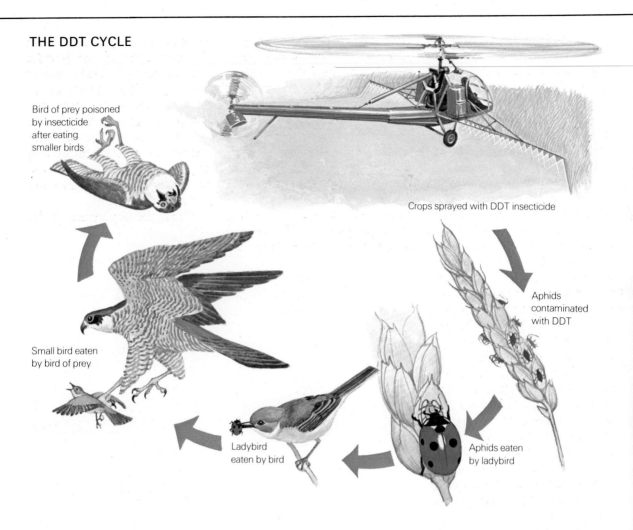

Bird of prey poisoned by insecticide after eating smaller birds

Crops sprayed with DDT insecticide

Aphids contaminated with DDT

Small bird eaten by bird of prey

Ladybird eaten by bird

Aphids eaten by ladybird

gated and discovered that, although the birds were laying the usual numbers of eggs, many of them were not hatching. Dead birds and unhatched eggs were tested and were found to contain large amounts of DDT. The birds had not been sprayed, so what had happened? The ecologists traced the birds' food chains back, and found the reason. The birds of prey were feeding on smaller birds that were feeding on the caterpillars and insects that had been sprayed. The birds ate the insects and used the chemicals in their bodies, but they could not use the DDT. They could not

break it down, and they could not pass it out of their bodies, so they stored it in their fat. As they ate more contaminated insects, the DDT in the fat became more concentrated. The small birds were eaten in their turn by the birds of prey, which then also took in more and more DDT. By the time that they had eaten a number of contaminated birds, the DDT became so concentrated that it made the eggs infertile. The Peregrine Falcon, *Falco peregrinus*, almost became extinct in the British Isles until the use of DDT was stopped and the bird was saved. An American ecologist,

Rachel Carson, wrote a book called *The Silent Spring* which described what the world would be like without birds. This captured the imagination of the Western world, and the use of DDT was reduced. The insecticide is now present in the ecosystems of the planet, however. It was washed into the rivers by rain and flowed into the sea. There the currents have spread it round the world. It is now found in the fat of Antarctic penguins, thousands of miles from the fields on which it was first used. It may take millions of years before a decomposer which can break down DDT evolves.

Food Webs

Food webs and food chains show how energy is passed around the natural world. In its simplest form, a food chain is a straightforward sequence of events. A grass plant grows and develops its seeds. An animal such as a Harvest Mouse eats the grass seeds. Then a Fox may eat the Harvest Mouse. That is a food chain. The sun's energy was used by the plant to store chemical energy in its seeds. The mouse eats the seed, and uses the chemical energy, and stores some as fat. The fox eats the mouse and uses some of the stored energy and stores some as fat. Energy is lost at each stage of the process, and only a tiny fraction of the energy stored by the grass reaches the fox. The food chain can be written: grass → mouse → fox. It would need a large number of grass seeds to provide enough energy to keep the fox alive.

There are longer energy chains: apple → insect larva → blackbird → cat is an example. In natural conditions chains are much longer and more complex. Harvest mice eat other things besides grass seeds and foxes eat other animals besides harvest mice. In reality the energy passes along food webs, not chains.

These webs are in layers, depending on how far from the source of energy they are. The bottom layer consists of the plants. They convert the sun's energy to chemical energy and they are called the *producers*. The plants are then eaten by the herbivores. They are called the first, or *primary*

consumers. The primary consumers are eaten by carnivores which are called the *secondary consumers*. If those secondary consumers are eaten by another carnivore, then that one is called the *tertiary consumer*, and so on. It takes a large number of producers to support a tertiary consumer, which is why large predators, such as tigers and eagles, do not live in large groups. The energy involved in all these stages can

be shown as a pyramid, with the producers at the bottom and the tertiary consumers at the top. The quantities of energy involved and the amount of energy that is lost can also be calculated. The energy loss is not vital as long as the sun shines on us and replaces it, but man must not upset the process.

From the beginning of the

A food cycle.

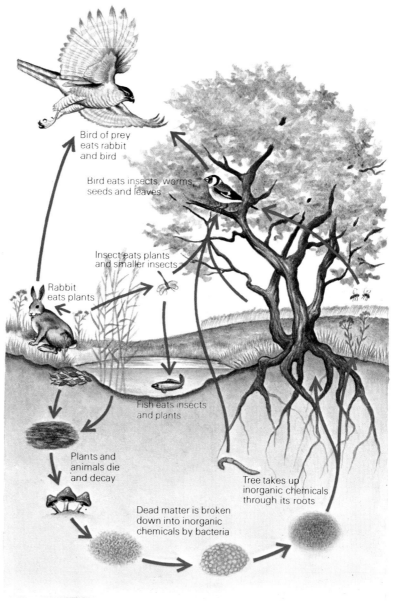

Bird of prey eats rabbit and bird

Bird eats insects, worms, seeds and leaves

Insect eats plants and smaller insects

Rabbit eats plants

Fish eats insects and plants

Plants and animals die and decay

Dead matter is broken down into inorganic chemicals by bacteria

Tree takes up inorganic chemicals through its roots

planet until about 2000 years ago, the plants and animals lived together in natural communities. The modern world was divided into geographical regions called *biomes*. These were caused by the shape of the planet. The Equator received the direct rays from the sun at right angles and it is much warmer than the poles, where the rays arrive at an obtuse angle and less energy is received by the plants. There are nine major land biomes in the world: the polar regions; the tundra; the coniferous forests; the deciduous, mixed forests; the tropical rain forests (also called jungles); the temperate grasslands; the tropical grasslands; the dry scrublands and the deserts. There are three water biomes, the fresh waters, the salt waters and the sea shores.

Now man is busy changing the face of the world. He builds towns which heat the air and the waters and change the climate. He cuts down forests which supply vital oxygen to the atmosphere and causes the soil to erode without the trees' protection. He plants great fields of crops and harvests them before they can return the precious trace elements to the soil, for the next generation of plants to use.

Man is upsetting the balance that has taken so long to evolve, without thinking about the results. Man has evolved very quickly and learnt much in a relatively short time. It is to be hoped that he will realize what he is doing and set about correcting the errors and problems he is causing before it is too late.

MAJOR LAND BIOMES

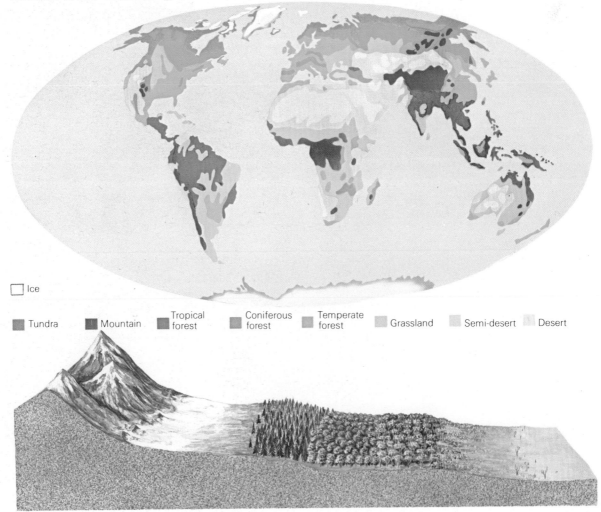

☐ Ice

■ Tundra   ■ Mountain   ■ Tropical forest   ■ Coniferous forest   ■ Temperate forest   ■ Grassland   ■ Semi-desert   ■ Desert

Mountain   Ice   Tundra   Coniferous forest   Tropical forest   Temperate forest   Grassland   Semi-desert   Desert

Arts and Entertainment

Contents

René Magritte (1898–1967), Time Transfixed, *(1932)*, Art Institute of Chicago.

Painting

'Modern Art' seemed to burst upon the Paris art world in the early part of this century. Some of the new painters were labelled 'wild beasts' by the critics, while others were condemned for their ugly contortions of the human body. Yet looking back from the present day, we can see that the apparently totally new techniques of these painters were based on what had gone before.

Throughout the history of art, there have been painters who have developed new ideas – the modern artists of their day – influencing the whole future course of painting. In the 14th century, Giotto broke away from the stylized form of painting which he had inherited from Byzantine culture and painted Jesus and his disciples as ordinary people. He rediscovered *perspective* – the way in which a three-dimensional scene is recreated on a flat surface – the first man to do so for nearly a thousand years. In the 16th century El Greco used the legacy from Byzantium in a different way, distorting and elongating the human body to tremendous effect. In the 17th century Rembrandt used colour in perfect harmony with the emotions that he expressed in his paintings. It is these two themes of perspective and the emotional use of colour that have dominated 20th century painting.

Two great English painters, John Constable and Joseph M. W. Turner, who painted landscapes in the early part of the

19th century, are now seen to be forerunners of the great French *Impressionist* movement. The effects of light and movement achieved by the Impressionists seemed to young painters like Pablo Picasso, Georges Braque and Henri Matisse, working in Paris at the turn of this century, to be the high point of purely representational art. Yet the way that the Impressionists placed brushloads of pure colour side by side on the canvas so that they merged a few feet away, completely revolutionized painting and

Left: Vincent Van Gogh (1853–90), The Sower, (1888), Rijksmuseum Vincent Van Gogh, Amsterdam. Van Gogh was one of the pioneers of Expressionism and influenced the Fauves and other experimental groups.

Left below: Henri Matisse (1869–1954), Red Studio, (1911), Museum of Modern Art, New York. Matisse's most characteristic paintings display a bold use of brilliant primary colours within a two-dimensional design.

Right: Paul Cézanne (1839–1906), Sous bois, (c. 1895), Private collection. Cézanne said he wanted 'to make Impressionism something solid and durable like the art of the old masters'.

forced young painters to re-examine their approach to art.

Fauvism

The first revolutionary movement to come before the public was *Fauvism*. In 1905, Matisse and a group of friends which included André Derain, Maurice de Vlaminck and Georges Rouault contributed a roomful of pictures to a Paris exhibition. They were immediately labelled *Fauves* (les fauves is French for wild beasts) and their work was described as 'the barbaric and naive splotches of a child playing with his box of colours.' Strong, unnatural colour was certainly one of their characteristics, and in this, they were influenced by two 19th century painters: Paul Gauguin who used strong, unnatural colour and Vincent Van Gogh who applied his paint to create effects of great force and strength.

Matisse and his friends had moved on a stage further from the Impressionists. The Impressionists painted what they saw, the Fauves added to this by using the impact of colour in a purely *subjective* way. They did not paint in the colours they saw, but in the colours they felt. Matisse's younger contemporaries, however, felt that the way in which he painted was *too* subjective and they experimented to find a new, more *objective* way of painting.

Cubism

The death of the painter Paul Cézanne in 1906, and the great retrospective exhibition which was mounted in 1907, illustrated the way in which he had been able to create a new relationship between his pic-tures and the objective world. It is not an over-simplification to say that Cézanne is the 'Father of Modern Art'. He broke entirely new ground by finding new ways to represent three-dimensional objects on a flat canvas, and his work had a tremendous influence on two young painters, Picasso and Braque. They worked together for four years, from 1907, rejecting colour, as used by the Fauves, in favour of form – the structure of their subject. Following the lead of Cézanne, they abandoned the tradition of a single viewpoint for a picture, painting several views of the same object at once,

Above : Robert Delaunay (1885–1941), La Tour Eiffel, *(1910), The Solomon R. Guggenheim Museum, New York.*

Above right : Georges Braque (1882–1963), Composition with the Ace of Clubs, *(c. 1911), Musée National d'art Moderne, Paris.*

breaking it down into planes. Their paintings of this period were monochrome and their dramatic, new style became known as *Cubism*.

Disruptive and cool, Cubist paintings can sometimes look wonderfully sculptural, but the idea of breaking the subject down into a series of planes, can, when taken to excess, lead to an almost unrecognizable picture. In 1911, Picasso and Braque abandoned their obsession with form for form's sake

and explored new ideas of colour and texture. They were joined by Juan Gris, a Spaniard, who was the intellectual of the group, writing about their ideas, linking Cubism with modern scientific development. He hated the idea that a spectator could take part in a painting by making his own interpretation of the picture. Very different from Robert Delaunay, another painter associated with Cubism. Delaunay started working in a more and more abstract style, drawing no point of reference from the world that he saw around him. He tried to use colour to create the harmony of music – colour interacting upon colour in the same way that notes make up the wonderful flow of sound in

great music. Delaunay was an artist who had a considerable influence on his fellow painters, and today, his work seems as fresh and as vibrant as the day that he painted it.

Expressionism

While all this exciting work was going on in Paris, supported by a few critics, including the poet Apollinaire, another group of painters were coming together in Germany. They met in Dresden in 1905, and their aim was to form a bridge between all the revolutionary movements in art. They had all trained in architecture and they rejected everything that was taught in the academic art world. We do not think that they knew what was happening in Paris, but

Right: James Ensor (1860–1942), The Astonishment of the Mask Wouse, (1889), Musée Royal des Beaux Arts, Antwerp.

Below: Wassily Kandinsky (1866–1944), Black and Violet, (1923), Collection of Hans & Walter Bechtler, Zurich.

their work has the same intensity as the Fauves, heavily tinged with the anguish and pessimism of German society at that time. They owed much to two earlier northern painters, Edvard Munch and James Ensor, and they called themselves Die Brücke – The Bridge. Their movement became known as *Expressionism*. About 1910 the group left Dresden for Berlin, but by 1913, they had ceased to function as a group.

Munich was the home of another group of painters, and their ideas are found in a famous book of essays called *Der Blaue Reiter* (The Blue Rider) which was published in 1912. About 1896, the Russian painter Wassily Kandinsky moved to Munich where he was greatly excited by the Art Nouveau movement. While he was there, he was influenced by Fauvism, and combined this with his own personal mixture of Art Nouveau, Russian folklore and the folk art of Southern Bavaria. Fascinated by colour, he developed the style known as *Abstract Expressionism*. In 1912, he edited Der Blaue Reiter (with his friend Franz Marc) which, illustrated with examples of the old and the new art, formally laid down their ideas. The First World War, which began in 1914, destroyed the group. One artist, who was loosely connected with them, Paul Klee, continued working in their spirit. He believed that colour was the key to painting, and experimented continually.

Dadaism

The First World War put an end to all this wonderful creative work, except for a group of anarchists living in neutral Switzerland. They came together in 1916, and wishing to show the bankruptcy of western civilization, they wrote poetry, painted pictures, produced magazines–all to satirize art and literature. They called themselves *Dada*, the most meaningless word they could

Above : Paul Klee (1879–1940),
Child consecrated to suffering,
*(1935), Albright/Knox Art Gallery,
Buffalo, New York. Klee created
fantastic, small-scale, mainly
abstract pictures, giving the effect of
inspired doodling. He was associated
with the Blaue Reiter group and
taught at the Bauhaus from 1920 to
1932.*

Below : Pierre Bonnard (1867–1947),
The Café, *(c. 1914), Tate Gallery,
London. Bonnard was a highly
individual painter who seemed to
expand the Impressionists' ideas of
colour and texture in his own way.
Ignoring the movement towards more
abstract works, he painted interiors
and landscapes, concentrating on
subtle light and colour effects.*

find, and paradoxically their
literary nonsense had a liber-
ating effect on writing. In art,
the effects of choosing objects
at random opened up so many
possibilities in the relationships between one object and
another that many painters
are still exploring this today.

Bauhaus

In spite of the terrible tragedy
of the First World War and
the mood of depression that
settled on the art world, there
were two events that took
place afterwards which were
tremendously important in
the history of art and design.
In Germany, the architect
Walter Gropius founded the
design school called the
Bauhaus in 1919. First of all,
it based its teaching on the
ideas of German Expressionism, and then moved on to

explore ideas of basic shapes and colours. Posters, typography, furniture design and architecture have all come under its influence, even to the present day.

Surrealism

In 1920, the second important event took place. The group of painters who called themselves Dada moved from Zurich to Paris. There, they found that a group of writers were exploring Sigmund Freud's new theories of psychoanalysis through spontaneous writing. The whole group was organised by the poet André Breton and included painters, writers and sculptors. They called themselves Surrealists. As far as art is concerned, Surrealism is based upon the idea that there are moments in our lives, sometimes during dreams, sometimes during our waking lives, when the imagination overwhelms our intellect, and these images, and the associations which go with them coming from our subconscious, mean much more than the everyday world which we normally accept. Men like Max Ernst and Salvador Dali delighted in this revolt against rational painting and their work is full of uncertain ideas which lead to unlimited meanings. The most important painter of this group is the Spaniard, Joán Miró. He often used colour-washed canvas as a background to his highly individual and childlike images of people and things.

Pablo Picasso

Picasso is one of the great masters of our century and cannot be labelled as belonging

Top: Joán Miró (born 1893), The Carnival of Harlequin, (1925), Albright/Knox Art Gallery, Buffalo, New York. One of the foremost Surrealists, with a highly personal style, Miró used pure colours and dancing shapes.

Above: Pablo Picasso (1881–1973), Demoiselles d'Avignon, (1907), Museum of Modern Art, New York. This is an early Cubist work – an attempt to render the three-dimensional, without resorting to perspective.

to one particular school of art – but like many others, he absorbed some of the ideas of Surrealism. In 1937, he produced one of his greatest masterpieces, *Guernica*, to commemorate the destruction of this village during the Spanish Civil War in 1936 and to symbolize the evil of man's inhumanity to man. This great painting, which is accepted as one of the masterpieces of European art, shows how Picasso absorbed elements from all the groups of painters working around him, and fused them into his own, highly personalized statement of the tragedy of his native land, Spain.

War in Europe

At this time, the whole climate of Europe was once again moving towards war. In Russia, Germany and Italy totalitarian governments had clamped down on what they believed to be revolutionary art, labelling it degenerate. Paintings were removed from museums, galleries and private collections. Adventurous directors of public galleries were dismissed – many avant-garde artists emigrated to the safety of Britain, France and America, while those who remained were forbidden to work. Paris regained its title as the centre of the art world, but Britain and the USA benefited most from this influx of foreign painters.

In Britain, this was particularly fortunate, because it coincided with the emergence of the first great British painter of international repute since Turner, Ben Nicholson. In 1934 and 1935, he visited the

Above : Ben Nicholson (born 1894), Painting, (1937), Tate Gallery, London. As well as producing purely geometrical paintings, he also uses conventional still-life objects as a starting point for finely drawn and subtly coloured works.

Left : Piet Mondrian (1872–1944), Composition London, (1940–2), Albright/Knox Art Gallery, Buffalo, New York. His abstracts in black, white and primary colours have had a considerable influence on other artists.

great Dutch abstract painter, Piet Mondrian, in Paris and was deeply impressed by his painting. Mondrian came to London, and lived there from 1938 to 1940, and his presence must have given great encouragement to English pioneers of abstract art. The 1930s saw the emergence of Henry Moore and Barbara Hepworth as outstanding sculptors, but the most powerful movement in British art was Surrealism. In 1936, an important exhibition of international Surre-

alism was mounted, but some painters like Paul Nash, had already fused romantic English landscape painting with Surrealist elements. After 1939, when the Second World War dispersed the various groups working in Britain and isolated her from the continent of Europe, several painters, including Graham Sutherland, worked independently in styles that moved between Romanticism (a return to nature – to imagination and feeling) and Surrealism.

Left : Andy Warhol (born 1928),
Green Coca-Cola bottles, *(1962),*
Private collection.

Art in America
After the Second World War, New York became the new centre of the art world. The Americans had always been aware of the developments in European art, indeed, American collectors had been among the first to buy the works of Picasso, Matisse, Braque and others. American painters had continually crossed the Atlantic to find out what was going on in Paris, but the Depression had put a brake on artistic activity. Many European artists fled to the safety of the USA on the outbreak of war. Mondrian, Max Ernst and many others worked in the States during the war years, and the effect of their presence was immediate. American painting did not, as might have been expected, develop along European lines. Instead, it attempted to find a style that was truly American, and this new painting which startled the art world between 1948–50, prided itself on re-

jecting European traditions. Jackson Pollock was its hero, and in 1947, he began to produce his drip paintings, dribbling strands of paint onto a canvas stretched on the floor so that it could be worked on from all sides. Working on impulse, he let the pictures form themselves – 'When I am *in* my painting, I'm not aware of what I'm doing', he wrote in 1947. The American critic, Harold Rosenberg named it *Action Painting.*

At the same time, another more passionate and violent type of Action Painting was being developed by the American Willem de Kooning. His aggressive, threatening paintings are so physical that they seemed to free painting from the inhibiting influence of 'taste' and 'fine art'.

Pop Art
Pop Art was the next movement to make its appearance. Here a loosely-based group of mostly American and British

painters borrowed ideas from the mass-media – from comic-strips, advertizing and poster design. The two most famous names are Roy Lichtenstein with his famous comic-strip-like painting *Wham!*, and Andy Warhol with his series of paintings of tins of Campbell's soup. The one thing that is really interesting about Pop-Art is the speed with which these painters' ideas have been re-used by the mass-media, so that the style and time-gap between art and commercial art has been closed for the moment. The cinema, fashion and graphic design have all been affected by Pop Art.

The future
What is the future going to hold? How will painting develop over the next decade? It is hard to say, although it does seem as if the long period of entirely abstract painting since the Second World War is over and there is now a return to figurative art. This is seen in the work of two of the most important painters of the present day, Francis Bacon and David Hockney. Bacon's paintings are not easy to look at, the artist's anguish and despair seem to scream from the canvas, unlike the cool, spacious, deceptively simple work of Hockney. What both these painters embody is a return to the traditional values of draughtsmanship, which, with the experience and energy of what has gone before, is probably where the future of 20th century painting lies.

Literature

Today, modern printing techniques and modern means of distribution mean that all kinds of books are widely available. In the 1930s and '40s publishers discovered that paper-bound books (the books we now know as paperbacks) could be produced very cheaply and, because of their low price, sold in huge quantities. Many countries now have public libraries where, even if you cannot afford to buy a book, you can borrow it free of charge. Before the development of printing in the 15th century, all books had

An illustration from the Codex Amiatinus (8th century) in the Biblioteca Laurenziana, Florence.

to be produced by hand. With the very few copies made available by this means confined to the Church and to very wealthy families, very few people could read or write. Stories and poems were passed on by word of mouth. This led to what is known as the *oral* tradition, and naturally, stories came to exist in many different versions as every storyteller could add his or her own details.

Of course, not every piece of printed material in existence today is 'literature'. Literature is generally regarded as writings which people want to return to again and again, each time learning more and finding more meanings in what they are reading. Literature lasts

James Joyce (1882–1941) Virginia Woolf (1882–1941)

for centuries, having ideas and messages which are always relevant and important. It is very unlikely that anyone would want to read, for example, an advertizing leaflet many, many times, or treasure it to lend to their friends to enjoy! Great novels, plays and poems are generally included under the heading literature, and also some factual prose works which are so well written that although the facts may become out of date, the books are still read for the beauty of the words. People have always had disagreements about whether particular works are, or are not, literature, and they probably always will.

This century has seen many great changes which have destroyed established ways of

*William Faulkner
(1897–1962)
Marcel Proust
(1871–1922)*

life and forced people to rethink ideas which past generations have taken for granted. These changes have affected all the arts, making artists look again at the traditional ways in which they have expressed themselves.

The Novel

One of the most important forms of literature writers have used to express their ideas in over the last two centuries is the novel. Traditionally a novel is a story about a group of characters, where and how they live, and their relationships with each other. Usually the story has a beginning, a middle and an end. That is – some kind of problem is stated in the opening of the novel which is worked out through the book and solved at the end. By the time the novel is finished all the loose ends are tied up and often, the good live happily ever after and the bad are punished. In this century some writers began to feel that this was not a true way of representing life. People's lives, they believed, do not fall into such neat patterns. What is more, some modern novelists felt that it was wrong for one person (the writer) to create characters and pretend to know all their thoughts and feelings, because in real life we can never know everything there is to know about another person.

New developments

Writers in this century have tried out many new techniques to overcome what they saw as weaknesses in the traditional novel form. In doing so some writers have created radically new forms of novel. Ideas have spread quickly from country to country because artists all over the world face the same problems and many travel about, carrying new ideas with them. One important new technique, developed in the first decades of this century, by which novelists tried to represent people's lives more accurately, was called *stream of consciousness* writing. When we think we do not usually follow a distinct train of thought for very long; our minds wander everywhere and we can end up thinking about a very different subject from the one we started on. Various novelists used this technique, reporting the confused and random thoughts of their characters. The Irish novelist James Joyce (1882–1941) used the idea in his novel *Ulysses*. Virginia Woolf (1882–1941) also adopted it – in particular in her novel *The Waves*. In America William Faulkner (1897–1962), as well as using the stream of consciousness technique, used more than one character to tell the story, in such a way that the reader cannot always tell straightaway which character is speaking or thinking at any one time.

To avoid the traditional form altogether writers like James Joyce tried to find other structures around which to build their novels. Instead of the beginning, middle, end, technique of earlier writers, Joyce wrote his novel *Ulysses* using episodes from the Greek myths about the adventures of Ulysses to parallel the happenings of one day in the life of a group of characters in Dublin. As this novel shows, if a writer actually describes every single thing a character does throughout one day, that one day can easily produce a whole long novel.

The French writer Marcel Proust (1871–1922) created a series of connected novels called *À la recherche du temps perdu* (In search of times past). In these novels Proust made time present and time remembered (events from his childhood) appear simultaneous. Again, a writer was trying out new ways of representing people's lives and thoughts, for often we do, in the middle of doing something else, vividly remember a past episode. Later French novelists like Alain Robbe-Grillet and

Alexander Solzhenitsyn (born 1918)

Michel Butor, have gone even further in developing the novel, producing what have been called *anti-novels* because they are so unlike the traditional novels of the 19th century. These anti-novels describe surroundings in very minute detail and often report the characters thoughts so carefully there is no place in the book for any 'action'. The English novelist John Fowles in his novel *The French Lieutenant's Woman* has written an apparently more traditional novel but the usually 'invisible' novelist appears as a character – following his characters and checking up on their movements!

Traditional forms

Alongside these new developments, other writers have continued to use the traditional novel form, some sticking with accepted ways of writing to get over certain political beliefs or criticisms of society to a wider audience. In 1932 *Brave New World* by Aldous Huxley was published, warning how Huxley feared the future could be for man – with drugs to make people happy. *1984* by George Orwell was another novel warning of a possibly horrific future. Published in 1949 the book points out the danger of the state gaining too much control over people's lives. Both these novels get their message over through telling a very interesting and absorbing story.

Recently the writer Alexander Solzhenitsyn was forced to leave Russia because he wrote novels criticising the state and had them published in the West. One of his novels *A Day in the Life of Ivan Denisovich*, describing one day in the life of a prisoner in a labour camp, has been filmed. Solzhenitsyn's novels show how an absorbing story can be used to get over many important ideas.

Poetry

As with the novel, poetry has undergone many changes in this century, and individual poets have chosen many different ways in which to express themselves. *Free verse* is by no means a modern invention, but it has been much used in this century as part of the revolt against fixed and rigid forms. Free verse lacks regular metre, rhyme and other formal devices, relying for its structure on rhythms natural to speech and appropriate to the subject matter of the poem.

Poets, and most other artists this century, have been divided in their attitudes to modern life. Some have retreated entirely into themselves and made it clear that their views are personal and subjective. Others have tried to be objective and to take into account what is happening in the world and the past traditions of literature. W. B. Yeats (1865–1939), the Irish poet, was involved in the struggle of his country for independence, but his greatest poetry is his later works which are a very personal vision of life. Paul Valéry (1871–1945) in France, and Rainer Maria Rilke (1875–1926) in Germany, were also concerned with very personal forms of self-expression, producing poetry which was often very complex and difficult to understand. T. S. Eliot (1888–1965), an American-born poet who spent most of his life in Britain, was a more 'public' poet. He wrote of things which affected him personally but he also made constant references to the works of past great writers. He believed in the importance of tradition: that every artist made a contribution to a continuing and living culture, which was greater

William Butler Yeats
(1865–1939)
Paul Valéry
(1871–1945)

Thomas Stearns Eliot
(1888–1965)
Wystan Hugh Auden
(1907–1973)

Rainer Maria Rilke
(1875–1926)
Robert Frost
(1874–1963)

than any single artist.

In the 1930s many poets were united by their fear of the spread of Fascism in Europe. Some of them believed for a time that Communism was an answer to the social problems of the '20s and '30s but most were disillusioned by the end of the '30s by the events in Russia. W. H. Auden was probably the best known of this group which included Stephen Spender, C. Day Lewis, and Louis MacNeice. Auden's poetry in the '30s reflected his concern with the social problems of that time. He emigrated to New York in 1939 and during the 1940s was converted to Anglicanism, his poems becoming more restrained and less openly political.

After the Second World War poets tended to be much less clear in their political beliefs and more tentative in their writing. In England Philip Larkin is perhaps the best known of a more conservative school of poets called *The*

Movement. In America the poet Robert Frost (1874–1963) achieved popularity with his quiet but strong poems concerned with the countryside and its people.

Poets all over the world are always re-examining the traditional speech patterns and traditional rhymes of their countries, and producing new work, but poetry today is perhaps a minority interest. Not many people buy books of poetry and few poets become national figures or best sellers in the way that some novelists do. All kinds of literature have now to compete for public attention with television and films which can often present the same ideas in a more immediate way. This has affected the kind of books writers produce – novels and poems are usually much shorter today than in the 19th century. Sometimes books and films work together when a novel is filmed, or the storyline of a successful film is published as a book.

Children's literature

One very important development this century has been the growth in the number of books written specially for children. For a long time children did not really have a literature of their own. They could, of course, listen to the stories told by adults and read some adult books, but until the middle of the 18th century children were not really regarded as a separate group to be allowed their own style of clothes, books and behaviour. Children were treated as tiny adults and expected to behave like adults. The 19th and 20th centuries have seen a complete change in this area. Paperbacks mean that more children can afford to choose and buy their own books and books for children are much more highly illustrated now that new printing techniques mean colour pictures can be reproduced cheaply. There are now classic stories for children in the same way as there are classic stories for adults.

Theatre

The living tradition of contemporary theatre stems from ancient forms of music and dance, and from primitive religious ceremonies. The ancient Greek and Roman civilizations first formalized these early forms of drama. Greek theatres were open to the sky and set into hillsides. Built of stone and semi-circular in shape, they had steeply-tiered seats surrounding a central, flat space, which was the main performing area. The audience, up to 16 000 sometimes, came from all sections of the community and were admitted free. Actors wore ornate costumes and masks which enabled them to play several parts in one play. The Roman theatre was less respected and culturally less important. Spectacles – gladiator sports and violent athleticism – replaced the plays of the Greek theatre.

The church has always been connected with the theatre, either as its severest critic, or, paradoxically, in the 14th century, as the source and inspiration of its main dramatic material. The *Mystery Plays* of York, Chester, Coventry and Wakefield in England, were staged on carts which travelled around the towns and countryside. The language was contemporary and colloquial and though the themes were religious, the style of production was often comical and satirical. The tradesmen's guilds soon began to involve themselves. The skills of the craftsmen – carpenters, nail-makers, cobblers, helped to

The theatre built by Polycleitos the Younger in the 4th century B.C. in Epidaurus, Greece.

make the scenic effects more spectacular and the language soon became richer and more poetic.

In Europe, the ancient tradition of *commedia dell' arte*, with its well known, popular stories and characters such as Arlecchino and Pulcinella (known later in England as Harlequin and Mr Punch) was the most widespread form of theatre.

Italian architecture produced the *proscenium* theatre with its picture-frame stage and horseshoe-shaped auditorium, while Italian artists and designers were creating brilliant painted scenery and costumes.

It was the fusion between the Italian architectural revolution and the theatrically aware English audiences that led to the extraordinary flowering of dramatic literature in England in the 16th and 17th centuries. The tradition of the *masque* – song and dance, beautifully costumed and presented – led to the popular stories of the day

being turned into plays as we know them. Shakespeare and Marlowe were soon writing full length poetic dramas.

Elizabethan theatres were roughly circular with galleries surrounding the open-air *pit*. The small stage was raised with a curtained area behind it, used for interior scenes. A balcony above was another acting area. Built onto the back was the *tiring house*, where the actors dressed and kept their costumes and props. The most famous theatre in London was *The Globe* on the south bank of the Thames. There were no actresses – boys played the women's parts – and scenery and costumes were contemporary and minimal.

In 1642, the Puritans shut down the public theatres and, until the Restoration of Charles II in 1660, the English theatres were silent. In France, Italy and Spain, however, the 'Golden Age' was flourishing. Lope de Vega in Spain enjoyed great success as a playwright in theatres not unlike Shakespeare's, while in France, Molière was leading an acting company which, under Louis XIV, was to become the world famous *Comédie Française*.

The end of the 16th century saw the rebirth of English Theatre, but the plays became more sophisticated and narrow in appeal. People even began to rewrite Shakespeare's great classics to suit their own tastes and the Restoration movement in dramatic literature led by William Congreve and William Wycherley was not widely popular. Some great performers emerged, among them David Garrick (1717–79) and Sarah Siddons (1755–1831).

The early 19th century was significant mostly for the career of Edmund Kean (1788–1833) perhaps the greatest of all English tragic actors. His *Macbeth* is legendary. Melodrama was very popular as were huge and complicated sets and spectacularly realistic effects with earthquakes, storms, and horses or bears on the stage. Though the theatre grew in technical expertise, it was not until much later that dramatic writing really flourished with the emergence of Henrik Ibsen, Anton Chekhov and George Bernard Shaw. Some great actors, like Henry Irving and Sarah Bernhardt played to audiences all over Europe and America.

Outside Europe and America, Japan's theatrical heritage is probably the most important. *Noh Theatre* in Japan has not changed for 400 years, although *Kabuki*

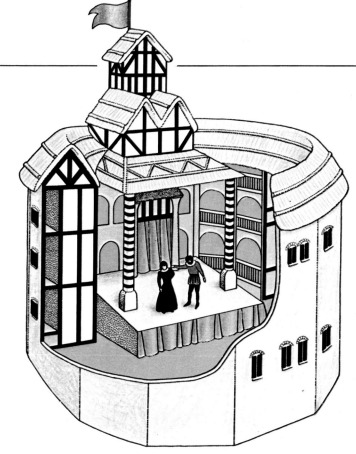

Above : An artist's impression of the Globe Theatre, London, 1589.

Below : Traditional Japanese theatre.

Theatre is more accessible (and popular in the West). The plays are highly stylized and traditionally formal. The actors pass their arts on through their families and it is not unusual to find two or three generations acting together in the same play. The Chinese Theatre is very spectacular with classical circus arts like acrobatics and group dancing.

The theatre today
The theatre of our time is in a state of constant and crucial change. The 20th century has seen alterations in the world that have radically affected society's artistic, social and in-

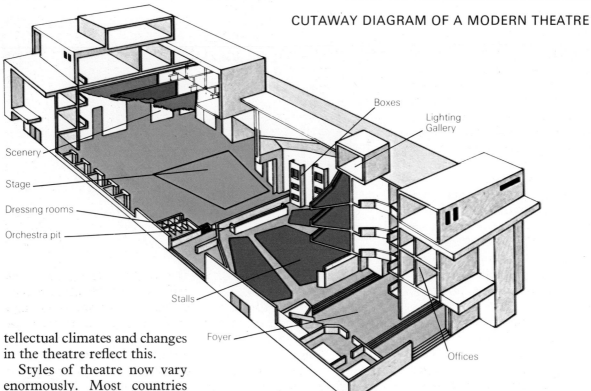

Boxes

Lighting Gallery

Scenery

Stage

Dressing rooms

Orchestra pit

Stalls

Foyer

Offices

tellectual climates and changes in the theatre reflect this.

Styles of theatre now vary enormously. Most countries have national companies which continue to explore their country's classical heritage in traditional theatres, but new and experimental work also takes place all over the world. In parts of Africa and Asia, Western directors, writers and actors have sought new forms of drama and new forms of language. Politics has been important in drama since before Shakespeare's day and the theatre in many countries continues to be politically involved, with authors using drama to express their views about society. Many small groups band together and travel about using rented halls and rooms to perform new and exciting plays. These groups are sometimes known as *Fringe* or *Off-Broadway* theatre. They are used by writers and performers to introduce unconventional, and sometimes controversial, works which

traditional, commercial theatres cannot risk staging. Some small companies have tried to reach a wider audience by devising ways of carrying their 'stage' with them – performing in their own portable tent, on the back of a lorry, or even on their own canal barge! Some groups do not even bother with an enclosed performing area at all and perform in the street.

The popular forms of theatre have changed too. The Music Hall, which reached its hey-day in the late 19th and early 20th centuries has really been supplanted by films and television. The circus and pantomime have survived, though both rely now on using popular stars from the film and television world. Some of the traditional theatre arts – puppetry and mime – are being kept alive by small groups but

Henrik Ibsen (1828–1906) Anton Chekhov (1860–1904)

Right : A street theatre group in action in London.

are not widely popular.

The professional life of the theatre has also changed immeasurably. Most large towns and cities have one or two theatre buildings, with perhaps a studio and experimental auditorium as well. State subsidy of the theatre has taken permanent root in some countries, though commercial theatre still thrives in major cities all over the world. America for example still depends on private finance and philanthropy to support its theatre.

Acting has always varied stylistically. Films made as recently as the '50s seem dated to us now and there is no doubt that the melodramatic acting

George Bernard Shaw (1856–1950)
Bertholt Brecht (1898–1956)

of the 18th and 19th century would be unacceptable now. This is partly because of the demand for naturalism in the theatre that began with the plays of August Strindberg and Henrik Ibsen. Konstantin Stanislavsky (1863–1938), the great Russian director who staged much of Chekhov's work, helped bring about greater social and psychological realism on stage. Other influences must also be acknowledged – the actor must be able to act in any media – there is no place for 'ham' acting in the modern world of film or television. Acting is still a precarious and taxing way of life, though its financial rewards for popular success can be great. Technical skills, like fencing, make-up, control of memory, proper and creative use of voice and physique all make great demands on actors.

Modern playwrights

The playwright's role has perhaps changed the most. He was once merely a 'wordsmith' responsible for writing down popular or familiar stories – often in verse. Shakespeare was the first great 'imaginative'

playwright. His genius has influenced the theatre for centuries and this shows no sign of changing, but it must be remembered that even he did not have quite the freedom to create and experiment as today's writers do.

At the turn of the century the plays of the Norwegian dramatist, Henrik Ibsen (1828–1906) had a great influence all over Europe. He wrote about realistic and often painful subjects, changing the emphasis in European theatres from light-hearted entertainment to more demanding and thought-provoking works. In Russia, Anton Chekhov (1860–1904) wrote plays which are known as *black* or *dark comedies*, observing the conventions of comedy but presenting a sombre and despairing picture of the world. George Bernard Shaw (1856–1950), the Irish born dramatist, carried on and developed Ibsen's ideas, using his plays to argue out important ideas, but often in an apparently light-hearted and entertaining way.

The German playwright Bertolt Brecht (1898–1956),

has had a considerable influence on 20th century theatre. In his plays he concentrated on putting over clearly and strongly his political beliefs. He used songs, brilliant lighting and short scenes to keep his audience's attention. In Italy Luigi Pirandello (1867–1936) wrote a play called *Six Characters in Search of an Author* which explored new methods of dramatic writing.

In America Eugene O'Neill, Tennessee Williams and Arthur Miller have been very influential. Eugene O'Neill began writing plays for amateur groups and went on to become one of America's greatest dramatists. Tennessee Williams had great success with plays like *The Glass Menagerie* and *A Streetcar Named Desire*. Arthur Miller wrote an extremely powerful historical play about the trial of a group of girls accused of witchcraft called *The Crucible*.

Contemporary French theatre has evolved what is known as *theatre of the absurd*, with plays which are strange fantasies without plots and often without normal conversation. Playwrights in this school include Eugene Ionesco, Samuel Beckett, Jean Genet, and, in England, Harold Pinter.

The director's role

The person who links the intentions of the playwright (as he sees them) with the energies of actors is the *director*. It is a relatively recently evolved profession, but none the less important. The director's job is to interpret the play – and a good play may have any number of different themes in it, as a piece of music

can. Shakespeare's *A Midsummer Night's Dream* was recently given a new and revolutionary production by Peter Brook with England's Royal Shakespeare Company. The set was a white box with doors and trapezes; Oberon and Puck did circus tricks, symbolizing their magical powers, while the costumes were all of brightly coloured silks. It was a completely novel reading of the play but the world-wide popularity of the production proved how a director's vision, with the support and commitment of his players, can totally change an audience's perception.

The director is responsible for the overall product. It is he who must communicate and discuss with the author, designer, actors, and technical experts in order to achieve a successful whole. There has always been a 'producer' figure in the theatre – 'Actor Managers' were businessmen as well as artists – and Shakespeare was certainly involved in a directorial capacity, but it is only recently that the director has become so prominent. America's Elia Kazan, Italy's Giorgio Strehler and Franco Zeffirelli, Peter Stein in Germany and England's Peter Hall and Peter Brook

Above : Britain's new National Theatre and (right) the Olivier Theatre inside.

Below : A scene from Peter Brook's production of A Midsummer Night's Dream.

Above : A scene from Samuel Beckett's Waiting for Godot.

are all acknowledged leaders of their profession and internationally respected.

Theatre buildings

The contemporary theatre building is a very complex structure and organization. Britain's National Theatre (in London), for instance, opened in 1976 and has three auditoria: the Olivier (named after Laurence Olivier) which is an amphitheatre (not unlike a Greek stage) seating 1200; the Lyttleton, a conventional end stage proscenium theatre seating 880; and the Cottesloe which is a flexible and experimental space seating up to 460. The building also houses all the administrative offices, workshops, costume departments, electrical staff and equipment, music and recording studios, dressing rooms and rehearsal rooms that a performing company of up to 130 may need. The stages themselves have to be adaptable to accommodate different styles of play and set in 'repertoire' (perhaps two or three plays playing in a two or three day cycle). Productions are planned far ahead and rehearsals are usually eight or ten weeks long. Of course, not all theatres operate on this scale, but even the smaller provincial theatre has a great many expenses to meet and many theatres have a struggle to keep going.

The future of the theatre depends on its ability to reflect the issues of its own society. Great plays and great theatre, whether comic or tragic must always entertain and stimulate or provoke the imagination of the audience. The theatre now has to compete with the cinema, radio and television, so reaching new audiences with exciting works is both its main aim and the key to its continuing future.

Music

Of all the arts in the 20th century it is perhaps music which has changed the most. Before the invention of the gramophone and the wireless (now commonly called radio) put all kinds of music within reach of a mass audience, music had only existed as a written score or as a live performance. The gramophone and the wireless made recorded performances available to huge numbers of listeners in their own homes.

The inventor of the gramophone, Thomas Edison (1847–1931), was an American, and it was in America that the record industry first became a powerful force. Mainly for this reason the history of popular music in the first half of the 20th century tends to be primarily a history of American popular music. Classical music was slower to adapt to the new technology. It was not until the development of radio broadcasting and satellite transmission that classical music became widely

Thomas Edison and an early gramophone.

available to a large audience. An important reason for this slow development of recorded classical music is that a classical work exists as a written score open to interpretation rather than as an immediate and particular performance by a recognizable individual or individuals.

Popular Music

The gramophone was becoming popular by the turn of the century in America and its development allowed 'folk' music, previously confined to small groups and areas, to reach the mainstream of listeners. Folk music in America covered a wide spectrum from the music of the Appalachian mountains played on accordion and fiddle and based on Celtic harmonies, to the African-derived music of the Southern negroes who had been plantation slaves. Different forms of traditional folk music were eventually blended together to produce a popular music which was listened to by millions in America and Europe.

Jazz

Jazz, with its strong dance beat, was the first expression of new popular music to reach an audience through records. The bright tone of the small jazz band's instruments was ideally suited to the crude reproduction of the wind-up clockwork gramophone with its papier-mâché horn and ivory stylus. Jazz evolved in the 1920s from the clash between two cultures – that of the former African plantation slaves, and that of the white American South.

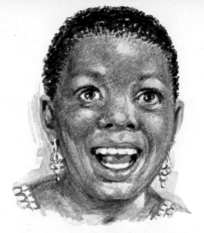

Bessie Smith

Through jazz black Americans, an oppressed minority, found a way of expressing their feelings.

Jazz centred around the Louisiana port of New Orleans. The first New Orleans 'street-band' to get a hit in the Northern States of America was *The Original Dixieland Jazz Band*, who played a date in Chicago, where singing star Al Jolson saw them in 1916 and invited them to New York. Jazz embraced a wide variety of sounds – from the wild and

Louis Armstrong   King Oliver   George Gershwin   Duke Ellington

jumping five and six pieces, often fronted by strong-voiced women like Bessie Smith and Sophie Tucker – to the symphonic lushness of George Gershwin's composition *Rhapsody in Blue*.

The Depression

In the late '20s came the Depression, when few Americans had money to spare for buying records. Although electronic sound recording had now arrived, improving the quality of the gramophone's reproduction immeasurably, record sales slumped catastrophically – from their high point of 110 million in 1922 to only 600 000 in 1932. The Depression brought sweeping changes to the face of America. Many families abandoned trying to make a living in the countryside and emigrated, either towards California, or towards the cities of the North like Chicago. These migrations were reflected in the music of the '30s.

The poor whites brought to general attention *hillbilly music*, now known as *country and western*, with its whining, nasal vocals accompanied by fiddles, accordions, and harmonicas. The blacks from the South brought to Chicago and New York the *blues*, music based on a solo singer's working on a small repertoire of familiar phrases and inflections to create an entirely personal sound. Often blues singers accompanied themselves on

A typical St. Louis street jazz band.

a guitar. In the 1930s these different forms of music were still strongly regional, although the spread of radio and juke-boxes was beginning to break down the separateness of the regions and beginning to weld a national identity for American music.

After the hard times of the Depression however, most customers wanted smoothness and sophistication. The sentimental song performed by an anonymous swing orchestra and sung by a faceless crooner proved most popular in the 1930s. Gradually the faceless crooners became popular in their own right, and singers such as Bing Crosby and Frank Sinatra came to overshadow the big bands in which they had started as side attractions.

By the end of the Second World War the popularity of the big bands had started to wane, while the popularity of individual singers continued to grow. Frank Sinatra's success marked a turning point: for the first time a singer was as popular as a Hollywood star. At last it became clear what records had done – they had made the singer far more popular than the song. The recording industry was back in business after a long, slow recovery from the Depression.

Rock and roll

Frank Sinatra and other singers like Perry Como, Dean Martin and Johnny Ray, had a huge following, but their music was not demanding and energetic enough for many young listeners. In the late '40s and early '50s, white teenagers in the Southern states started to tune in their radio sets to stations where the disc jockeys – then a new breed of radio presenter – had started to play black and hillbilly music, available on records from small independent labels which had sprung up during the war. This music had become known as *rhythm and blues* and *country and western*. Rhythm and blues had its origins in black jazz, developing when the old rural blues of the American South were transported to the urban environment of Chicago. Country and Western had its origins in hillbilly music.

It was a disc jockey called Alan Freed who made the first breakthrough for rhythm and

Bill Haley

blues. He was the first to call it *rock and roll*, and he had soon moved from Cleveland, Ohio, to New York, to fill the airwaves with the new sounds. Young people responded immediately to this change from the smooth unaggressive music of Sinatra and his followers.

Bill Haley was the first artist to record a song which specifically used the term rock and roll – *Shake, Rattle and Roll*. Haley was typical of the new movement because he crossed his own roots – a white hill-

Bing Crosby

Frank Sinatra

Chuck Berry

billy style – with the uptempo beat of the black rhythm and blues. In Haley's wake followed more rebellious and controversial exponents of rock music. Elvis Presley was perhaps the most notable white singer to appeal to young audiences, developing his own unique style from the traditions of black music.

Other performers followed Elvis Presley: Jerry Lee Lewis, a white Southern pianist and singer; Little Richard, a black singer who was wilder on stage than any previous stars, and Chuck Berry, a brilliant guitarist and song writer. All of these performers had a great influence on popular music in Europe and in particular, in Britain. Rock and roll caught on in Britain and its followers adopted a special uniform – the Edwardian drapes of the Teddy Boys.

Developments in Britain

In the 1960s the exciting new developments in popular music came from Britain. A new generation of British teenagers had gone back to the rhythm and blues sources of rock and roll and emerged with a curious amalgam of American and British music. In Liverpool the Beatles established their own rock style and gained immense, often hysterical, popularity. In London, the Rolling Stones learnt from authentic rhythm and blues artists like Muddy Waters as well as black rock

Elvis Presley, who died tragically young in 1977. The considerable industry generated by his music has continued to grow even after his death.

and rollers like Chuck Berry. Through their records and tours the Beatles and the Rolling Stones (and their many imitators) re-exported their music to its original home in America. By the end of the '60s both groups had developed their style far beyond their original sound. The Beatles in particular displayed extraordinary inventiveness in writing songs.

In the early 1970s rock music became more melodic, with the trend being set by groups such as Fleetwood Mac, the Bee Gees and Abba and by singer-songwriters such as David Bowie, Elton John and Rod Stewart. However, this was shattered in the mid-1970s by the appearance of Punk Rock led by the Sex Pistols, and with this came a whole new generation of rock groups.

In the 1980s many of these groups became successful in the USA as the Beatles had done 20 years earlier. They included the Boomtown Rats, Adam and the Ants, Police and Duran Duran. However, America still had many native stars such as Billy Joel and

Michael Jackson.

In this century popular music has come a very long way. Today there is a huge variety of musical styles, and recording techniques are getting better and better.

Above : The Beatles – Ringo Starr (drums, vocals), John Lennon (guitar, vocals), Paul McCartney (bass, vocals), George Harrison (guitar, vocals).

Right : Bob Dylan – born Robert Allen Zimmerman in 1941. In the mid 1960s Dylan withdrew from the music scene, but ten years later he was back producing brilliant new albums.

REGGAE AND BOB MARLEY

The 1970s produced a major talent representing both a new music and a new country in *Bob Marley* — a black Jamaican musician whose reggae sound was an amalgam of West Indian rhythms and American New Orleans influences. Bob Marley and his group The Wailers, were committed to the cause of freeing black people from oppression, and their performances took this cause as their inspiration. Reggae is now widely popular.

Classical Music

New sounds were produced at the turn of the century in the works of Claude Debussy and Béla Bartók. Debussy, a Frenchman, developed a striking new musical 'language', which he used to create an impression of a scene: *Prélude a l'après-midi d'un faune* conjures up a hot, drowsy summer afternoon; *La Mer* uses the most subtle and exciting sounds to suggest the play of light on water and the feel of the wind and waves. In Hungary, Béla Bartók was studying Magyar folk songs and dances. He experimented with *polytonality*. This means writing a piece of music in which different instruments are playing in different keys at the same time.

Debussy and Bartók both broke away from the traditional system of scales and keys, but the composer Arnold Schoenberg went further and invented an entirely new musical 'grammar'. He developed what is known as *atonal* music, music not written in any particular key. This music was so different from the sounds produced by composers in the previous three centuries that many people still find it difficult to understand and appreciate.

Igor Stravinsky's *The Rite of Spring* met with shouts of protest at its first performance in Paris in 1913, and the occasion ended in a public riot! Stravinsky had been commissioned by Serge Diaghilev, who ran a famous ballet company, to write music for three new ballets: *The Firebird*,

The instruments of the orchestra, and their normal positioning. Orchestras can vary greatly in size from under 20 to over 100 members.

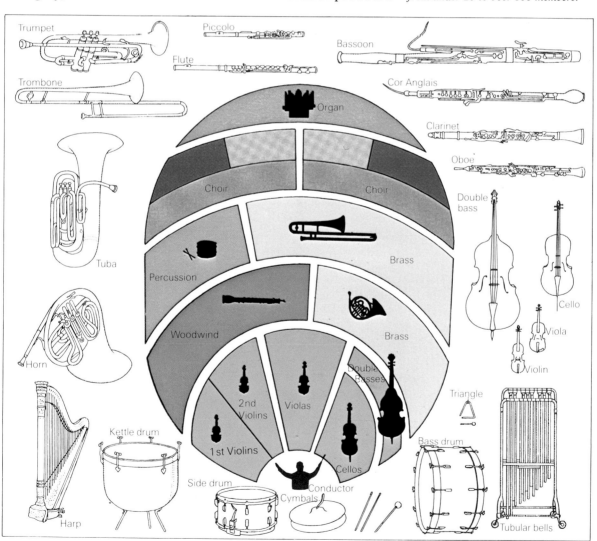

Béla Bartók (1881–1945) *Claude-Achille Debussy (1862–1918)* *Igor Stravinsky (1882–1971)* *Edgar Varèse (1885–1965)* *Benjamin Britten (1913–1976)*

Petrouchka and *The Rite of Spring. The Rite of Spring* contained some passages of deliberate harshness and discordancy which infuriated the audience.

Avant-garde composers like Edgar Varèse, Pierre Boulez and Karlheinz Stockhausen have experimented with music still further – to the extent that their work can only be appreciated by the few. Other composers have further developed Stockhausen's ideas of atonality, and gone on to think of ways to create entirely new sounds, by using electronics for example.

There have, of course, also been composers in this century who have tried to develop traditional methods of composition further. Paul Hindemith in Germany and Francis Poulenc in France are two such composers. Benjamin Britten in England wrote a number of fine choral works and operas. Britten had a particular interest in working with children and writing music for them to perform. Sergei Prokofiev and Dimitri Shostakovich in Russia have both kept to conventional methods of composition.

The developments in classical music in this century have been overshadowed by the enormous increase in the amount of popular music available, but there have been important developments in both spheres. Certainly a great many more people can listen to classical music if they choose now that the radio and record player are common fixtures in many homes, and classical music of this and past centuries has been widely recorded.

Cinema

The number of people who go to the cinema has declined since the great days of Hollywood in the 1930s and '40s. This is probably because of the ever-growing popularity of television although there is now evidence to show that the cinema audience is gradually returning. Perhaps this is because the cinema today is truly international, with films being made and distributed all over the world, and reflecting many different interests and cultures. The enormous variety of films now shown, will surely help to bring back audiences to the 'movies'.

How films are made

Moving film, does not in fact move at all. It is made up of a series of still pictures, each one minutely different from its predecessor. When these are projected onto a screen at a rate of 24 pictures every second they give the impression of movement. A cine camera, therefore, is simply an ordinary camera adapted to take 24 pictures every second instead of one at a time.

The sound for a film is recorded on a tape recorder. At the beginning of each section of filming (or slate as it is known) two pieces of wood, hinged together (a clapper board) are banged near a microphone and in view of the camera. This enables the sound on the tape and the pictures on the film to be matched to one another, or synchronized.

The producer

The producer is the man or woman who starts and controls the whole process. He may buy the film rights to a book or employ a scriptwriter to write a script. He employs all the staff, both technical and creative involved in the making of a film, including the director. He is also in control of the finances of the film and it is his responsibility to see that the cost does not exceed the budget allowed. In the golden age of Hollywood in the 1930s and '40s, the famous names were the producers like David Selznick and Samuel Goldwyn and not the directors.

The director

The director is probably the most important person on a film set. He helps the producer choose the cast and technicians, is constantly in close consultation with the writer and envisages the form and structure of the finished film. He rehearses the actors and supervises the entire shooting and editing of the film. Famous directors today include François Truffaut, John Schlesinger and Martin Scorsese. Sometimes the director will also be the producer but the two jobs are entirely different.

The lighting cameraman

The lighting cameraman with his team of camera operators, grips, focus pullers and so on, supervises the lighting and the photography of a film. In consultation with the director he sets the style and look of a film. Directors often try to work again and again with the same lighting cameraman once a rapport has

been achieved. David Lean, the director, for example has worked with the cameraman Freddie Young on *Lawrence of Arabia*, *Dr Zhivago* and *Ryan's Daughter*.

The editor

The editor of a film is the final link in the chain. It is his job to take all the film that has been shot, often as much as 20 or 30 hours of it, and cut it together to produce the completed film. When filming conversation between three people a director may shoot a scene five or six times from different angles, and it is the editor, under the director's supervision, who cuts these together into one smooth-running sequence.

Glenda Jackson being made up to play Queen Elizabeth I.

The cast

The cast of actors and actresses are the stars of the industry, the faces seen by the public. Many are able to command huge salaries and some, such as Robert Redford or Barbra Streisand, can almost guarantee a film its success by their appearance in it. Theirs is not by any means an entirely glamorous life. Shooting often starts very early (six or seven in the morning) and the stars will have to arrive a couple of hours earlier to be costumed and made up. The day is a long one and often boring, and the film is more often than not shot out of sequence (ie. the

Paul Newman and Robert Redford in The Sting.

Olivia Newton-John and John Travolta in Grease.

Tatum O'Neal in International Velvet.

The film studio

The film studio is almost a city in miniature. Everything necessary for the making of the film is there. All the different departments – make up, props, costume, set builders are readily available and not surprisingly many producers prefer to work in studio as their job is made so much easier. Some films, however, are made on location. The great advantage of location filming is the much greater sense of reality

end first, the beginning in the middle and so on).

in the final film.

Most films use a little of both studio and location which leads to other problems. For example, if an actor in a scene walks out of a house into a street, and if the house interior is in the studio and the street is on location, the two shots may be filmed many weeks apart. It is then the job of the *continuity girl* to ensure that the actor is wearing the same clothes, that his hair is the same length and so on.

The final stages

In the cutting room the film is finally put together. All the film that has been shot ends here. Every shot has a slate number and every attempt to film it has a take number. This means that any piece of the film can be found at any time by referring to the script and finding out the numbers, for example slate 196 take 5. The editor and the director view all the film as it has been shot. This is known as *the rushes*. Between them they decide which slates to use and which takes are best and the film is thus slowly assembled. It can take many weeks of hard work to produce *a rough cut* of a film which may even then be an hour or so too long.

When the film is completed, it is the job of the producer to sell it to one of the distribution companies who own the cinemas, before it can be seen by the public.

To make an animated cartoon, a series of drawings have to be made, each slightly different from the last. When they are projected at the rate of 24 per second, the cartoon figures appear to move. In the early days a separate drawing was made for each shot, but now a system is used where only small parts of one background picture are made 'mobile'.

Television

Television means literally, seeing at a distance. Pictures and sound from all over the world can be seen and heard on a small screen in your own home. This is achieved by translating picture and sound information into ultra high frequency waves that can be transmitted (like radio) and then re-translated into picture and sound through an electronic gadget – the television set.

There are two basic ways of creating these pictures and sounds. One is through film – as explained in the previous section on cinema – and the other is an electronic method.

The television camera, unlike the film camera, translates the images that it sees, into high frequency electronic information. This can then be transmitted 'live' or can be recorded onto video tape in much the same way as sound is recorded onto tape on an ordinary tape recorder.

A television studio

A television studio seems at first to be very like a film studio set, but there are two important differences. Firstly, there are several different cameras, maybe as many as five or six, which are arranged to obtain as many different shots (wide shots, close ups and so on) as required. This means that instead of shooting a scene many different times as happens on film, it can be shot by the different cameras all at the same time.

Secondly, the director does not operate from the floor of the studio. He is in a separate control room, *the gallery*, where

he can see the pictures from each individual camera on a row of television screens. His assistant works on the studio floor, and through a radio link can issue the director's instructions from the gallery to the actors, presenters and technicians in the studio. As the programme is rehearsed, the director can decide which camera to use at which moment and an extra television screen shows him how this intercutting from one camera angle to another will look. The pictures which appear on that screen will make up the finished programme, which will either be transmitted live or recorded on video-tape to be shown later on.

Above: A television studio and director's gallery.

Below: An outside broadcast camera.

Outside broadcasts

Many programmes come to us via outside broadcasts which are the television equivalent of filming on location. As in films, all the equipment and personnel have to be transported to the location, as also does a mobile gallery from which the director can supervise the shooting in the same way as he does in a studio.

Special effects

One of the advantages of the electronic medium is the ease with which certain special effects can be arranged. For example, the pictures which appear behind a newscaster as he reads the news can come from many different sources and are fed through an electronic machine so that they seem to appear on the screen behind the newscaster. This screen is in fact bright blue. The trick lies in the colour. The two pictures (the newscaster and the background shot) are fed into the machine, and the background picture will appear anywhere in the overall picture where this bright blue colour occurs. For this reason newscasters never wear bright blue. If they did their clothes would seem to disappear and only the background picture would be visible! This process is known as *colour separation overlay*.

The two disciplines of film and electronic (usually video tape) recording are often used in the same programme. In the news, for instance, news reports are often on film, whereas the newscaster is in an electronic studio. In some drama programmes the interiors are created in the studio while the exteriors are shot on film. This is common practice in Britain, but in Australia and the USA there is a stronger tradition of making drama programmes entirely on film in much the same way as feature films for the cinema are made.

If a programme is recorded onto video tape, it may be recorded rather like a film in small sections. These have to be edited together to make a completed programme. However, unlike film, the tapes are not actually cut. Sections are recorded one at a time onto a master tape in the exact order required. This can be done very quickly. Some sporting events can be edited and transmitted only an hour or so after they have finished.

There are many different types of programmes and the distinctions between them can be confusing. Basically, they can be divided into two categories – 'entertainment' and 'fact'.

Entertainment

There are two different areas here: drama and light entertainment. A television drama

It is important to plan a set carefully before filming begins, so time and money are not wasted.

will usually be made in much the same way as a feature film, but whereas a film may take months or even years to complete, a television drama can normally be completed after two weeks rehearsal and two or three days in a television studio. However, some television drama is shot entirely on film and this *does* take much longer.

Light entertainment programmes such as variety or quiz shows, chat shows or comedy series are usually much simpler and cheaper to produce.

Fact

This also falls into two categories: news and current affairs, and documentaries. News and current affairs departments are probably the most hectic in any television company. Programmes have to be assembled right up until the last minute because of last minute changes in the news. There is therefore a much greater chance of error.

Documentaries are not quite as difficult to compile because they are not so topical. They are programmes about real people and real-life situations and are normally produced on film on location. They will usually be re-assembled and edited after shooting to produce the desired impact without distorting the facts.

Television is a very powerful medium but it is still very young – barely 30 years old. It is changing all the time. New ideas and equipment, home video recorders, digital studios – all these new developments, will help television keep abreast of the times.

Ballet

The story of ballet begins about 500 years ago, when lavish entertainments of music, dance and song were provided by the kings of Italy for visitors to the royal court. This soon became fashionable and spread throughout Europe over the next 200 years. Louis XIV of France, in particular, had a great love of dancing and founded an academy for the training of dancers. The language of ballet reminds us today of the important part played by France in its history: all steps, positions and movements have French names.

At the same time as Louis XIV (1643–1715) was encouraging ballet in France, Peter the Great was doing the same in Russia. Soon the first dancing school was opened, and by the beginning of the 19th century the Imperial Ballet was firmly established in Russia. Many dancers and teachers came to Russia from Italy and France, and at the time of the Russian Revolution, several Russian dancers in turn fled to France, where they passed on their skills to others.

The man who did the most to introduce Russian ballet to the world was Serge Diaghilev, a theatrical impresario who formed a ballet company and took it to Paris in 1909. For the next 20 years the Ballet Russe toured the West with immense success. Two of the dancers who worked with Diaghilev were Anna Pavlova and Vaslav Nijinsky, two of the greatest dancers ballet has ever seen. Russians have always excelled in dancing and Russia's two

Madame Anna Pavlova

ballet companies, the Bolshoi and the Kirov, still produce outstanding dancers.

The birth of ballet in Britain took place in the 1920s, thanks to the inspired dedication of two women – Ninette de Valois and Marie Rambert. Both had trained as dancers and worked with Diaghilev, and both started ballet schools in London.

Ninette de Valois joined forces with Lilian Baylis, who was then putting on operas and plays at the Old Vic Theatre in South London, and from providing small dance pieces where necessary in these productions, the dancers went on to present entire performances. When Lilian Baylis opened a new theatre, the Sadler's Wells, in Islington, the dancers formed themselves into the Vic-Wells Ballet, and appeared at both Sadler's Wells and the Old Vic. Their leading *choreographer* (the person who 'writes' the ballets) was Fred-

erick Ashton, who is still creating wonderful ballets today and has to his credit such works as *La Fille Mal Gardée*, *The Two Pigeons*, *The Dream* and *A Month in the Country*. Not long after the Vic-Wells Ballet was formed, Margot Fonteyn joined as a young star and proved a great inspiration for Ashton, who wrote many ballets especially for her.

In 1946 the Sadler's Wells Ballet, as it was then called, moved to a theatre in Covent Garden and opened a second, touring group, and in 1956 the entire company was finally named The Royal Ballet. Throughout most of the company's history Margot Fonteyn has been the leading ballerina. In 1961 she began a highly successful dancing partnership with the brilliant young Russian Rudolf Nureyev, a member of the Kirov Ballet who defected while his company was on tour in Europe. In 1970 another dancer from the

Margot Fonteyn and Rudolf Nureyev dancing together.

Above left : The Tales of Beatrix Potter, *performed by The Royal Ballet.*

Above : The shows staged by Maurice Béjart are a mixture of song, dance, speech, music and acrobatics.

Left : A Month in the Country, *choreographed by Frederick Ashton.*

Kirov, Natalia Makarova, defected to the West, followed in 1974 by Mikhail Baryshnikov.

If you go to performances by The Royal Ballet today, you will be able to see fine dancers such as Lynn Seymour, Merle Park, Anthony Dowell, Maina Gielgud, Antoinette Sibley, David Wall and Wayne Eagling in ballets such as *Swan Lake, The Sleeping Beauty, Giselle, La Sylphide, Coppelia* and *La Fille Mal Gardée.* Past Royal Ballet dancers have sometimes gone on to open new companies elsewhere, among them Celia Franca and Peggy Van Praagh, who founded the National Ballet of Canada (1951) and the Australian Ballet (1962) respectively.

Meanwhile, back in 1927, Marie Rambert's husband, who was a playwright, opened a theatre in Notting Hill Gate called the Mercury. This was Ballet Rambert's first home. In 1966 the company was whittled down to 17 dancers, and began to concentrate on presenting modern ballets. Today you can see a repertoire of exciting modern dance, very different in style from the classics. Many of Ballet Rambert's current works have been choreographed by Christopher Bruce, formerly a dancer with the company.

The third major British ballet company is the London Festival Ballet, founded in 1950. Based at the Festival Hall in London's South Bank complex, it presents full-length classical ballets as well as newer material. Its Artistic Director, Beryl Grey, was for many years a star dancer with The Royal Ballet.

The Scottish Ballet, based in Glasgow, is a small company producing a mixture of classical and modern works, while the London Contemporary Dance Theatre concentrates on modern material and has many talented choreographers in its ranks.

Ballet-lovers today are lucky in that so many dance companies go on tour. A chance to see the Russian Bolshoi Company is not to be missed, and other companies to look out for are the Stuttgart Ballet, run by its leading dancer, the talented Marcia Haydée; the Nederlands Dans Theater from Holland, which dances exciting modern works; Maurice Béjart's Ballet of the 20th Century from Belgium, which presents ballets using speech, song and all kinds of special effects; and the New York Harlem Dance Theater, a young and lively all-black company. Classical ballet in America has two marvellous outlets – the American Ballet Theater and the New York City Ballet. The American Ballet Theater has produced a lively American style that is born of strict classical training joined with fresh American vitality.

Ballet is increasingly shown on television in many countries, so that even those of us who cannot possibly see all the world's most brilliant companies, can learn something of this fascinating art form.

Commerce and Industry

Contents

An interdependent world

Technology has made the world seem a much smaller place and this is particularly noticeable in the fields of trade, industry and finance. In fact, it has often been because countries have wanted to extend their trading areas that 'earth-shrinking' developments have taken place.

As the world gets 'smaller' we can see the similarities between peoples and notice how some countries are at similar stages of development. Some are advanced industrial countries, like the USA, many of the European countries, Japan and Australia. Others it is harder to classify because less is known about their development. This applies particularly to the USSR, China and countries in Eastern Europe. Then there are the developing countries, like most of those in Africa, South-east Asia and South America. The oil-rich countries of the Middle East form a class of their own.

However developed they are, all countries depend on each other to a greater or lesser extent and in different ways. Some are rich in basic *commodities* like ores for iron, copper, lead, zinc and tin, or foodstuffs like sugar, coffee or tea. But these countries may lack the technology to manufacture goods they need. So they *export*, or sell abroad, the commodities they have and *import*, or buy overseas for home use, the manufactured goods they want. Ideally a country's exports should be worth the same as, or slightly more than, their imports. If this happens, the country is said to have a favourable *balance of trade*.

Unfortunately, one country's exports are another country's imports. So not all countries can earn a trade *surplus*. But it is possible to earn money abroad in other ways. If companies make *overseas investments* by building factories abroad they can send home part of the *profits* in the form of *dividends*. Such non-trade items can be very important. For example tourists bring in foreign money and so help to pay for imports into the country visited.

The total value of all a country's dealings with the rest of the world are summed up in figures called the country's *balance of payments*, which add the value of non-trade items to the trade balance figures.

THE BALANCE OF TRADE

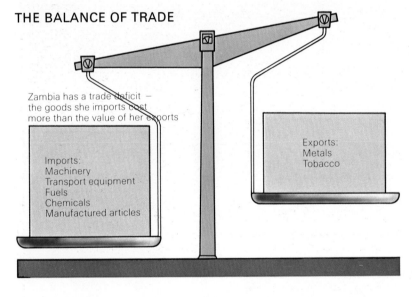

Zambia has a trade deficit — the goods she imports cost more than the value of her exports

Imports:
Machinery
Transport equipment
Fuels
Chemicals
Manufactured articles

Exports:
Metals
Tobacco

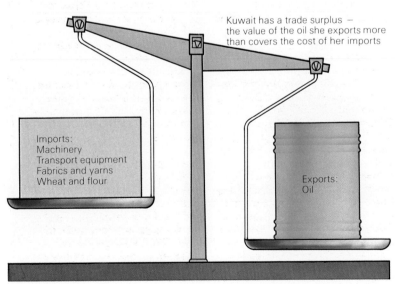

Kuwait has a trade surplus — the value of the oil she exports more than covers the cost of her imports

Imports:
Machinery
Transport equipment
Fabrics and yarns
Wheat and flour

Exports:
Oil

INTERNATIONAL ORGANIZATIONS

A good indication of the way the world is becoming a more unified place is the fact that there are now a large number of international organizations. Through these organizations individual countries give up some control over their own affairs to achieve the greater benefits which can come from being in harmony with the rest of the world. For example, it is better to accept other people's rules about postal services than to get no mail from abroad. Some of the more important organizations are listed here.

The United Nations (UN)
Formed 1945. Nearly 150 member states. Headquarters in New York, USA. Founded to prevent war, its aim is to 'reaffirm faith in fundamental human rights, in the dignity and worth of the human person, in the equal rights of men and women and of nations large and small'. More political than economic, but it does gather and publish statistics.

The Food and Agriculture Organization of the UN
Formed 1945. Nearly 140 states are members. Founded to increase productivity in agriculture, fisheries and forestry. Collects and publishes technical and statistical information.

The General Agreement on Trade and Tariffs (GATT)
Came into force in 1948 after an attempt to set up a stronger trade ruling arm of the UN failed. Over 80 countries are committed to following GATT rules for the conduct of world trade and they account for well over four fifths of world trade.

The International Monetary Fund (IMF)
Established 1945. Founded to promote international monetary co-operation. Supervises the ways countries change the exchange rates of their currencies. Acts as a bank to member countries.

The Council for Mutual Economic Assistance (COMECON)
Founded 1949. Members are USSR, Eastern European countries, and Cuba. Formed to promote co-ordinated expansion of members' economic and technical progress.

The European Economic Community (EEC)
Started in 1958. Merged, in 1965, with European Coal and Steel Community (ECSC) and European Atomic Energy Community (Euratom). In January 1973 Denmark, Ireland and the United Kingdom (confirmed by referendum in 1975) joined. Other members are France, Italy, Germany, Belgium, Luxembourg, the Netherlands and finally Greece which became a full member in 1981. Seeks to establish a common European economic framework.

Top: The UN Assembly, New York.
Above: The EEC Headquarters, Brussels.

The Organization for Economic Co-operation and Development (OECD)
Formed in 1961 as successor to an organization that helped administer American aid to Europe after the Second World War. Now an influential policy review body with 24 members – most of the developed Western countries.

The Organization of Petroleum Exporting Countries (OPEC)
Formed to promote interests of countries which originally had oil and few other resources – the Middle East and Venezuela. In 1971 OPEC countries acted together to impose a massive increase in the price of crude oil.

The role of governments

As the world has become more highly industrially developed so governments have played an increasingly active and important part in daily life – and in economic matters in particular.

Today nearly half the working population in some countries work for the state – as policemen, social workers, soldiers, administrators and employees of state-owned businesses.

As a result, governments have to meet the very heavy costs of keeping a country going. In most advanced countries the major items of government expenditure are: defence and the armed forces; internal security and the police; education; health care; communica-

Governments have to meet the very heavy costs of keeping a country going. This diagram shows the areas in which the British Government was spending most money in the late 1970s. The rate support grant is money given by central government to local authorities to help them meet their expenses.

tions facilities and roads, railways, airports and telephone networks.

To pay for all this, governments impose a variety of *taxes* and *duties*. Direct taxes are those charged, for instance, on an individual's or a company's income and paid directly. Indirect taxes are those paid as part of the price of something else. Sales taxes and value added tax (VAT) are indirect taxes. Duties are charges raised on goods imported or charges on drinking spirits, like whisky, administered by customs officials.

Like households, governments have to balance their spending against their income. This is usually attempted by an annual *budget* which sets out what expenditure is needed and how money will be raised to meet it. If income is the same as expenditure, the country is said to have a balanced budget. But most governments tend to have a *deficit* – they spend more than they receive.

Governments are a major influence on their country's economy. For example, if a

government decides to re-equip its army, it will buy weapons, vehicles, clothing and so on in huge amounts. Manufacturers, in turn, need to buy large quantities of raw materials and often hire new workers to fulfil the orders. So government spending can boost employment and prosperity.

Governments use their powers as big participants in, and regulators of, the economy to help shape prosperity by stimulating or dampening demand. If taxes on basics like food, clothing and petrol are suddenly raised sharply people have less to spend on 'luxuries' like new cars, jewellery, furniture, holidays and so on. The companies providing non-essential goods are then not so busy and reduce the number of workers they employ. Unemployed workers have less money to spend and so the impact of a tax change spreads right through the system. So raising taxes on essentials could help, for instance, to cut spending on luxury imports and restore a country's balance of trade.

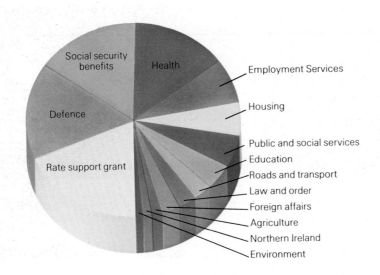

Different economic systems

The extent to which governments can shape their country's economy depends on the kind of political system they work under.

Communist countries tend to work with a *planned economy*. They try to direct production in all parts, or *sectors* of the economy, in order to produce what the government planners decide is needed.

The opposite kind of system is known as a *free market* economy. Here the idea is that everything is left to the forces of *supply and demand*. If people want a certain product they will pay higher prices for it which tempts businessmen to build factories to supply it. As more and more of the product is made, the demand is satisfied and traders have to lower prices to encourage even more people to buy the product. As prices come down so other businessmen realise that it is not so profitable to make this product any more. So no more factories are built to make it.

The level of supply settles at a point which satisfies demand at prices people are willing to pay.

That is the idea, but it does not exist completely freely anywhere. In practice most industrial countries are organized as *mixed economies*. That is to say there is some central planning and control of production and prices (of electricity, for instance) but many industries are allowed to compete freely.

The method and extent of central planning and control, however, does not really change the aims and purposes of governments in trying to direct the economy. Most governments want to achieve full employment, stable prices, rising standards of living and a satisfactory balance of external payments.

These aims are often in conflict and one of the most difficult problems for governments is to balance stable prices and full employment.

Most economists believe that there is an important connection between prices and employment. If wages increase

then some workers are better off for a while. But the companies they work for have to pay more wages and therefore have higher costs so these companies put up the prices of the goods they make. This in turn makes other companies and workers buying those goods put up their prices or ask for more wages. And so it can go on in a *spiral* of one wage or price increase triggering off another.

A situation where prices are tending to rise is called *inflation*. Very occasionally it can get completely out of control, as it did in Germany in the 1920s when people had to take baskets full of notes to buy a loaf of bread. Today it is not so bad, but it remains a serious problem, particularly for people living on fixed incomes which buy fewer and fewer goods each year.

Far left, left, and centre : Among the many calls on government money are defence, education and road building programmes.

Below : Inflation in Germany in the 1920s was so bad, that money was practically worthless and notes were sold as scrap paper.

International trade

The modern world could not survive without international trade. Every day the seas are full of ships carrying commodities and manufactured goods around the world. The most important commodity in international trade is oil, followed by coffee.

There will always be a need for shipping companies to move bulk commodities like oil, minerals and basic foods around the world, simply because they are found or grow best far from where they are wanted.

An important factor in determining what is worth exporting is what is known as the *volume : value ratio*. This simply compares the size of a product to its value. Two items of furniture may take up as much space as a car, but they would be worth less. So cars get traded around the world but furniture tends to be manufactured locally.

Above : Loading a cargo plane.

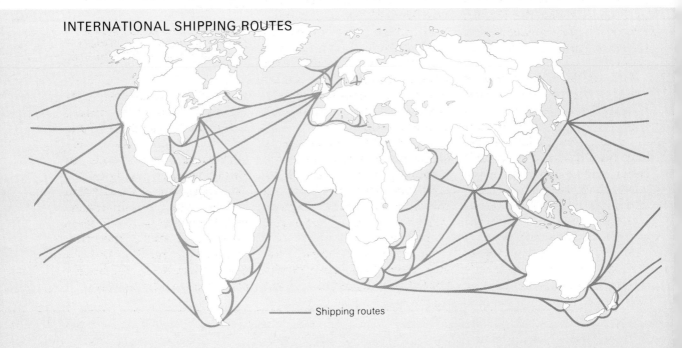

INTERNATIONAL SHIPPING ROUTES

—— Shipping routes

All round the world there are invisible highways formed by the pattern of shipping lanes, which lead from port to port. These lanes gradually shift with time because of changes in the way things are transported, in the routes available and in what countries need and with whom they wish to trade.

Some of the biggest physical obstacles have been removed with major feats of engineering. The Panama Canal links the Atlantic to the Pacific with an 80 kilometre (50 mile) channel, while the Simplon Railway Tunnel links Italy and Switzerland with a 20 kilometre (12 mile) shortcut through the Alps. The Suez Canal, which is 160 kilometres (100 miles) long, saved ships the enormous journey round Africa.

The Suez Canal was closed to traffic because of ships sunk during the Egyptian-Israeli war of 1968. By the time it re-opened in 1976 transport methods had changed. So where previously oil tankers had used the Suez Canal to bring oil from Saudi Arabia to Europe, today the tankers are too big for the Canal, and they have to go round Africa again.

One of the biggest factors affecting the pattern of trade has been the creation of the EEC and other similar groups of trading countries. These have been designed to make it easier and cheaper to move goods about within the group. The main way this is done is by the member countries agreeing to a common external *tariff*. A tariff is a kind of tax that countries charge on goods coming into the country.

For example, New Zealand may wish to discourage a certain kind of product coming into the country to protect its own manufacturers. It can impose a heavy tariff which adds to the cost of the import which then becomes very expensive by comparison with the local product.

So the EEC now charges a single set of tariffs on goods coming into the EEC countries. But there are no tariffs on movements of goods between member countries within the EEC.

When Britain joined the EEC it gradually changed the special arrangements it had

Top: Containerization means that goods can easily be transferred from ship to lorry.

Above: The Suez Canal links the Red Sea and the Mediterranean. It is about 160 kilometres (100 miles) long.

with other countries. Previously it had given special treatment to members of the Commonwealth who were allowed to send goods to Britain without paying tariffs. By joining the EEC Britain had to treat the Commonwealth countries as outsiders in the same way as the other members of the EEC did. As a result the pattern of Britain's trade changed dramatically.

Population – the most important resource

The driving force behind the economic success of any country is its population. It is the people that make good or bad use of available natural resources. And it is the needs of the population for goods and services which create the demands that businesses supply.

It is not only the total number of people that matters. Populations grow at different rates and have different proportions of old or young people. Some countries have proportionally more children and old people than others, which makes it harder for the working members of the population to support the rest.

Modern medicine and expertise has played a major part in shaping populations. It has brought under control all sorts of diseases that used to be fatal. Now all over the world more babies survive and people live longer. Thus, populations can increase even if the same or a smaller number of babies is born. All these people need food, clothes and shelter. Increasing numbers means that there is an increased demand for goods.

The culture, development, traditions and the religions of peoples affect the kinds of goods they will want. People in poorer countries still need the basics – food, housing, clothing and medicines. In the developed countries, people want cars, washing machines, holidays and luxury goods such as fur coats and jewellery.

Many people worry about whether we will be able to go on providing for a world population which seems to keep growing faster and faster.

Right : Rush hour crowds at a Japanese station.

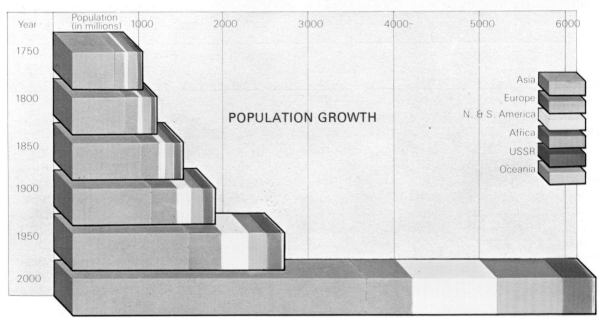

POPULATION GROWTH

Business organizations

Many different kinds of group or organization are involved in contributing wealth to nations.

There are, first, the people who do not join any group but work on their own, as *sole traders*. These can be craftsmen with their own workshops, like cabinet makers or watch repairers; and there are traders like the families who run local shops or cafes; and there are *professionals* like lawyers and journalists who hire out their skills.

Sometimes people join together in a *partnership* to pursue a common enterprise. They share any profits and losses and people can join or leave the partnership. But, under many legal systems, partnerships do not enjoy the two most important benefits which make *companies* the most important form of organization in Western countries.

Companies are organizations that have legal existence independently of those who work for them. If all members of a partnership die then the partnership ends. If all the directors and employees of a company were to die, the company would continue to have legal existence and someone would be called in to look after the business. Some companies in existence today were founded hundreds of years ago.

The other important legal feature of companies is that they can assume responsibilities for which the owners are not personally liable. This is what the English term

Small businesses can grow into international concerns – the Coca-Cola bottling plant in its early days and, inset, the company H.Q. today.

'Limited' or 'Ltd.' means after a company's name or the American term 'Incorporated' or 'Inc.' The owners of a company have a *limited* liability in the affairs of the company. If someone starts a company with £1000 or $1000 that is the extent of his or her risk. If the company fails, or goes into *liquidation*, he or she has lost the £1000 or $1000 *equity capital* and that is all. If the company owes other people more money they have to do their best to recover the debt by arranging for the company's *assets*, such as properties, to be sold.

Not so long ago most companies were family affairs – owned by different members of the same family, and some still are. But now many companies have survived the founding families and grown into big organizations which own *subsidiary companies*.

These companies operate in other countries to form *multi-national* groups, such as the big oil companies like Shell or Esso, and the big car manufacturers like Ford. The big multi-national companies each control more money than many countries do. All these organizations exist to make *profits* for their owners or *shareholders*.

Some nations, however, increasingly feel that it is wrong for certain industries to be managed solely in order to increase profits for owners. They may feel, for instance, that railways should be run for the benefit of the nation, even if they run at a loss. Many countries have bought out the owners of basic industries and created *nationalized industries* and state-owned corporations, for example: railways, coal, oil and postal services are state-owned in many countries.

Oil

Oil is the world's biggest business and it is one of the most varied. The raw product is found and produced in quantity in only a few countries, but it is made into thousands of products besides petrol or gasoline and used right around the world.

The first commercial oil wells were developed in the USA in the last century. The USSR is now the world's largest producer of crude oil with over 500 million tonnes per year. Saudi Arabia is, however, the most important oil producer in many ways because the Saudis export most of their oil and they produce over 420 million tonnes per annum. The USA is the third largest producer with over 400 million tonnes followed by Iran (300 million tonnes), Venezuela (150 million tonnes) and Kuwait (110 million tonnes).

Countries in the Middle East now dominate world oil exports to such an extent that they were able, in 1971, to impose a massive increase in the price of their crude oil. They effectively formed a *cartel*.

The income now coming into the tiny oil-rich country of Kuwait is so big that if it were distributed to all the population, each person in Kuwait would have more income per year than the population of any other country in the world.

Production of oil from the major oil fields of the Middle East has been relatively constant but demand for oil has steadily increased. So the oil companies have been ready to explore for oil in more remote places. The big successes have been discoveries of large fields under the North Sea and on the northern shores of Alaska.

Such exploration is extremely expensive but the oil companies are able to afford this because they are very big

An oil pipe line stretching across the desert in Saudi-Arabia carries oil to the nearest refinery or port.

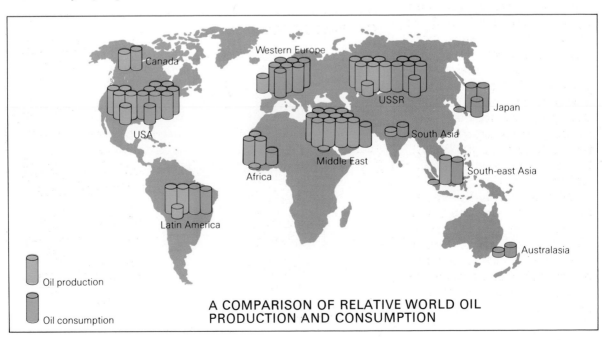

A COMPARISON OF RELATIVE WORLD OIL PRODUCTION AND CONSUMPTION

organizations. The leading ones run virtually every stage of the business from looking for oil, through transporting it, refining it and selling it to the end consumer.

You can see the symbols of the big companies like Esso, Mobil, Texaco, BP and Shell on ships, refineries, tankers and gasoline or petrol stations. This type of business is said to be *vertically integrated* since the companies run all the stages of production, distribution and marketing for themselves. By contrast, manufacturers of most household goods buy the parts they need from other companies and let shops do the final selling to the end consumer. They concentrate on manufacturing. The integrated oil companies do everything.

One of the most important things about oil is that it is the main ingredient in the manufacture of plastics and all kinds of other synthetic materials. The big refineries of the oil companies heat up the thick crude oil and 'crack' it down into different substances. Some become kerosene, gasoline or petrol, and others become ethylenes or 'feedstocks' for factories which produce polythene for bags, vinyl for floorcoverings, and nylon for clothing. The list for oil-based products is enormous and keeps growing.

Oil is the truly indispensable material of the modern world. We rely on it to keep most of our transportation systems going, we burn it to generate power to keep us warm and we modify it to make many products we rely on in everyday life.

Above : Oil is now in such demand that it is worth the expense of extracting it from beneath the sea.

Left : An oil refinery in Saudi-Arabia.

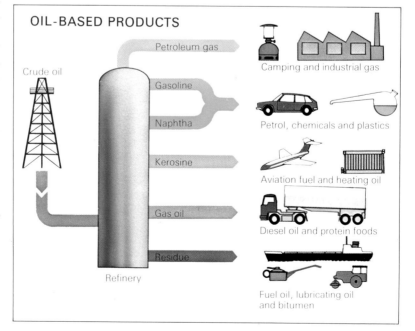

OIL-BASED PRODUCTS

Crude oil

Refinery

Petroleum gas — Camping and industrial gas

Gasoline

Naphtha — Petrol, chemicals and plastics

Kerosine — Aviation fuel and heating oil

Gas oil — Diesel oil and protein foods

Residue — Fuel oil, lubricating oil and bitumen

CHANGING SOURCES OF POWER IN THE USA

Energy industries

Oil is the main source of energy in the modern world, but many people are working hard to make better use of it and to replace it with other sources because there is only a certain amount of oil under the earth and at some point in the future it will run out.

So other sources of energy are actively pursued despite their disadvantages. Water can be used to generate electricity when it is harnessed behind dams and released through small tunnels so that it turns turbines to generate electricity. *Hydro-electric* schemes, as they are called, are very expensive to start, when dams have to be built, but relatively cheap to

run since fuel does not have to be bought. Unfortunately, not many countries have the geography to exploit hydro-electric power.

In some places energy from the sun and wind can be converted into electricity through *solar cells* and *windmills*. But this depends on the weather and is expensive.

Coal is still an important power source for the countries which have it. It is difficult and dirty to work but a kilo of coal does produce a large amount of heat when compared with wood, oil or gas.

Nuclear power is growing in importance as a source of energy. The expense (and dangers) of building nuclear power stations however, means

The considerable changes in sources of energy over the last century (especially in industrialized countries like America) will have to continue as oil supplies are running out.

that only governments can provide the necessary investment.

Energy industries are usually owned or tightly controlled by government. In America independent companies buy fuels, generate electricity and supply it to homes and factories. These are big companies, but their activities are carefully controlled by government to ensure that people pay a fair price for their light and heat. In most other countries the energy industries are completely run by the state.

● Major coal producing areas

● Major iron ore producing areas

● Major copper producing areas

● Major gold producing areas

Above : Drilling underground at Mufulira mine, Zambia. The increased use of machinery underground speeds production.

Left : Steel is not a pure metal but an alloy of iron. Until the middle of the last century steel was difficult and expensive to make. Then a man called Henry Bessemer invented a way of making steel which brought the price down drastically. This meant that steel – which is much stronger – could replace iron in many cases.

Mining

The modern world depends on mining and allied industries to supply basic materials which have to be dug out of the earth. Coal was one of the first minerals to be mined on a big scale, to provide fuel for heating homes.

In England in the 1800s coal was found conveniently close to deposits of iron ore. So it was comparatively easy and cheap to make large quantities of iron – burning the coal to melt down the ores.

Today matters are seldom so easy. Conveniently located deposits of important ores have been used up. Mining companies now have to spend a lot of money *prospecting* in inaccessible places.

Mining is a difficult business because it is very expensive to find ores and build the necessary plant to get into production on a regular basis. Mining companies have to hope to recover their *investment* and make profits by mining for as long as the ores last. This might be more than 20 years. During this time the selling price, and so profits, will go up and down depending on world demand. For countries like Zaire, for instance, which depends on exporting copper to pay for imports, it is very difficult to cope with the way sales fluctuate.

Although many mining companies are international, many of the useful minerals are concentrated in just a few countries. Most of the world's gold comes from South Africa. Iron ores are mined in Australia, Brazil and the USA. Copper ores are important in the African countries of Zaire and Zambia, and in Chile and Peru.

Modern manufacturing processes

The engineering industry

There are two kinds of achievement behind the existence of cars, sewing machines, drills and other machines. First there is the skill of the inventor who has the idea and knows how to fit gears, levers and so on together to make a machine work.

Second, there is the skill of the organizer or *entrepreneur* who arranges the required operations and creates a business to make the machines. He or she is helped by three ideas.

First, there is the idea of *division of labour*. A craftsman might be able to make one chair a day doing all the jobs himself. But the work goes much faster if one man spends all his time making the legs, another the seats and a third the backs. Together the three would make more than three chairs a day.

Second is the idea of *interchangeable parts*. This was invented by the American Eli Whitney around 1800. He won a contract to make guns for the government using a system which would overcome what he knew to be the main problem – a shortage of skilled labour.

He equipped his factory with special jigs and machines, such as saws with automatic stops so they would cut just the right amount and no further. Ordinary workers could guide the machines to make musket parts which were exactly the same each time. At the end of the day there were separate piles of all the parts – butts, barrels, triggers etc. – and muskets could be *assembled* by picking any part from each pile. This was revolutionary. Previously guns

Above : Eli Whitney (1765–1825). As well as developing the system of interchangeable parts, Whitney invented the cotton gin.

INTERCHANGEABLE PARTS

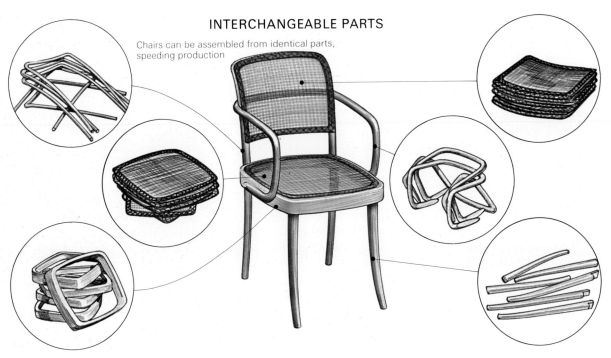

Chairs can be assembled from identical parts, speeding production

were individually crafted and each was, in its way, unique. Now working guns could be assembled even from the parts of others broken on a battlefield. The idea of interchangeable parts become known as the 'American System' and it was adopted to make rifles for the British army some 50 years later.

The system, of course, can be used to make other things besides guns. And it leads to the third idea on which modern manufacturing depends: the *assembly line.*

This starts with the frame of a product being placed on a conveyor belt which carries it past the workers. They each add a part or perform some small task until the finished product emerges at the other end. Cars are made like this and the line can be set fast enough in a modern plant to make 100 cars an hour. This is what is meant by *mass production.*

The same principles can be seen in the most advanced industrial *robots.* These replace humans on certain assembly line jobs. They are like any other part of a big machine because they will do the same limited action over and over again in time with the rest of the machine. But robots can be re-programmed so that the next day they can be doing something else. It is as if a lever can be told to be a cog-wheel for a few hours and then to act like a crane.

Modern manufacturing processes mean a lot more goods can be produced, but they also mean that many workers may have to do very boring and monotonous jobs.

Automation speeds production:
Right: An automated canning plant in a brewery.

Below left: A car assembly line in Detroit, USA.

Below right: A motor cycle assembly line in Japan.

The chemical industry

Big chemical plants are like big cooking pots kept permanently bubbling. They are so expensive to build that they have to be kept going 24 hours a day for 365 days a year. They employ the principle of *continuous processing*.

The chemical industry is large and varied. There are giant multi-national companies with huge plants in many countries and there are tiny, local concerns. At the same time the industry can be divided into those dealing with *inorganic chemicals* which derive from minerals and those concerned with *organics*, which include everything extracted from living things.

The industry has made spectacular contributions to the ease of modern life with

Above: Automated manufacture and packaging of pills.

Below: A chemical plant keeps working 24 hours a day. It is too expensive to start and stop processes at the beginning and end of each day.

fertilizers and pesticides for farmers and gardeners; detergents, plastics and synthetic fibres, like polyester, for the household; and raw materials of all kinds for industry.

Developments in the industry are sometimes the result of a happy chance and sometimes the result of determined, exhaustive search. In the drugs industry, for example, it was a brilliant observation by Sir Alexander Fleming that led to the discovery of the antibiotic qualities of penicillin. But massive research programmes after the war were required to expand the range of antibiotics.

For the big companies making widely used chemicals the main resource required is money committed to the company for an indefinite period. They form a *capital intensive* industry: it takes a lot of capital or money to build one of the huge plants required. It is often true that the bigger the plant the cheaper the end product. There are *economies of scale* which simply means that things get cheaper if they are made in bulk.

The electronics industry

Another kind of manufacturing situation is referred to as a *job shop* and certain parts of the electronics industry are good examples. Here the key is that the company uses a number of people with specialist skills and some fairly general-purpose machines to produce *batches* of a product.

An electronics company, for instance, may be asked to make controllers for a manufacturer of textile printing machinery. The order would probably in-

volve only some hundreds to be delivered over a few months before a new design would be required. So it is not worth the company investing in specialized machinery which could make thousands of parts to fulfil one order in a few weeks, but then be useless.

Electronics companies in fact live with constant change, and the need to produce only small batches of their products. Research laboratories keep coming up with new inventions – for example valves have been succeeded by transistors and now transistors are being replaced by integrated circuits etched into chips of silicon.

Below : The manufacture of integrated circuits under clean room conditions.

And new uses are constantly being found for electronics, from traffic lights to space flights.

Making electronic components needs very unusual methods and the factories often look like surgical operating theatres. Workers are dressed in special gowns, and even the air and water has to be carefully conditioned to remove dust and other particles and impurities. One speck of dust and a circuit can be rendered useless.

Building

The world's tallest inhabited building is the Sears Roebuck Tower in Chicago, USA. It is 533 metres (1749 feet) high and uses enough electricity to light a small town. There are many other notable achievements of the construction industry around the world, but the bulk of the work is more ordinary – building houses, factories, offices, roads, bridges and tunnels.

Construction companies do not have to spend large amounts of money on special factories of their own, nor do they employ large numbers of permanent staff. Instead they have a number of experts who know how to assemble staff and materials for specific building projects. Once the building is finished the workers will be paid off – unless there happens to be another project just starting.

Project management, which is what construction companies have to be good at, requires different skills from those needed in mass production and continuous process industries. The manager in charge of a project usually has the power and responsibility of a ship's captain. He or she has to know how to make sure that all the machines, materials and workers needed are available on the site at the right time. Ways have to be found to prevent delays with one job holding up another. You cannot put the roof on a house until the walls have been finished, but if workers have been employed to build roofs before the walls are finished much money is wasted unless

alternative work can be found for them to do.

As projects get bigger it gets harder and harder for the experts to estimate in advance how much they will need to charge. Companies need to have a lot of spare capital to pay for the costs of building until the work is sufficiently far advanced for the customer to begin paying. So while there are lots of local companies able to build small things like family houses there are only a few big construction companies that can tackle large projects such as skyscrapers, or major civil engineering projects like dams or bridges.

Below : The National Westminster Bank Tower under construction. It is the tallest office block in London.

Agriculture

The most important business in the world is agriculture since all human beings need food. In the past agriculture was a straightforward business. Farms grew the mixture of foods possible and needed in their location. Surpluses could be sold outside for cash or bartered. But as cities and populations grew, farmers had to grow more foods and they became more *specialized* and expert. Instead of growing food to be eaten by their neighbours they grew foods for sale as *cash crops*. Now, in the West, a farm with a full mixture of livestock and crops available for year-round harvesting is the exception.

Science and technology have been very important in making better use of the land. Machines enable one man to do the work of several. Chemical fertilizers stimulate plant growth while special poisons can destroy just one kind of pest in a field. Careful breeding produces special varieties of plants which may, for instance, grow to a more regular height and so be easier to harvest.

Powerful machinery is too expensive for every small farmer to own. Often it is necessary to have huge fields and farms to make it economic to buy and use new machines. The wheatfields of North America, for example, can extend for miles.

Terraced rice fields in the Philippines.

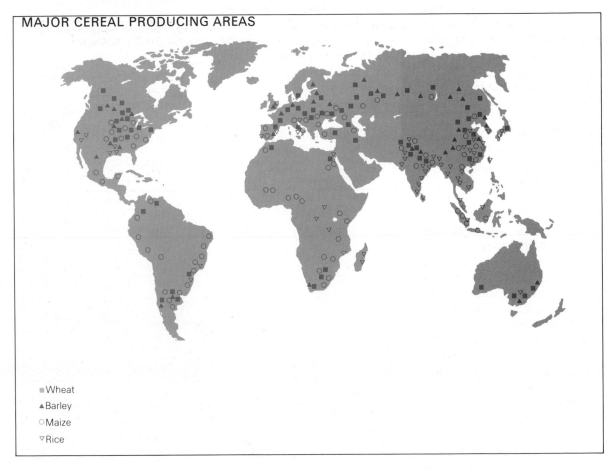

MAJOR CEREAL PRODUCING AREAS

■ Wheat
▲ Barley
○ Maize
▽ Rice

Food

Although much food is grown, harvested and distributed without being 'treated' in any way, there are many food companies which can be classified as manufacturers, particularly since the invention of food preserving processes like canning and freezing.

The techniques of mass production have now been applied to baked goods, vegetables, fruit and meat products. Big companies sign contracts with large farms to supply so many tonnes of vegetables each year. They have special arrangements to rush the vegetables straight from the fields to the canning or freezing stations. Huge warehouses, which can be like enormous refrigerators, are used so that the companies can hold the frozen food until it is needed in the shops.

Manufacturers are always looking for new ways to present foods in more convenient ways. Packets of the right ingredients, ready mixed, take labour out of making cakes and other foods.

Technology too plays a major part in the food industry. There are specialist chemical companies who can produce smells and tastes in the laboratory. So a manufacturer of ice cream can buy liquids to add, for instance, a strawberry flavour.

One of the most spectacular achievements of the modern business world rests on a secret recipe. Coca-Cola is a drink known and made all over the world, but only a handful of people at any one time know exactly how to mix the in-gredients together in the right proportions and the right way. Other companies have chemists who can analyze Coca-Cola and produce good drinks very like it. But devotees will be able to tell the difference. This fact has been enough to make the drink a worldwide success – helped of course by a lot of other business skills, like advertizing.

Most other beverages, including beer, wine, whisky and other alcoholic drinks also depend for their success on subtle variations of taste.

A crucial skill in many branches of the food industry is that of *blending*. Scotch whisky is made by blending up to 100 different whiskies from all over Scotland. Even butter is made to achieve a consistent quality by blending. And it is vital in achieving consistent taste in tea and coffee, which continue to battle for favour around the world.

Above : Producing large quantities of food at low prices means employing 'factory farming' techniques.

Below : A refrigerated warehouse means that huge quantities of food can be frozen and stored.

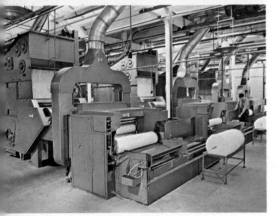

Textiles

Along with food and shelter, clothing is one of the essential requirements for survival. But many textile and clothing companies have found it hard to make profits.

The first problem is that people want individual clothes and follow fashions. A modern trend has been jeans and denims but there are still many different styles. And fashions change very quickly. So companies have to make great efforts to keep up.

Yet more problems are caused by the interplay between fashion suggesting what people want and technology dictating what is available. Cotton is a fibre derived naturally from semi-tropical plants. Compared with synthetic fibres like polyester and acrylics, it is relatively expensive but usually more comfortable. Companies need to know which factor is most important to their customers: comfort or cheapness.

Clothing manufacture is a business that is very easy to enter. You just buy a sewing machine and some cloth, make up the garments and go out and sell them to the shops, hoping that you are the first with your ideas.

Companies which wish to become big can expand production by hiring more people – textiles is a *labour intensive* industry employing a lot of people. What has happened is that new factories have been started in Asian countries like Taiwan, Hong Kong and Korea where wages are much lower than in Europe and America. So the Asian countries now supply many of the clothes worn in Western countries, because they are much cheaper.

Stages in cotton processing :
Top : Bale blending and opening.

Above : Bales are fully opened and cleaned in the blowing room.

Below : The carding room – fibres are separated.

Right : The spinning mill.

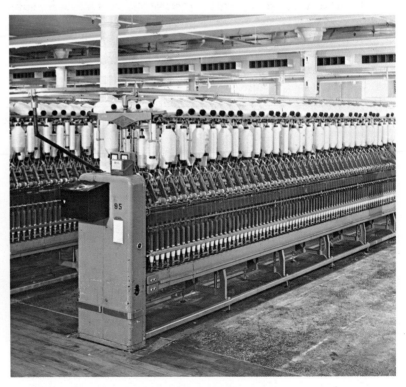

Travel and tourism

Today hotels, catering, travel and tourism are big businesses dominated by *chains* of facilities run by large companies.

Companies have been able to grow big thanks to the *franchise* system. They find people who wish to operate an hotel or restaurant and sell them the right to use the name of the operation. The individuals run their businesses according to set procedures written up in a big operations manual. They know that businesses managed according to these procedures tend to be successful and they join a club which is advertised on a scale that they could not afford themselves.

Most of the costs of keeping a hotel open have to be paid whether there are any guests or not. They have high *fixed costs*. So hotel owners are very anxious to keep their hotels full and they are prepared to let their rooms at cheaper rates to organizations who can guarantee to fill a lot of rooms.

Airlines are similar and have high fixed costs from owning the aeroplanes and flying them on set timetables whether there are passengers aboard or not. They also are prepared to give *discounts*, or lower prices, to companies buying a lot of tickets.

Travel companies can buy tickets from the airlines and reserve hotel rooms in such big quantities that they can buy them very cheaply. So they put together *packages* of what is required for a holiday – travel and accommodation. People can then buy a complete holiday for less than what it would have cost them as individuals just to travel to the resort.

Everyone benefits out of the business. People have more exciting holidays, the hotels and aeroplanes are full and the countries visited enjoy tourists bringing in money and spending it. In fact for some countries tourism is an important part of the economy, providing employment for thousands of people and bringing in significant amounts of money.

Above left : Foreign tourists bring money into the countries they visit.

Above : The demand for holidays abroad increases the demand for air travel.

Below : In Spain enormous hotels have been built to accommodate the large numbers of holidaymakers.

Marketing

It is usually not enough now for a company to have a good product or service and just wait for people to come and buy it. There are so many competing products that companies have to spend money on *marketing*.

A company's marketing force will include salesmen, advertizing experts and people who know other ways of promoting products – by organizing demonstrations, competitions and so on.

Of these, advertizing is the most noticeable. It is particularly useful for promoting different makes of *consumer*

Left : From small, local beginnings, advertizing has developed into an important international industry, as these posters illustrate.

goods, such as foods and soaps as well as cars and other *durables* like washing machines.

Every year millions of pounds and dollars are spent in making advertizements and arranging for them to be printed in the press or shown on television. Advertizing is a big industry in its own right.

For industrial products a different approach is used. These are more complicated products, like lathes, machine tools, electrical components and so on. There are fewer possible customers, numbered in hundreds or thousands rather than millions, and they tend to want much more detailed information. So marketing is done by personal visits from salesmen together with displays at special trade exhibitions.

HOW GOODS REACH YOUR HOME

An easily over-looked business is that of distribution. Goods are often most conveniently made in one factory and they have to be transported to the people who want to buy them. To actually shift goods from producers to consumers there are companies which have fleets of general purpose lorries, and there are others with specialized fleets – large tankers for oil products, or refrigerated trucks for food.

Distribution involves not just the means of transport but also other businesses which the final customer does not see. Many companies sell their products not direct to shops but to *wholesalers*. A company making pots and pans for instance, will make a single big delivery to a wholesaler who will then divide it up into smaller loads for individual shops. Wholesalers keep their stocks in warehouses which can be

enormous, using computers to keep track of stock movements.

Wholesalers deliver to *retailers* who generally have shops where customers can look at and choose the goods they want to buy. Businesses can by-pass shops altogether and go direct to the consumer either by post, using catalogues, or by sending salesmen around from door-to-door, but most people go into shops to buy.

In some respects a flourishing retail trade is necessary for towns and cities to survive. The growth of department stores during the last century went hand in hand with the growth of towns. In this century towns have increased in size and have been able to support new kinds of stores: supermarkets that are like department stores for food. They have a complete range of food in the store so that customers can buy everything they need in one place rather than visiting separately a baker, a butcher, and a grocer. As supermarkets spread in post-war years, people predicted that small

local stores would go out of business. In fact many small shops were forced to close but others have become very successful by specializing and by providing their customers with a more personal service than a big store can.

A big change in shopping habits has been brought about by the spread in car ownership. As parking is difficult in many towns big shopping centres with huge car parks are being built outside towns. In America these centres tend to include a variety of stores run by the big *chains* – companies who have many shops throughout the country all selling similar goods.

In Europe there has been a slightly different solution. *Hypermarkets*, enormous single stores run by one company and selling everything from food to garden equipment, are built out in the countryside, preferably near an intersection of a motorway, and have enormous car parks. People will travel many, many miles to visit them.

Money

Money is essential in the modern world but it remains a confusing subject best appreciated by realising that a coin has *no* use or value in itself but only as a *means of exchange*. The only reason for having money is to be able to acquire, conveniently, something else.

In some cases people do not bother with money. Neighbours help each other with different jobs which one may be better at than the other. And a certain amount of swapping and bartering still goes on. Swapping half a chicken for a few pints of milk is easy enough but there are problems if one wants to swap a pig for a bicycle. Who is to say they are worth the same? If they are not worth the same, how do you give change?

Having standard symbols of value, or money, solves these problems. All sorts of things have been used as money – shells, stones, iron bars, pressed tea leaves and cigarettes. As long as everyone is prepared to accept the items in exchange for other goods whose values, in terms of shells or cigarettes, is agreed, then there are no problems.

Today money comes in different *currencies* – dollars, pounds, francs, pesetas and so on – and as coins and notes. But it also exists as figures in bank accounts.

A bank may say it holds a million units of currency for its customers but it would actually hold only a small part of that as notes and coins in its vaults. The customers only need cash for a small part of their business and prefer to keep the rest as *deposits* in the bank. The point is that the word 'money' means more things than just coins and notes, and money is actually created in the banking system.

If a customer deposits 1000 units of currency, the bank knows that only about 100 units will be required by this customer for things which have to be paid for in cash. The bank also may know nine other customers each of which would like to borrow 1000 units of currency to buy, for example, some new furniture or a new car. These purchases would be made by cheque, so again each of the customers would need only a little bit of cash for day-to-day items. The bank can allow these customers to have the use of the spare 900 units deposited by the first customer and it can literally *create* new money by making loans of 1000 units each to the nine customers who want to borrow money. Each customer then has 1000 units in *money*, all recorded in the bank. And the bank has available 100 units for each customer's minor expenses.

This 'creating' of money is controlled by governments in one way or another, principally by setting rules for what proportion of customers' deposits may be used for loans.

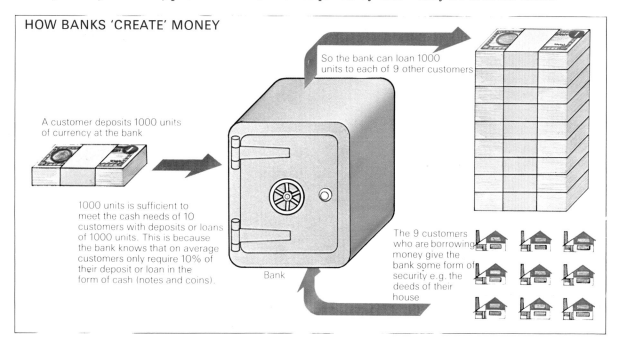

HOW BANKS 'CREATE' MONEY

A customer deposits 1000 units of currency at the bank

1000 units is sufficient to meet the cash needs of 10 customers with deposits or loans of 1000 units. This is because the bank knows that on average customers only require 10% of their deposit or loan in the form of cash (notes and coins).

Bank

So the bank can loan 1000 units to each of 9 other customers

The 9 customers who are borrowing money give the bank some form of security e.g. the deeds of their house

STOCK EXCHANGES

Stock exchanges exist to provide a place and a means for people to buy and sell, not food or other goods normally found in markets, but *securities*. These are certificates issued by governments or companies to raise money. The certificates are evidence of an obligation by the *issuer* to the holder.

A government can create *bonds* which it will issue for a price. By doing this it creates an agreement to borrow money from people on set terms. It sells a certificate for a set amount which it undertakes to buy back for the same amount in, say, 20 years (this is the *term*, or life of the bond), during which time it pays interest to the registered holder of the certificate, whoever he is. The certificates are bought, at a stock exchange, by people wanting to invest money.

In such a situation where new issues are being made, the stock exchange acts as a *primary* market. If the first buyers of a security later wish to hold cash rather than the certificate, they can sell to other savers on the floor of a stock exchange, which then acts as a *secondary* market. This trading does not affect the issuer, which still has the use of money raised in the first place.

It is not only governments which raise money by selling securities in this way. Companies issue and sell new stock or *shares*, which literally represent a share in ownership of the company. Big companies are actually *owned* by the thousands of people who have shares in them, which is why they are called *public* companies. If companies do well, savers are usually prepared to pay a higher price to own shares in them. And since there are always people trading in shares, some wanting to change their holdings, others wanting to put money into the market and others wanting to take cash out, so the prices of shares goes up and down, reflecting whether people think companies are doing, or going to do, well. When prices rise, this indicates confidence and a fall indicates a lack of optimism.

Observers usually watch the performance of just a few shares – those of the biggest companies which indicate the behaviour of the market as a whole. In the USA the top 30 industrial companies' shares are grouped into the *Dow Jones Average*. In the UK the *Financial Times Index* has the same function.

The biggest stock exchange in the world, in terms of the value of trading, is the New York Stock Exchange. There are two other big exchanges in the USA – the American Stock Exchange and the Over the Counter market – and many local exchanges, in Philadelphia, Boston and so on. The oldest exchange is that in London. There are exchanges in all major financial centres.

The Stock Exchange in London.

Banks

Every person or organization sometimes has more or less money than they immediately need and that is why banks exist. Banks have big vaults to hold spare cash safely and they make loans to individuals and companies who need money immediately, which they will be able to repay over a period of time.

A person borrows money to buy a car, for instance, and agrees to pay *interest* on the money borrowed as the cost of being able to use the money.

A major part of the bank's business is lending money and interest payments are a main source of income.

Banks, of course, have to be careful and they almost always require *security* for their loans. A company for example, borrowing money, will pledge a factory to the bank so that if it fails to re-pay, the bank can sell the factory to someone else.

More and more business today is done without cash but with *cheques* and *Giro payments*. When a shop buys goods it will issue a cheque to its supplier. The two banks (the bank to which the shop belongs, and the bank to which the supplier belongs), will process the cheque by transferring the funds from the shop's *account* to the supplier's account. Each bank keeps a careful record of all the money put into and taken out of accounts.

Payments are being made even faster by the method of *Electronic Funds Transfer* which uses computers and communications links to move funds from one account to another. Banks are also introducing *automation*, with machines which people can use to deposit or withdraw cash.

Credit cards also help people to buy things without actually handling cash. If a bank thinks a customer with money in his or her account is trustworthy, it may issue a credit card to the customer. That person can then present the card to a shop to pay for goods. The shop gets its money direct from the bank, having presented a copy of the bill signed by the customer. The bank takes the money out of the customer's account to pay the shop.

Cash dispensers mean that money can be withdrawn outside banking hours.

PAYING INTEREST

If you borrow money, you are likely to have to pay *interest*. It is important to check how it is calculated and what kind of charge is being made.

There are two kinds of interest – *simple* and *compound*. The first is straightforward. If you borrow 100 units of currency (for example £100 or $100) at five per cent 'simple' you will pay back the 100 units (known as the 'principal') together with five additional units per year in interest for the use of the money until you have repaid the 100 units borrowed. Per cent simply means 'per hundred' so that five per cent is the same as five per hundred. And it applies in proportion to amounts different from 100. So five per cent (or per hundred) of two hundred is five per hundred twice, ie 5 × 2 = 10. In simple interest sums the amount of principal borrowed stays the same until repaid.

Compound interest is more complicated. If you save 100 units of currency and leave it on *deposit* with a bank, the bank will usually assume that you do *not* want to take out the interest each year. So it is added to the principal and for the next year a new 'per hundred' or per cent calculation will be made on the new amount in savings. If you save 100 units and are paid five per cent compound by a bank the sums will be as follows. At the end of one year, you will have earned five units interest on 100 units. The two are added together so that you start year two with 105 units and this is the amount on which the next five per cent interest figure will be worked out. Five per cent of 105 is $\frac{5}{100} \times 105 = 5.25$.

Over five years the sums work out as in the table. So interest payments add up to 27.63 units instead of 25 units which is what five years of simple interest would be.

Year	Principal at start	Interest Rate	Amount of interest	Principal at end
1	100.00	5%	5.00	105.00
2	105.00	5%	5.25	110.25
3	110.25	5%	5.51	115.76
4	115.76	5%	5.79	121.55
5	121.55	5%	6.08	127.63
			27.63	

Insurance

Insurance is almost as important to business as banking. It works quite simply by spreading over a large number of people, the costs or the losses which otherwise would fall on the few who actually suffer them.

Fire, for instance, normally damages only a few businesses each year but almost all companies buy insurance to protect themselves against it. What happens is that most companies pay regular small amounts of money, called the *premium*, to insurance groups and so a large pool or fund of money builds up. Then the few who have suffered fires *claim* the cost of the damages. After investigation, the claims are paid out by the insurance companies.

For the operation to work, insurance companies have to calculate what is the chance or *probability* of certain events happening, and what the cost of making accidents good will be, and how many people will pay, what rates, to have protection. Premiums are fixed in proportion to the risk involved.

There are four principles backing up every insurance contract. The first, known as *indemnity*, is that the insured should get back the same value as was lost. If you insure your watch against the risk of its being stolen then the insurance company will only pay out the cost of a similar, second-hand watch unless you make a special agreement with them.

The second principle is that of agreeing that the insurer has to own, or have *the insurable interest* in, the property covered, *both* at the time of effecting the insurance *and* at the time of loss. This is usual for policies covering fire; but the insurance on ships and their cargoes can be transferred to new owners if required.

Third it is necessary that the agreement be concluded in *good faith*. Generally the company providing insurance cover, or the *underwriter*, charges a premium based on what he is told. If a company fails to mention that a warehouse sometimes contains explosives the underwriter may declare the contract void and refuse to pay a claim if the warehouse blows up.

Finally, insurers distinguish between *remote* and *immediate* causes of an event. If there is an earthquake and a house is damaged, catches fire and is flooded by firemen when putting out the flames, the compensation due will depend on the exact words used in the detailed insurance contract. Usually companies do not provide cover against earthquake damage, so the house-owner may not get any compensation for the effects of the fire or water, as these were a direct result of the earthquake.

The Queen Elizabeth *on fire in Hong Kong harbour. It is to cover the cost of accidents like this, that owners insure their property. Claims are always investigated carefully by the insurance company concerned.*